Teaching Children about Physical Science

Also by Elaine Levenson
Teaching Children About Life and Earth Sciences:
Ideas and Activities Every Teacher and Parent Can Use

Teaching Children about Physical Science

Ideas and Activities Every Teacher and Parent Can Use

Elaine Levenson

Illustrations by Debra Ellinger
Foreword by Mary Budd Rowe, Past-President
National Science Teachers Association

TAB Books
Division of McGraw-Hill, Inc.

New York   San Francisco   Washington, D.C.   Auckland   Bogotá
Caracas   Lisbon   London   Madrid   Mexico City   Milan
Montreal   New Delhi   San Juan   Singapore
Sydney   Tokyo   Toronto

© 1994 by **Elaine Levenson**.
Published by TAB Books, a division of McGraw-Hill, Inc.

3 4 5 6 7 8 9 10 11 MAL/MAL 9 9 8 7 6 5

Library of Congress Cataloging-in-Publication Data

Levenson, Elaine.
    Teaching children about physical science : ideas and activities
every teacher and parent can use / by Elaine Levenson.—2nd ed.
        p.   cm.
    Rev. ed. of: Teaching children about science. c1985.
    Includes bibliographical references (p. 169) and index.
    ISBN 0-07-037619-0 (pbk.)
    1. Science—Study and teaching (Elementary) 2. Activity programs
in education. I. Levenson, Elaine. Teaching children about
science. II. Title.
LB1585.L395 1994
372.3'5044—dc20   93-34326
                                                          CIP

Acquisitions editor: Kimberly Tabor
Editorial team: Robert E. Ostrander, Executive Editor
                Sally Anne Glover, Book Editor
Production team: Katherine G. Brown, Director
                Wanda S. Ditch, Desktop Operator
                Joan Wieland, Proofreading
                Stephanie Myers, Computer Artist
                Jodi L. Tyler, Indexer
Design team: Jaclyn J. Boone, Designer
                Brian Allison, Associate Designer   GEN2
Cover design and illustration: Sandra Blair Design, Harrisburg, Pa.   0376190

Dedication

In loving memory of MaryBelle Jackson, a retired engineer from IBM, for her ingenuity and creativity. Despite her loss of sight due to diabetes, she was able to observe her surroundings more clearly than most sighted people. Her warmth, courage, strength, and bravery were inspirational to all who knew her.

I dedicate this book to my mother (Sadie Moss), to parents and teachers who feel insecure about teaching science subjects, to the young children they teach, who ask, "why?" and "how come?" and to my own very special children, William and Emily, whose curiosity and thoughts helped inspire many of the ideas put forth in this book, as well as to Jean Harlan whom I have never met, but whose book greatly influenced me.

"Teaching Children About Science is a good resource for persons in both school and nonschool settings who are helping children learn science ... much more functional than other activity-oriented books."
— *Curriculum Review*

"An excellent source of ideas presented in a simple, sound format. It belongs in the library of every science curriculum lab, school, and teacher .... Levenson's work could be the key to running an exciting, effective science program."
— *Science and Children*

"This author knows what scientific information children need and how that information is successfully transferred to the child .... She is involved in improving the quality of science instruction on a grand scale with this wonderful book."
— *Science Activities*

"Highly recommended."
— *Science Books & Films*
   Children's Science Booklist (Education)

" One of the best teacher reference books I have found. Her approach is so well structured that a parent, novice teacher or seasoned science teacher would have no difficulty bringing science education into the home or classroom. The hands on and interdisciplinary approach fit right into our Montessori classroom."
— Terry Cook, Educational Director
   Montessori Elementary School of Blacksburg, VA

"If a parent or a teacher could buy only one book about exploring science with children, there is no doubt that TEACHING CHILDREN ABOUT SCIENCE is absolutely, wholeheartedly the book I would recommend."
— Julie Fudge Smith
   Volunteer scientist for the Boston Museum of Science, Science-by-Mail program, Science Curriculum Consultant and science writer for parents and children.

"We highly recommend this book for teachers, home-schooling families, and parents who want to stimulate and enrich their children's view and understanding of their world."
— Harriet Eskridge, Lead Teacher
   Faith Christian Academy

Contents

Foreword

One afternoon I went to a rural first-grade classroom, invited by the young teacher who was doing the "career education" part of the curriculum in that district. The program called for a visiting scientist (me) to whom the children were to ask a set of questions about careers in science. They sat on tiny chairs in a semi-circle around me. Finally, in dutiful fashion the questions began. No children in first grade would ever have thought of them: "Do you have career satisfaction? How many years of training did you have? Are you satisfied with your job? Would you advise others to go into science?" There were ten questions. It took five minutes to answer them. Then we sat facing each other. I finally said, "Are there any questions you always wanted to ask a scientist? I can't promise to answer all of them—maybe there are no answers yet. We keep learning new things every day. What I can't answer I will try to find out by asking other scientists."

They sat for a moment in silence. Then the first hand went up and a small boy said, "Why is it that every time just before I start a fight, I sweat?" I answered that, and the next question was, "I watch preying mantises eat some leaves and he looks like it's good. But when I try chewing those leaves I get sick. Why is that?" Another asked, "Are we sort of a sack of blood? It seems like any place you get cut blood pours out. What good is that?" And so the questions came—for nearly two hours.

There is a great drive on the part of children to know, to get answers. They have to learn, however, that the way we explain things today might change tomorrow. New discoveries lead to new ways of thinking about the facts. As the children themselves mature, their conceptions of the world and their ability to deal with abstraction expands, just as science does. We need to nurture the ability of children to ask questions and seek answers, to compare competing ideas, and to learn strategies for finding out which explanations are more likely. It is characteristic of scientists to ask questions, to continually challenge ideas. Children start life that way, but somewhere many of them appear to lose it. (Actually, we now know they go "underground;" they get answers, sometimes from undesirable sources. The questions do not stop.)

Once during a trip to China I met a history teacher who was teaching science. He knew very little science and a great deal of history, but he preferred to teach the science because, "They keep changing the version of history to be taught. But science doesn't change. You can count on it," he said wistfully.

He is wrong, of course. Science is always changing. Someone challenges an interpretation; that prompts a basketful of questions, and these are usually followed by experiments meant to provide evidence that favors one of the competing interpretations. Our explanations are continually subject to new interpretations. Science thrives on argument, on resolving conflicting views through experiment and observation, on exploration, and on asking questions. That is one thing little children do with great gusto if anyone will listen—they ask questions!

This book provides three things to adults who work with young children: a large set of science activities that do not require any sophisticated equipment, guidance about how to conduct the activities, and some relevant science content to help answer questions.

Be careful in using the information provided. The temptation is to tell it all before its pertinence ever occurs to students. One second grader in a class I was visiting sat without doing anything during a science class, despite the fact that he had materials on his desk. When I asked him why, he shrugged, "What's the use. They don't care what I think or what we find out ourselves—just what they think. They always tell you what that is, whether you believe it or not. I have lots of questions, but who cares?"

For very young children, nothing is ordinary. Everything is worthy of their attention. They have no hard-and-fast rules about priorities, about what is important and what is not. They have a million questions for anyone who will listen. Remember that about the questions; listen to their questions as you start to use this book. There is a host of simple activities and little explorations in this book that you can use to provide occasions for children to do some "sciencing." Warning: Do not turn these occasions into inquisitions. Let the questions come from the children. Answer them when you can; encourage them to find answers on occasion by asking other people; and help them plan activities that will produce both answers and more questions. If you do not know answers, do not worry about it. Let them help you find out.

Use this book as the valuable resource it is. Listen to the questions and the observations of children—that will show them you care. Besides, it's great fun. They do see the world in a different way. One young child gazed up at the contrail of a jet and said, "Look how that plane is scratching up the sky." She needed no comment, just someone to see it, too.

Enjoy using this book. Science ought to be fun and adventure. More learning takes place when we are having fun, when we feel compelled to find out something or to make something work. Once, while doing some science problem-solving activities with a small group of first graders, I asked if they wanted to come back for another session. One of them said, "I had a good time and I learned how to make that system work the way I wanted it to. But my mother didn't send me to school to have a good time. I'm supposed to get into Stanford and I have no time for fun in school." (First grade!) This mother did not understand that there is a close connection between what information people have and how they learn it. We all know people who are virtually walking encyclopedias but who cannot seem to do anything with the information. The ability to solve problems is closely related to what you know and how you came to know it. Science is best learned through involvement, by talking over what happened, by arguing and experimenting until some satisfactory explanation emerges—and by holding on to ideas tentatively until something better comes along. Science is fun, and the bonus is that it is the most successful device we know of for developing language comprehension.

Mary Budd Rowe

About the second edition

While in the process of writing a revision of *Teaching Children about Science*, it seemed that I included so many new activities that the publisher decided it would be best to divide it into two books. That meant two new titles needed to be created for what I had envisioned would be a single book. Thus, we decided on the titles: *Teaching Children about Physical Science* and *Teaching Children about Life and Earth Sciences*.

I did not feel entirely comfortable with these titles because I was concerned that some might find the titles to be misleading. So, I am writing this note to the reader to clarify what this book contains and what it does not contain. *Teaching Children about Physical Science: Ideas and Activities Every Teacher and Parent Can Use* does not include extensive coverage of the following topics: simple machines, gravity, balance and motion, current electricity, and simple circuits.

This book about physical science does cover:

- Magnetism, which includes activities on observing and using material and human-made magnets, observing magnetic force, observing magnetic strength, observing lines of force, observing a magnetic field surrounding a magnet, observing temporary magnets, making a magnet, observing the laws of magnetism, playing with and making magnetic toys, observing magnetic poles.

- Static electricity, which includes activities on: creating static electricity, understanding force, observing the very small, lightning, and playing with static electricity.

- Sound, which includes activities on: how sounds are made when something vibrates, how we can see things vibrate, how we can feel things vibrate, observing how vibrations can cause other things nearby to vibrate, observing how vibrations can be absorbed and stopped or left free to bounce, observing how resonance and echoes cause amplification of sound vibrations, observing how sounds are able to travel through things, observing how different sounds can be made with the same objects if they are different sizes, and observing how sounds can be made to move up and down the musical scale.

- Light, which includes activities on: observing sources of light, observing that light reflects and/or absorbs heat, observing that light can go through some materials and not others, observing and playing with shadows, observing that night is earth's shadow, observing that light can bounce (reflect), observing refraction (the bending of light), making and using lenses, separating and combining colors, and observing that the energy from light can affect plants and animals.

- Air and water, which include activities on: air being virtually everywhere, air taking up space, air having force, air having pressure, observing that air streams and air currents can cause movement and/or lift, observing water pressure, observing surface tension, observing and describing the properties of water, making boats, and observing and experimenting with balance and buoyancy.

Both *Teaching Children about Physical Science* and *Teaching Children about Life and Earth Sciences* have the same introductory chapters. When I found out that this new, original manuscript was to be divided, I felt that these chapters were a necessary part of each book, as they explain my philosophy of how to do science with children.

The first three chapters deal with the concepts that integrate physical, life, and earth sciences. Please know that, in everyday life, sciences do overlap. They are not isolated subject areas. There is an interrelationship between the sciences. It is important for children as well as adults to become aware that systems and measurements can and do connect the sciences. Both books contain an introduction to science, a chapter on models, and a chapter on the five senses. (Developing quality observation skills by using our appropriate senses is an essential skill when doing a scientific investigation, and/or a science experiment.) Each book is now a complete entity, and I believe your experience of each will be a thorough one. (The margins and blank pages in the back of the book are for your notes.)

Preface

To a young child, the unexplainable is magic. Experiments and activities that help explain physical phenomena help children understand their environment better and help them to have a sense of mastery over it. Children should be encouraged to observe and to compare, to predict and test their ideas. They should be encouraged to repeat an experience or an activity several times to see if the results are always the same or if they vary. In learning about the process of inquiry, you can encourage children to question their results and to try varying their experiences or "experiments" to find out if their results change. You can encourage children to devise ways to measure, record, and arrange their findings in an orderly way, and to think in a logical way when they try to find answers or try to set up experiments.

When science ideas are presented to young children, the experiences need to be real, concrete, tangible experiences with real materials. The ideas and experiences need to be presented in a way that will allow children to feel a connection to them. Avoid presenting information, ideas, or activities in isolation. Try to tie them to a child's life so that the child will feel a desire to know.

As adults, we often become carried away with content and facts. Try to remember that, for a young child, less is more. It is more important for young children to be actively involved in science experiences than for them to learn all of the facts. They will learn and remember what they choose to and that for which they are ready.

My goal is that, through the activities in this book, children will see that learning about and understanding science is simply a matter of looking at the world a bit differently. Science is thinking about the world in terms of how and why. It is seeing relationships between common occurrences and looking for patterns in these common occurrences to help make the world make sense. Science helps young children learn to control their world and to develop a better understanding of natural and physical phenomena. It is exciting for young children to understand that some things are yet to be discovered and understood—and that someday, when they are older, they themselves might be the very ones who find the answers to today's mysteries.

During the past ten years, there has been a boom in the development—and the availability—of useful and innovative science books filled with science activities and experiences for young children. Most of the newer children's books have beautiful, life-size, colorful photographs, and/or wonderful diagrams. With that in mind, I have decided to update this book to include some of the newer ideas that I have discovered, and also to share with the reader some of the more current quality science books now available.

In general, a high-quality science book is one in which: the author is reliable; the science content is accurate and interesting; the sequence is logical; the format is attractive; the illustrations enhance the text and are accurate; the safety precautions and pertinent background information are included in the text; and, finally, the materials used are readily available. Often, thought-provoking questions are included in the text, as well as suggested ways or places to find the answers. Usually, an outstanding science book has received a "very good" or higher rating from a science specialist, or a librarian, who has written a published review in a respected periodical.

Please be aware that when a publisher prints a suggested age of reader or audience in a book, it is merely a "suggested" age. When you visit the libraries and book stores, do not be influenced by the suggested age. Picture books with labels can be of great value to both adults and children to increase their understanding or awareness of a system, a structure and its function, a cycle, a pattern, and sometimes properties of an object.

Because the primary audience for this book is adults who use it as a resource book for young children, I have included Additional Selected Resource Books for Parents and Teachers, as well as Additional Science Books for Children and Their Parents at the end of each chapter. Another list of generic titles for adults and for children appears at the end of the book.

A bibliography of Suggested Literature Connections has been added to the end of most of the chapter bibliographies. These particular fiction books have been listed because when they are read to children, their contents and their illustrations can be used by parents and teachers as a resource to spark interest in and/or discussion about science topics. The list of books in the Suggested Literature Connections are merely a sample of some of the beautiful trade books that are in existence today.

It is not my intention to overwhelm the reader, so I have not attempted to make the lists in the appendices or the bibliographies complete. They are merely a sample of the possibilities. As this book goes to print, other new books will be "emerging." The only books that appear in this book's bibliographies are the ones I have actually been able to put my hands on and have opened, or books that I have not seen but have been highly recommended by other respected sources.

Workshops at your school

The author offers hands-on workshops and seminars for teachers and parent groups, and parents-with-their-children groups, on the activities written about in this book, as well as other topics. She can be reached at Levenson Communications, First Colonial Professional Building, 921 First Colonial Road, Suite 1805, Virginia Beach, Virginia 23454, or telephone (804) 496-0745. FAX (804) 491-0389.

A special note to parents

In the past ten years since I first wrote this book, I have been pleasantly surprised to find out that it has been used as a supplementary methods text in many college courses to train both pre-service and in-service teachers who plan to teach kindergarten through third-grade children, as well as in graduate classes to train special education teachers. I have also learned that it has been a useful source book for sixth-grade children who are able to read this book on their own.

Ten years ago, I had intended that this book would be used by parents, and perhaps a few teachers. It has been my hope that more parents would begin to take a more active role in the education of their children. My own view is that science is intellectually stimulating and can be so much fun. It presents a wonderful opportunity to share your own knowledge of the world, to rediscover the world through the eyes of your child, to slow down from your own hectic pace, and to observe what your child observes.

Parents have a great opportunity to spend special "awareness-time" and "story-time" with their children. As a practical matter, the school and the child's teacher cannot provide children the same kind of science experiences that their own parents can. Often, in a school setting, children do not get that "special time" to be alone with their teacher in a one-to-one experience for longer periods of time.

Unfortunately, in most schools, because of the necessary push for literacy, science activities are neglected or fit in only at the end of the day. Although I love to do science with children, I am as guilty as other teachers are of not devoting more class time to science. Perhaps, if children come into our classrooms more enthused about science, teachers might make the time for more science activities.

As for literacy, as your children are learning to read, or even having difficulty, the experiences with science that you share together can surely enhance their interest in wanting to read "to find out more." Your children can easily make the connection that reading is of value because it allows them to become independent and to try out science experiences for themselves. Science activity books contain exhilarating activities and interesting information with which to play. Science observation skills can enhance auditory discrimination (which is important for repeating sounds with phonics), as well as perceptual discrimination skills (being able to distinguish letters and words).

Please remember that collecting exact measurement and data is for older children. Younger children should be encouraged to keep a journal of their science experiences. For younger children, the journal of their science experiences can be pictures that they draw of what they "did" or "found out," with a caption they dictate to their parent or teacher about their observation or their results. Such a journal of their observations is called recording. Scientists who are serious about their work always record what they do. It helps them to remember what happened, and what they attempted. If you copy down your children's exact words, later, the child will be able to review and read back their own captions. This will encourage the development of their reading skills. Older children who are more capable can do their own writing. Their journal entries can be written about:

- What they already think they know about a science concept.
- What they would like to find out.
- What they learned or found out from having done "some things."

Some of the reasons hands-on science activities are often omitted in schools include:

- It takes a good deal of teacher preparation time—let alone storage area—to gather materials for a class to have ongoing science experiences. A teacher might need to gather twelve of everything, so that children could work, say, in twelve pairs; in contrast, the parent only needs to gather one of everything.

- When children do science activities at school, they often become excited and loud, and sometimes they are difficult to bring back to order. When such chaos results, teachers feel uncomfortable, losing momentary control of their class. The more time it takes to settle children down, the more time is wasted from doing other important school activities. Parents need only to deal with the excitement elicited from one or two children.

- Science activities usually result in making a "mess." For a parent, cleaning up one mess is less time-consuming than cleaning up a mess created by twelve pairs of children.

- Often a complete science experience takes time. Observation of events or changes do not always occur rapidly; some take "awhile" to occur. It is easier for a parent and child to leave something on display for "awhile," to observe a change without worrying that the custodian or another child might shift or inadvertently move materials that were being observed. When a parent engages in science activities with their children, the parent has more space to store materials and more control over the environment.

- Sometimes teachers neglect science because they feel intimidated and uncertain about their knowledge of science, and they prefer to teach units of study with which they are more familiar. Teachers have lots of pressure on their time and, although their intentions are good, the time is not always available to them to read or study about specific areas they know they will need to learn more about. As a parent, you can afford the time to learn with your child and have an enjoyable time in your "second childhood" discovering what you missed the first time around. It's a great opportunity for you to experience what you missed.

I am a kindergarten teacher, not a scientist. I happen to enjoy doing science with children. As a student in high school, I did not have an extensive science background. My math skills were inadequate to continue taking "serious science" classes. I avoided science courses in college in that I was too concerned about a grade-point average. Looking back on my earlier years, it seems rather dim-witted to be more concerned about grades than with obtaining knowledge. Fortunately for me, I had an opportunity to take several graduate-level science classes in a noncompetitive setting through the National Science Foundation and to enjoy learning about all the wonders I missed the first time around.

Of course, we are never too old to learn. As we grow older, we realize that there are many things we do not know. If we stop learning, we stop growing. We are all living entities, and when living entities stop growing, they die. Eleanor Roosevelt, whom I have always greatly admired, is said to have written in her daily column: "Living is learning, and learning is living. When we stop learning, we stop living a vital life."

This book is a result of my having a chance to have a "second childhood" (in league with my own children), who are now quite grown up and in their twenties. This book is filled with happy memories; it is my journal of my own science experiences.

Enjoy your children while they are still young and while they "believe everything you say," but please let them make their own discoveries. Your knowledge will help guide them.

Happy "sciencing!"

About the icons

 Whenever you see this icon, it is meant to be a safety tip.

 This icon indicates that this information is meant as an additional piece of information. It is not necessarily meant for the children. Most of this information is too abstract and too complicated for young children to understand or comprehend. It is included to enhance parent or teacher background.

Other respected sources

Appraisal: Science Books for Young Children, Boston University, School of Education, Science Education Program, 605 Commonwealth Ave., Boston, Mass. 02215.

Brainard, Audrey. A bibliography of children's literature connections that she compiled.

Butzow, C.M. and Butzow, J.W. *Science through Children's Literature*. Englewood, CA: Teachers Ideas Press, 1989.

Cordel, Betty. A bibliography of children's science books that she compiled.

Harwayne, Shelly. *Lasting Impressions: Weaving Literature into the Writing Workshop*. Portsmouth, NH: Heinemann Educational, 1993.

Kramer, Pamela A. and Smith, Gail. Presentation entitled, Science and Literature: Linking and Loving Them. Eighth Annual STS Meeting/Technological Literacy Conference, Arlington, VA, Jan. 1993.

National Science Resource Center. *Science for Children: Resources for Teachers*. National Academy Press, Washington, D.C., 1988.

Paula, Nancy and Margery Martin. *Helping Your Child Learn Science*. Office of Educational Research and Improvement, U.S. Dept. of Ed.: Washington, D.C., September, 1992.

Science and Children, March issue, published annually by National Science Teachers Association (NSTA), lists outstanding trade books for children, NSTA, 1742 Connecticut Avenue, Washington, D.C. 20009.

Teachers' Clearinghouse for Science and Society Education Newsletter, edited by Irma Jarcho at 1 West 88th Street, New York, NY. 10024

The Korbin Letter, Concerning Children's Books about real people, places and things, 732 Greer Road, Palo Alto, California 94303.

The Science Book List for Children, published by the American Association for the Advancement of Science (AAAS), 1515 Massachusetts Ave., Washington, D.C. 20005

Acknowledgments

For this second edition, I wish to acknowledge the following people for their assistance and help in the preparation of this book.

I am greatly indebted to Ralph Brainard, Ph.D., for helping me better understand the nature of atoms, static electricity, weather, sugar crystals, and glaciers, and above all for taking his time to explain concepts to me and to clarify my thinking; I also thank him for editing and helping me to clarify my text so that it would be scientifically accurate; to Audrey Brainard for sharing her knowledge of "literature connections" to science activities and for her guidance and support, for regularly lending me so many great publications, and for the science activities and experiences she was so willing to share at her Hands-On-Science seminars, as well as her Literature-And-Science seminars; to Marco DiCapua, Ph.D. for assisting me to better understand the use of models; to Edward E. Jones, Ph.D., Miami University, Ohio for helping me define density more accurately, for his suggestions on ways to improve this book, and for offering me moral support and encouragement; to Dianne Q. Robinson, Ph.D., Director of the Interdisciplinary Science Center, Hampton University, for her guidance. I am also indebted to my special friend Estelle Feit, a terrific editor, for willingly volunteering to edit this second edition as well as the first one.

I am grateful to my special friends and colleagues from Virginia Beach Public Schools: Sarina Coffin, from Thoroughgood Elementary School, for her patience, suggestions, and words of encouragement; Judy Lewis, Ph.D., Principal, Trantwood Elementary School; Melanie Malbon, Julie Hallberg, Lynn Gibson, Kim La Ferriere, and Alice Walsh, from Linkhorn Park Elementary School, for their support as well as my supervisors at Linkhorn Park Elementary School: Carroll W. Monger (Principal), Julie Risney (Assistant Principal). I am also grateful for having many special friends who provided me with needed breaks: Julia and Harvey Pearce, Marie Biggers, Rose and Manny Meyer, Nat and Georgia Kramer, to Eileen Bengston, CESI President, for listening to me and helping me come to a decision about staying a kindergarten teacher, to Kay Kent, an AIMS workshop leader for taking her time during her workshop to answer my many questions, to Debbie Deyer, Ph.D. for her contagious energy, to Shalini Perumpral, Ph.D., (my son William's finance professor) from Radford University for sharing the first edition of *Teaching Children About Science* with her child's Montessori teacher, to educators across the country who reached out for me and gave me "warm-fuzzies," in particular: Beverly Perna, from Boston, Mass.; Julie Fudge Smith from Colombus, Ohio; Kathleen Greene, Ph.D., Director of Science Education, Beloit College, Beloit, Wisconsin; Terry Cook, Educational Director Montessori Elementary School of Blacksburg, VA; Sandi Schlichting, Educational Director of the Idea Factory, Riverview, Florida; Nancy Jones, Director of Resource Center, Wheelock College, Boston, Mass.; Harriet Eskridge, Lead Teacher, Faith Christian Academy, Cheraw, S.C.; and to Mary Kennan Herbert for helping connect me to Kim Tabor at TAB Books; to Kim Tabor for her patience with me, and for keeping this book "alive," to Andrea Sykora, an instructor at Electronic Systems in Virginia Beach and the support people at WordPerfect who answered so many of my questions about word processing procedures.

My greatest acknowledgment goes to my family for their love, understanding, and support. I am especially indebted to my daughter, Emily, who is currently in her junior year at James Madison University, for researching the bibliographies from the first edition to find out if the books listed were still in print (to my surprise most of them were not) and for assisting me with the preparation of this manuscript, and from whom I have learned so much over the years; to my son William, who graduated from Radford University this past year, and who has always been helpful at assisting me in organizing my thoughts; most of my thanks goes to my husband of thirty years, Hal, for giving me the space and time to work on this revision, for his insights, support, encouragement, understanding, and above all his ability in the last decade to cope with being neglected for long periods of time.

1

Introduction to science

How to use this book

At the beginning of each topic, you will find "Objectives," followed by "General Background Information for Parents and Teachers" about the science content and concepts.

The chapters are divided into several concepts for each science topic. The concepts are further broken down into numerous sequential activities. In the "Activities and Procedures" section of chapters 3–13, you will find numbered sequential activities. They progress from simple, concrete experiences to more complicated, abstract ideas. I suggest that this sequence be fol-

lowed. The activities have been arranged to progress from simple ideas to more complicated ones in a sequential order. Try to present the activities in order, even if you skip some.

Materials

Materials are listed at the beginning of each procedure.

Procedure

Each procedure in an activity begins with a bullet (•).

Questions

All suggested questions are italicized.

( )

Items inside of a parenthesis after a question or a suggested discussion indicate to adults a possible answer or a direction in which to lead children. These answers are provided more for your benefit, rather than for the children. Children should be encouraged to discover their own answers. They also need to know that there can be more than one answer.

Vocabulary

Suggested vocabulary to use with children is included in the suggested possible answers and in the explanations.

Fine points to discuss with children

These suggestions are introduced occasionally when it will enrich an activity. They are usually meant to be discussed with older or more sophisticated younger students who are better able or ready to think and analyze on a higher level.

Going further

These are suggestions for further investigations usually meant for older children. They are the ideas I have come across that I have found to be especially good or innovative, that would extend the activity.

Older children

By older children I mean children in the third grade and up. The activities in this book are intended for children between the ages of four and ten.

You will notice that I have acknowledged the sources of "unique" ideas that I have not found to be redundant in other source books. This book is really a "science sampler" and a synthesis or "anthology" of science activities from many sources that I have found useful in helping young children to better understand science ideas.

An important note to teachers and parents about using this book

As you read this book, you will notice that many of the procedures have long explanations. These explanations to children have been included more for your benefit than for the children's. They are provided in the event that a child asks a question that you might not be able to answer. But, primarily, the explanations are included so that you, as adults, will understand the content of a procedure.

It is wise, if the children are intellectually able, to have them reason on their own and not to "tell them everything." Allow the children to come up with their own explanations whenever possible. Have children do the experiments or do research in age-appropriate reference books such as those listed in the bibliographies at the end of each chapter. Many of the explanations are included so that you, as an adult, will know whether a child is on the right track or needs to be guided to use more reason and systematic logic to solve a problem.

With older children or those who are able intellectually, show them the materials and let the children devise ways to use them, rather than telling them how to use everything.

The content of science is a wonderful tool for helping children develop their reasoning and thinking skills. Reasoning is the fourth "R," along with reading, writing, and 'rithmetic. Help children develop themselves by allowing them the freedom to think problems out on their own and to test out their ideas.

To do many of the procedures in the book, you will need to assist many of the children, but remember not to over-assist.

Science journal

1-2 Science journal.

Do encourage all children to keep a science journal. A science journal is a personal log written by and about what each child is experiencing.

Younger children can draw pictures, and adults can take down the children's dictations. Keeping a journal will help children remember what they did. It will encourage children to take a closer look and to think more carefully about what they see.

Children should be encouraged to write or draw a picture of anything that catches their attention and that they personally find interesting. When they write in their science journals encourage them to ask themselves:

"What do I already think I know about this?"

"What do I think will happen?"

"What did I do?"

"What did I really see?"

"What really happened?"

"What else would I like to find out?"

For a mnemonic device for assisting a child to make a journal entry, see Table 1-1.

Table 1-1 Science journal entry

Encourage children to write or draw a TT-DD-K in their journal.
T– 1. What I THINK I know.
T– 2. What I THINK will happen.
D– 3. What I DID.
D– 4. What I DISCOVERED.
K– 5. What I now KNOW I know.

Answers

Please be aware that when you do activities with children and ask questions of children during an activity, there are no wrong answers. Every answer a child volunteers or that you yourself think of should be considered and investigated. Creativity should be encouraged.

Questions

All questions in this book that are meant to be asked of children are usually italicized. When you begin any new activity, it is usually good to review what knowledge your child(ren) already has by asking a few simple questions to recall previous information.

When you formulate your own questions during a science activity, try to ask questions that start with "How" or "Why." "How do you know" questions help children to focus and assist them to give a logical explanation of their observations and encourage them to see the need for taking or recording measurements, either formally with a measuring device or informally by sight, sound, touch, or smell. "Why" questions are more open-ended and lead to more creative answers, but not necessarily logical ones.

When you are almost finished with an activity that your child(ren) or you have especially enjoyed, encourage your child (ren) to go further by asking some questions that start with:

"What if ......?"

"What do you think might happen if we (change a part of the procedure [that was just done] or use different materials) [other than the ones suggested by the author]?"

Demonstrations

Some activities in this book need to be demonstrated by an adult. When an activity is demonstrated, it should be followed up by encouraging children to repeat the demonstrated procedure on their own. In general, more demonstrations might be needed for younger children than for older children. (Older children usually have better hand-eye coordination, more control of their larger body muscles, a longer attention span, and more logic from experience about how to go about accomplishing a task.) As you read the directions in this book, use your own good judgment as to the appropriate approach to use. Whatever approach you decide to use, do remember to encourage children to repeat their procedures several times to find out if their results are always the same or similar and to discuss their results and the differences that they might notice in their results.

How to teach science

Young children (and those who have not been exposed to science) should learn about science through a multitude of hands-on experiences with real physical objects or models* or real things. The objects, ideas, and concepts presented should be placed in a meaningful context, so that a need is created within the child to want to know more. If a question or

*Models are representations of real things and can be much smaller or much larger than the objects' real-life size. A more detailed description of what is meant by models is presented in chapter 2.

problem can be created, the experience becomes more relevant and significant to the child's life. The information learned from the experience is more likely to be remembered.

Many adults feel insecure about their knowledge of science and, therefore, are uncomfortable teaching content areas with which they feel a lack of familiarity. In reality, most adults understand much more than they give themselves credit for. The basic problem is that of not knowing how to organize the science knowledge they already possess.

Science is "everything" and "everywhere." Just zero in on what you already understand and know a little about, or choose something you are already interested in and want to know more about. As parents and early childhood educators, you have the freedom to choose what areas to study in science and what you want to expose your children to. You have the total world to choose from; the natural world, the physical world, the ancient world, and the universe. The study of most science subjects at the early stages is merely a matter of looking at the content in a methodological way and organizing the content into classes and subsets so that a meaningful context and relevance can be set up for the information.

Teaching by contrasts and similarities

The easiest way to help children understand or learn something new is to expose them to sharp contrasts, so that differences will be obvious. Then they can try to find the similarities between objects that are different. For example, if you are looking at mammals, you might ask if the cat and the horse look alike: How are they different? How are they alike? How are their bodies like our bodies? How are they different? What special features do horses have in their anatomy that help them run faster than we can? What does a cat have on its feet that helps it climb a tree faster than we can, if we can at all? How do cats and horses stay warm? When we run, what part of our body starts to perspire first?

Teaching with a topic and a sequential plan in mind

Avoid a flamboyant "magic-show" style, one that creates mystery and awe. For example: one day presenting magnets, the next day making a cloud appear in a glass,

and the next day taking a flower apart. It is difficult to connect these three experiences. Instead, a more formal plan should be implemented. For example, decide on a science unit you or the children would like to investigate, and then spend a week or two doing activities related to the topic being studied so that a relevant context for the experiences can be created and built upon.

Teaching systems for categorizing

Help children develop a system for categorizing and classifying, so that they will be able to break down a large area of study into its smaller parts. Then create an order out of the chaos by grouping, sorting, matching, and positioning materials.

Teaching to discriminate among details

Help children develop their ability to discriminate among details by looking for attributes held in common. Compare likenesses and differences of size, color, shape, texture, age, sound, smell, and if possible, taste.

Teaching by helping children think and make discoveries

Ask children a lot of questions, rather than giving them information. Try to make them find the answers and think. Allow children the opportunity to feel, manipulate, and discover on their own, and then encourage them to share their thoughts. As an adult, help children make predictions, and help them design experiments to test out their hypotheses. Allow yourself and the children to make mistakes; then try to analyze the mistakes together. Stress the importance of testing something several times before drawing conclusions.

Teaching by using logic

Science is logical. Categories and sets need to make sense. Things are included or excluded for reasons, and sometimes sets can overlap and form a union or intersection of two sets. For example, animals can be categorized by two sets: those with backbones and those without backbones. An intersection can occur, however, between the two sets that consists of all animals with jointed legs. Allow children to form a classification system thought out by themselves. Question the child's logic. Ask, "Why is this included and why is that not included?" Ask if there is another way of sorting the items. "Can you make more piles or fewer piles that would make sense?" There is no right or wrong way, as long as there is a logical reason for inclusion or exclusion. All categories are artificial and arbitrary.

Teaching abstract thinking skills by discussing familiar objects

Discuss things around you that can be observed for likenesses and differences. For example:

Are tables and chairs alike?

How are they alike?

How are they different?

Are the floor and the ceiling alike?

How are they alike?

How are they different?

Are people and flowers alike?

How are they alike?

How are they different?

Then progress to:

What is like a pencil?

What is like a ball?

Scientific behaviors

While doing science activities with children, try to keep in mind that there are scientific behaviors that you should attempt to make your child(ren) aware of and to encourage.

- Encourage your children to use their observation skills by using their five senses to observe properties and to notice inconsistencies, (what a scientist would call a "discrepant event," then see if the discrepant event can be repeated).

- Encourage further investigation by asking—"What would happen if?"—by changing a variable (see glossary).

- Encourage your children to always find and use safe available resources or materials to find out answers to questions they might think about after making an observation; discourage them from ever tasting anything unless they know it is absolutely harmless to themselves.

- Encourage the development of logical thinking by asking questions about possible outcomes, making predictions about what might happen, and by carefully observing what does happen.

- Encourage your children's ability to develop and make inferences about his/her observations and the results.

- After your children have had many repetitious experiences and observations with various materials, encourage your child(ren) to think up new situations to see if a generalization he/she is creating can be formulated about a "phenomenon" or event.

- Encourage the refinement and enrichment of your children's logic by discussing: what happened, what worked, what did not work, why or why not, creating new problems to solve and then doing further investigations to find out possible answers or solutions to the problems.

- Encourage your children to construct models to represent or simulate a phenomenon.

I hope that, eventually, when children are doing science activities they will become aware of the importance of creating and doing investigations that can be replicated and repeated by another person, so that a generalization can be formed about an event they have discovered.

The big conceptual pictures

While doing science activities with your children, try to put your experience into a conceptual context. There are nine big conceptual pictures that the The National Center for Improving Science Education has recommended. Most science experiences you do with your children can fit into the framework of one or more of these nine large concepts.

Organization

Encourage your children to classify by: color, size, shape, kind, similar properties. Can they find patterns in the objects they have classified?

Changes

Encourage your children to observe and talk about changes. Is there an observable or measurable change? Has the change occurred rapidly or slowly? Has there been an observable change in any of the objects' properties (color, size, shape, odor, texture) position, (movement/position). Any change is an "event." Events take time to occur. Time is measured from one change until the next. Have your child observe repeatable patterns, cycles in nature: water cycle, lunar cycle, seasonal cycle, day/night cycle, growth cycle of a seed into a plant.

Systems

Make your children aware of systems. A *system* is a whole that is composed of many parts. Usually a hierarchy of interdependence between many systems exists. The "parts" of a system can be systems in their own right. A system occurs when two or more objects or parts of a system or systems interact in some way with each other.

For example: A wolf has many systems operating inside of its body in order to function (skeletal, digestive, reproductive, nervous-sensory, etc.). The wolf is part of a larger system and is part of a food chain. A food chain is part of another system called a food web. The food web is part of an ecosystem, which is part of a biome system. All of the biome systems are part of a still larger system. A change of energy or a "breakdown" in one part of a system over a period of time will have an effect on other parts of the system.

Cause and effect

Encourage your children to test their inferences to see if there is a predictable pattern. Have them observe and record repeatable patterns; predict; experiment; and record. Do they notice that there is a repeatable experience? Can a prediction be made based on repeated experiences with similar results?

Models

Models represent something real. They can be exaggerated in scale-size to be larger than life, smaller than life, or exact replicas of objects in size. Models can be created for things we have never seen. Examples of real things of which we often make models are: the solar system, buildings, cars, and insects. Models can help us look closely at objects or systems that are too big, or too small, to see. They also allow us to create images of what we see by drawing pictures of our observation. All illustrations, diagrams, maps, and pictures are models that are representative of reality. Encourage your children to construct models of what they observe or do by drawing pictures or by creating a three-dimensional representation out of paper,

plasticine clay, construction toys, etc. (See chapter 2.)

Structure and function

All living things consist of many parts. These parts make up a system. Each part or structure in the system has a function. By observing skulls, we can observe the kind of teeth an animal had, and infer the kind of food it ate. By observing the placement of the eyes on the skull, we can infer whether the animal was a predator or prey. We can observe a bird's feet and infer its preferred habitat. Encourage your children to make inferences about the function of structures he/she (they) observe.

Variations

There are no living things that are exactly identical. Two leaves from the same tree might look identical, but a closer look at their vein pattern will show distinctions. The same is true of our fingerprints. There are many similarities, but there are also distinct and subtle differences. Even amoeba have different shapes. Identical twins are very different to the discerning eye. Their mothers and close acquaintances can easily tell them apart. Encourage your child to observe, verbalize, and record variations.

Diversity

The natural world is filled with diversity. The world consists of innumerable kinds of animals, plants, and objects. The diverse creatures, plants, germs, protista, monera, and nonliving objects interact with themselves and with each other due to changes in systems. Rocks wear away due to the force of water, wind, and weather. Seeds fall into cracks in boulders and the roots of new plants can either "cement" the boulder together or force the boulder apart, allowing water to enter, freeze, expand, and break the boulder apart. Most events do not occur in isolation. In a laboratory setting, diversity (variables) can usually be controlled if we are aware of all of the variables. There are usually so many variables that it is difficult to isolate and control all of them. Encourage your children to observe, verbalize and record the diversity in nature that surrounds us.

Scales and measurement

Measurements and scales are relative. For measurement or scale to have meaning, there needs to be a context for a comparison to be made. For example: How big is big? Is an elephant big? If an elephant is big, what would you call the size of a brontosaurus? Yet, the word you choose to describe the brontosaurus' size is meaningless in comparison to the size of the solar system, or to the universe. What does big mean? Absolutely nothing unless it is placed into a context. The same is true of our perception. Our perception of what we observe and choose to measure is relative to our position. For example, a room full of children might seem noisy to a teacher who is in the room. A bystander outside of the building, observing the same classroom looking in through a window, might not notice the noise level at all. Encourage your children to talk about objects in comparison to other objects when they describe a property. For example: It was as dark as; it was as small as; it was as shiny as. Making comparisons will enhance your children's vocabulary, and improve their observation skills.

How to organize a science unit

When introducing a new unit, it is necessary to establish a context for the unit. Children understand new ideas better if they can relate them to a context. It also helps them remember what they learn. There are three basic approaches to organizing a science unit:

Moving from the familiar to the less familiar

Children are familiar with their own bodies but are less familiar with the structure of other organisms. For example, if you decide to investigate trees, you might want to compare our human body to the tree's "body:" Both, humans and trees, are alive. Both, humans and trees, become taller and wider as they grow. We have feet; trees have roots. We have skeletons; trees have trunks. We need to eat food and cannot make our own food; trees are able to make their own food. We have veins and tubes going through our bodies; trees also have veins and tubes going through their "bodies." Veins and tubes carry liquids. Liquids can flow.

Or you could compare our bodies to an insect's body: We both have eyes, jointed legs, and are able to walk. Our skeleton is on the inside of our body; the insect has an exoskeleton on the outside of its body. We

are unable to fly unless we take an airplane ride. We have senses in our ears and noses that an insect has on its antennae.

Another choice might be to compare our human body processes to that of an exploding volcano. If we hold our breath, we, too, will need to let the air (which is a form of gas) out of our body. Like a volcano we cannot hold it in. Eventually, our body will force air out, just as a volcano must ventilate its accumulated gases.

Moving from the beginning of a process to a result with a tangent or two

Children are familiar with many things that are made from lumber, but they might not understand where the lumber comes from, or how something is constructed. For example, you might want to investigate how wooden boats are made by examining the building process in detail. Trace a boat's origin from forest to log to mill to factory. Then go on a tangent and investigate the properties of wood, metals, and rocks. Try hammering a nail into wood, metal, and rock. Which is the easiest to penetrate? Which weighs the least and is the easiest to carry?

Or, take another tangent. Try to design a wooden boat that will float. Experiment with different designs. Add a sail. Find out if the sail can catch wind. Find out what kind of sail design is most efficient.

Or, you might want to find out where paper comes from by tracing its origin. As with boats, you might examine other kinds of materials from which books could be made, and determine which material is easiest to find and lightest to carry. Also, which would be the easiest to inscribe or mark?

Arranging information in chronological order

Children are familiar with life as it is today. They take it for granted that life has always existed as it does now. It is revealing and fun for children to think about how life might have been during prehistoric times or to think about how electricity might have been discovered. It is possible to trace the steps in human knowledge that eventually led to the discovery of electricity. It was not until the 1900s that electric companies came into existence. There was a long series of events, and much experimentation took place before electricity was harnessed. Many of those experiments can be duplicated. Especially easy are the Oersted and Faraday experiments dealing with electromagnetism.

There are many possibilities and ways to cover topics. The important thing is to design a cognitive structure that makes all the pieces of new information stick together. Moving from the familiar to the less familiar, following a process and/or a chronological order establishes a direction, a focus, and a relevancy, so that a context can be provided.

Skills to be nurtured and developed through teaching science

- Observation skills. Learning to use our five senses.
- Learning to classify. Identifying, matching, sorting, naming, comparing, contrasting, grouping, and distinguishing likenesses and differences.
- Learning to measure. Arranging objects in sequence by: length (shortest to longest); weight (lightest to heaviest); volume (least to greatest); chronologically (beginning to end); numerically (in ordinal order).

- Learning to communicate. By identifying, matching, sorting, naming, comparing, contrasting, grouping, and distinguishing likenesses and differences by verbalizing descriptions, asking questions, relating observations, and using words accurately.
- Learning to make predictions. By developing skills of thinking systematically and logically about what might happen next, and beginning to think about planning ahead.

In summary, an easy acronym to remember when doing science with children is the word NOTICE. (See Table 1-2.)

Role of parent or teacher in exposing young children to beginning science experiences

We as adults can greatly influence children's interests. Most children have a vast untapped potential. It is our responsibility to tap that potential and to expose children's curiosity to new and stimulating topics and to help them organize their knowledge. Knowledge that is not categorized, sorted, and classified in some internal way is not helpful. The knowledge is out of reach. It is useless trivia, meaning-

Table 1-2 NOTICE

Adult's role: Begin a science activity by: finding out what a child already knows, helping the child name their observations and organizing what they know.

  N – Naming observations
  O – Organizing observations with adult assistance

Child's role with adult guidance:
  To do the play or "tic" part of notice.

Find out what makes something "tic"

  T – Take apart and analyze what you observe
  I – Investigate your (child's) questions
  C – Change something and observe it

Adult's role: E – Extend and Enrich a child's observations, to create Accelerated Learning and correct any misconceptions.

Guide child's observations and help child place the observations into a meaningful context.

less facts, and unconnected thoughts, like the information on a television game show. The ability to generalize is based on our past experiences and the significance those experiences hold for us. If we can convey our enthusiasm about the topics we are interested in to our children, then we can arouse their curiosity and interest in those areas of science to which we expose them. Children's interests are acquired. If they are stimulated and exposed to "something," they become curious about the "something" and acquire an interest in it. It is easier for children to build future cognitive bridges* with ideas and topics with which they are familiar.

Try to see the world through a child's eyes, but try to add structure and organization to observations that are made. Children are experts at observing, but they lack analytical skills.

Our job as early-childhood educators is not to give an intense course in science, but rather to open doors and plant seeds of knowledge that will grow and will continue to excite children about the wonders of their environment. We want to encourage them to delve and be curious, to ask questions, to experiment, to learn, and to integrate knowledge from their own experiences.

* Cognitive bridge: When two seemingly unrelated ideas fit together to form a broader concept. For example: A young child learns the names of the basic colors. Later the child learns that by mixing and combining two colors, he/she will form a new color with a new name. A cognitive bridge is built. The idea forms that materials can be mixed and combined to form new colors and/or new substances.

Selected professional science resource books for parents and teachers (Dewey Decimal Number, 372.3)

**Abrucato, Joseph. *Teaching Children About Science*, 2nd ed. Englewood Cliffs, NJ: Prentice-Hall, 1988.

**Blough, Glenn, and Julius Schwartz. *Elementary School Science and How to Teach It*, 8th edition. New York: Harcourt, Brace, Jonovich, 1990.

**Carin, Arthur A. *Teaching Science Through Discovery*. New York: Macmillan, 1993.

*Claitt, Mary Jo Puckett and Shaw Jean M. *Helping Children Explore Science: A Source Book for Teachers of Young Children*. New York: Macmillan, 1992.

**Esler, William and Mary. *Teaching Elementary Science*, 5th ed. Bellmont, CA: Wadsworth, 1989.

**Gega, Peter C. *Science in Elementary Education*, 6th ed. New York: Macmillan, 1990.

*Harlan, Jean. *Science Experiences for the Early Childhood Years*. NY: Macmillan, 1992.

**Lorbeer, George C. and Nelson, Leslie W. *Science Activities for Children*, 9th ed. Dubuque, IA: Wm. C. Brown, 1992.

*Taylor, Barbara J. *Science Everywhere: Opportunities for Very Young Children*. New York: HBJ, 1993.

**Victor, Edward. *Science for the Elementary School*, 7th ed. New York: Macmillan, 1993.

**Zeitler, William R. and Barufaldi, James P. *Elementary School Science: A Perspective for Teachers*. New York: Longman, 1988.

Selected further resources

Hauser, Bernice. "Educating Parents About Educating Children," Teachers' Clearing House for Science and Society Education Newsletter, Vol. XII, No.2., Spring 1993.

*Kamii, C. and DeVries, R. *Physical Knowledge in Preschool Education: Implications of Piaget's Theory*. Englewood Cliffs, NJ: Prentice-Hall, 1978.

*McIntyre, M. *Early Childhood and Science: A Collection of Articles*. Washington, D.C.: National Science Teachers Association, 1984.

* Denotes adult resource books for younger children.
** Denotes that these books can be ordered from Science Supply Catalogue Companies, or your local book store. (College and university book stores often stock a few of them depending on which text is a required book for their science methods courses.)

*Pade, Alyson. *Science at the Sensory Table*. Early Education Materials, Denver, CO, 1991.

*Paula, Nancy and Margery Martin. *Helping Your Child Learn Science*. Office of Educational Research and Improvement, U.S. Dept. of Ed.: Washington, D.C. September, 1992. (A short, helpful guide for parents. Filled with great ideas.)

Petroski, Henry. *The Evolution of Useful Things: How Everyday Artifacts—from Forks and Pins to Paper Clips and Zippers—Came to Be as They Are*. N.Y.: Knopf, 1992.

Rowe, Mary Budd. *Teaching Science as Continuous Inquiry: A Basic, 2nd ed*. New York: McGraw-Hill, 1978.

Rowe, Mary Budd. "Wait-Time: Slowing Down May Be a Way of Speeding Up," *American Educator*, Vol.11, No.1, pp. 38–47, Spring, 1987.

The National Center for Improving Science Education. *Getting Started in Science: A Blueprint for Elementary School Science Education*. The NETWORK, Inc. Andover, Mass., and Washington, D.C.; and Biological Sciences Curriculum Study, Colorado Springs, Colorado. 1989.

UNESCO Source Book for Science Teaching. New York: UNESCO, 1976. (This book is a classic. It suggests inexpensive easy to find materials. It has been used in third world countries where materials are hard to come by.)

Weber, Robert J. Forks, Phonographs and Hot Air Ballons—A Field Guide to Inventive Thinking. N.Y.: Oxford University Press, 1993.

*Wilkes, Angela. *My First Nature Book*. New York: Knopf, 1990. (Contains beautiful, life-size drawings and activities appropriate for pre-schoolers as well as older children.)

*Williams, Robert A., Rockwell, Robert E., and Sherwood, Elizabeth A. *Mudpies to Magnets*. Mt. Rainer, MD: Gryphon House, 1987. (Contains activities that do not require special equipment.)

Young, Ed. *Seven Blind Mice*. New York: Scholastic Books, 1993. A beautifully illustrated children's book about the importance of seeing the whole before making conclusions about the parts. Seven blind mice observe different parts of an elephant, and each mouse comes to a different conclusion about what the elephant is.

2
Models

Objectives

The objectives of this chapter are for children to develop an awareness of the following:

- What models are.
- How and why models are used.
- What the words "science" and "observe" mean.
- That some events continually reoccur in cyclical patterns in nature.
- That living things have many parts to them, and each "part" is important to the "whole."
- That a "whole" that has more than one part is called a system.
- That objects and models can be arranged in an orderly way.

- That objects and models can be sorted or classified into groups.

General background information for parents and teachers

Models are representations of real things. They can be much smaller or much larger than the object's real-life size. Scientists and engineers build models or replicas of large and small objects to see if the objects or "things" are constructed well. They test, study, and observe working models close up. Many children's art projects are models they have constructed of real things in their world. Most toys are models of real things. Toy cars, trucks, houses, dolls, etc., are miniature models that represent reality. Many toys are models of the real things that children might not be allowed to touch and manipulate. For example, a child can "drive" a play truck, or play "parent" to a doll, "cook" dinner for the dollhouse people, or "mow" the lawn with a model of a lawn mower.

The wonderful part about introducing and using the word "model" with children is that it helps train them to think abstractly. They can learn to picture something in their minds that they are familiar with without having to touch it. When children do have a model to look at and to touch, they can study and observe the model to compare it to reality. How is the model like the real thing? How is it different? For example:

Does a real fire truck have only two doors and six windows like the toy model? (It depends on the model design of the real fire truck we are comparing it to.)

Does a real frog have four front toes as the rubber model shows? (Yes.)

How is the frog's body different from our bodies?

How is the frog's body like ours?

What body parts do frogs and people have on their heads?

Do frogs have ears? Where?

How can you find out?

Do the little wooden people found inside of commercial toys look like real people? What part of them is missing? (All of their joints are missing, including their arms, legs, fingers, and toes.)

Why are joints important?

Do all animals have joints?

Some models are much larger than reality, like rubber spiders and rubber insects. Their large size allows us to examine and observe things we might not have discovered if the creatures were moving or were too small to see. Some models are built in exact proportion to their real-life size, like silk flowers. A silk flower is a model representing reality. Usually it contains the stamen, pistil, calyx, stem, and leaves along with the flower petals to make it look real. Pictures are also models. A picture of a flower or a house can be seen as a model of the flower or the house. The picture helps us visualize what something looks like when we cannot touch it. Likewise, a cross-section diagram is a model of reality. It is a model representing a splitting open of a surface. It allows us to use our imaginations, and gives us the ability to think abstractly. We can look at a model and imagine that it has been cut open. A globe is also a model. A map is a flat representation or "model" of a globe (or part of a globe). Maps are models of models. They are flat representations of a curved surface.

A good reason to encourage children to use or construct models is that, as children grow older, their ability to construct abstract models will allow them to use their imaginations to visualize or to create tangible models of theories or systems that no one has ever thought of or seen before.

The television program Star Trek is based on a fantasy model of our world and the universe as it could exist in the distant future. The world of the starship U.S.S. Enterprise is a model. The stage-set represents a model of that fantasy. Does Star Trek exist in reality? No, but perhaps it could exist. It is a world that exists in the imagination of Star Trek fans and of the writer who has created it.

If children can be trained to visualize or think abstractly about a model of a theory, it will be easier for them to solve problems by finding up solutions or developing theories to test.

Albert Einstein visualized an imaginary model of a person riding on a light beam, and that image or mental model helped him to develop the General Theory of Relativity.[1]

When children are encouraged to predict (hypothesize or guess) what will happen if a variable is changed, they are actually generating a model based on a set of assumptions. It is through experimenting or testing their thoughts (models) that they are able to refine their thinking and their model to fit the features of the known data collected from their observations and to reach a conclusion or generalization.

As new information is gathered, models are altered and refined to be compatible with the more current information. The theory of what the model of an atom would look like has been modified many times since "scientists" first began to discuss it in ancient Greece.

Likewise, the model of the solar system has also changed periodically. In ancient days "scientists" believed the earth was the center of the universe and that the

---

[1] Please note: Atomic physics is beyond the scope of this book. However, if children become aware that their observations are based on their own relative position, perhaps, when they are older it might be easier for them to comprehend the relativity theory. What is observed depends on the observer's relative position to what is being seen. Terms such as: slow/fast; above/below; east/west are relative to the position of the observer in relation to what is being observed. Observations are meaningless without a frame of reference.

earth was flat. As "new" information was gathered or discovered over the centuries, the model did not account for that data, so the model was modified until it was able to represent the features of the known data. In the future, as more discoveries are made, the model will continue to evolve.

As models evolve, they change to include new features to explain data. Models are valuable tools because they give us the freedom to think abstractly, and to use our imagination to construct mental images. In the most general sense, practically anything that is not "real"* but a representation of something real can be called a model.

Note: As you do these activities with your children, do try to encourage them to keep a science journal of their observations and their thoughts.

Definitions of frequently used terms

Concept

A *concept* is a general idea or understanding, derived from specific instances or occurrences. It is important to try to establish the concept of what "model" means. It is a goal to be worked on all year. When children understand the concept of what a model is, they are free to develop their abstract thinking skills and to use their minds more effectively. They will not be constricted by needing concrete materials in order to think.

The concept of a model is a way of thinking about something. It allows children and adults to paint in their minds pictures of real things when the real things or objects are not available to touch.

Models in play

When children use their imaginations in playing house, building with blocks, and constructing in sand, they are creating models of things they are thinking about. Art activities and play activities are chances for young children to role-play, act out, build or construct, "pretend" play, and manipulate reality. They provide an

*"Real" in this sense means an object or thing that is tangible and three-dimensional, something that we are able to touch physically as a whole that is not a representation or model of "something" else.

opportunity to discover a problem or create a challenge and to try to solve the problem or meet the challenge.

Science

Science is the art of studying. It is also the study of observation, identification, description, experimental investigation, and theoretical explanation of those (observable) events. It is a methodological activity that attempts to answer and discover "why, when, and how" observable natural and physical events occur as they do.

The five senses

Seeing, hearing, smelling, tasting, and feeling. All five senses are located in our faces. Our senses help us make observations. (See chapter 3 for activities that develop an awareness of our five senses.)

Cycle

A phenomenon or event that repeats itself predictably.

Classification

The systematic grouping of objects or organisms into categories based on shared characteristics or traits.

Attribute

A quality or characteristic belonging to an object or thing. It is a distinctive feature that results in an object or thing belonging to a set or group.

Sort

Grouping similar objects together. Ordering objects according to some characteristic such as: size, weight, or alphanumeric designation.

Group

The assembling of objects or things into a set.

The short lessons that follow represent a "model" of how to present a science idea or concept to young children. Each mini-lesson takes about five or ten minutes to present. The model lessons include the kinds of questions you might want to ask, the kinds of comparisons you might want to make to induce a child to want to inquire further on his/her own, and the kinds of explanations you might give to children about a particular topic.

The model lessons have been included in this chapter on models to set the tone and to be a "model" or an example of how to present ideas. The model lessons do not need to be followed. However, the tone of "acceptance" the lessons try to demonstrate does need to be followed. Please feel free to develop your own style. Do remember to have a direction or a focus. Your focus or direction could simply be to develop observation skills, to heighten awareness and curiosity, and to help children develop an inquiring attitude.

The experiences and information gained by the children from individual science units and from the activities described in the chapters are important. However, they are not nearly as important as nurturing children to develop a desire and a need to know more about natural and physical phenomena, so that they will develop a positive attitude toward inquiry.

Eight model lessons

Lesson one: What is science?

Science is the art of studying. It includes everything around us: living, nonliving, and not living now.

Objective

For children to become aware of what the words "science" and "observe" mean.

Materials needed

The word "science."

Procedure

1 Hold up the word "science."

Does anyone know what this word says? (It says science.)

Does anyone know what the word "science" means?

2 *Explain*: The word science means the art of studying. It is a way of looking at everything around us that is living,

nonliving, and not living now. It is also the study of how things work and why things happen.

Are dinosaurs alive today? (No.)

How do we know they existed?

3 *Explain*: Scientists study and observe everything. They study and observe things that were never alive, like rocks and sound. They study and observe things that are alive, like plants and animals. And they study and observe things that are no longer living, like dinosaurs and other things that have died. Scientists also study subjects such as: why shadows are formed, how to make jobs feel easier, and why volcanoes erupt. Scientists try to answer why, how, and when things happen. The first thing a scientist does is observe.

What does observe mean? (To study carefully.)

What parts of our body do we use when we observe? (Our eyes help us see. Our ears help us hear. Our nose helps us smell. Our skin helps us feel. Our tongue helps us taste.)

4 *Explain*: We use our senses—eyes, ears, nose, skin, and tongue—to find out about things. Our senses help us observe. Sometimes we need to use all of our senses.

Conclusion

(See chapter 3, "The five senses," for activities and ideas on what to do with the children to make them aware of their five senses.)

Vocabulary

Science, living, alive, nonliving, once living, observe.

Evaluation

After this discussion, see if a child can name or point to something that is alive or was once alive and then to something that was never alive. Also, see if the children can point to a part of their body that helps them observe and to explain how that part enables them to observe: Eyes—see, ears—hear, nose—smells, etc.

Note: In most cases, italic type indicates questions to ask children. Material in parentheses indicates a possible answer.

2-2 *What is science? Science is everything around us (living, nonliving, and extinct).*

Lesson two: Identifying natural and human-made objects

Objective

For children to develop an awareness that all materials and things can be classified.

Materials needed

Assorted natural objects, such as: seeds, leaves, flowers, rocks, soil, bark, feathers, and chicken bones; Assorted human-made objects, such as: nails, bottle caps, paper, pencil, scissors, paper clips, and rubber bands.

Procedure 1

1 Place all of the objects in a container and then spill the objects out onto the floor.

2 Ask the children to find objects that grow on plants or can be found in the soil, and to place all of these objects in a pile.

What kinds of things are not in the pile?

3 *Explain:* All of the objects in the pile are called natural things. The materials not in the pile are things people have made with the help of machines.

Procedure 2

1 Ask the following questions:

Can you name something that is living? (We are living.)

What is something that we can find on the ground outside that is not alive and never has been? (A rock.)

Note: If children say "picnic table" or "chair" and the picnic table or chair are made out of wood, then ask them to explain from where the wood for the picnic table and the chair came. (From a tree.)

2 *Explain:* Even though the picnic table and the chair are not alive now, the materials they are made from were once alive. They have been made into a table and chair by people and machines. They are made by humans. Tables and chairs are often made from natural materials but would not be found in nature unless people made them.

3 Ask children to name on their own some things that are made by people and some other things that are natural or found in nature.

Conclusion

Take a nature walk with the children so they can collect natural and human-made objects. After the nature walk, ask the children to observe their collection and sort it into two piles: human-made and natural. Most human-made things that are found on a nature walk are called litter: bottle caps, paper, empty containers, nails, wire, etc.

Vocabulary

Nature, natural, human-made, machine-made, pile, litter, sort.

Evaluation

Ask children to sort all of the objects found in nature into three piles: See if children can separate the pile of natural objects into:

• Things that are still alive now.

• Things that are not alive now.

• Things that were never alive.

Lesson three: Awareness of cycles

Objective

For children to develop an awareness that some events continually reoccur in cyclical patterns in nature.

Materials needed

Fresh flowers, dead flowers, full seedpods, one paper plate labeled "seeds," one paper plate labeled "petals."

Procedure

1 Bring fresh flowers to class. (Marigolds are easy to study. They grow in abundance.)

Are these flowers alive now? (The children will probably say: "No, they have been picked and they can no longer grow.")

2 Hold up some dead flowers.

3 *Explain:* Even when flowers stay on a plant, they eventually die. They do not stay alive forever. If the flowers are not picked, they might look pretty longer, but eventually the flowers will die.

Are these dead flowers really dead? (The children will probably say, "Yes.")

4 *Explain:* The flower has died, but it has produced seeds that are very much alive. The seeds can create whole new plants that will flower again. The new flowers from the new plants will create seeds all over again for new plants.

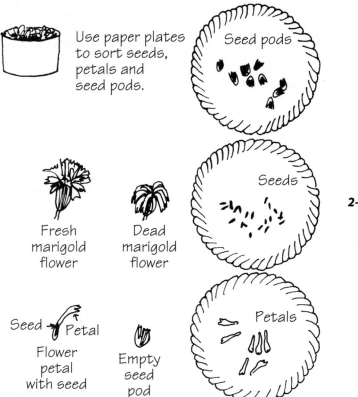

Use paper plates to sort seeds, petals and seed pods.

Seed pods

Seeds

Petals

Fresh marigold flower

Dead marigold flower

Seed — Petal
Flower petal with seed

Empty seed pod

2-3 *Finding seeds in flowers.*

Why do plants grow flowers? (To make seeds.)

Where do we look to find the seeds on a marigold flower? (In the seed pod at the bottom of the petals.)

5 Have each child open up a seed pod.

6 Pass out a petal with a seed attached to it to each child.

7 Ask children to find a similar petal with a seed attached from their opened seed pod.

8 *Explain:* The petal is the yellow part. The seed is the black part. Hold the petal with one hand and the seed with your other hand and pull.

What happens? (The petal separates from the seed.)

9 Set up two paper plates—one labeled "seeds" and one labeled "petals."

10 Ask the children to drop some of their seeds into the "seed" plate.

11 Ask them to drop some petals into the "petal" plate.

12 Have children check the placement and correct the placement of any misplaced seeds or petals.

Are the seeds alive now? (Yes.)

Are the petals alive now? (No.)

13 *Explain:* The plant grows flowers to make seeds so it can flower again next year. The seeds grow into new plants with flowers. When events or things occur or happen in a pattern over and over again, it is called a *cycle*. A cycle is like a bicycle wheel: it goes around and around and has no beginning or end.

Do all of the flower seeds become plants? (No.)

Why not? And what happens to them? (Some seeds are eaten by small insects and birds, and some decay. Many animals eat plant seeds for food.)

What kinds of seeds do you eat?

Note: The topic of seeds can be expanded. Various edible nuts and seeds can be tasted: peanuts, almonds, sesame seeds, poppy seeds, caraway seeds, sunflower seeds, etc. The diets of animals like squirrels and other small rodents can be discussed to see the relationship and interdependence that exists between plants and animals for food, and seed dispersal of plants by animals. (See chapter 12 for activities to do with seeds.)

Conclusion

Ask children to explain what is inside a dead flower. Show them another kind of dead flower like a dandelion or a zinnia. (Ask them if they find a seed and separate it from the petal). *Note:* Different species of plants vary in the length of time that it takes to produce seeds from flowers.

Vocabulary

Alive, dead, plant, seed(s), flowers, marigold, seed pod, petal, cycle.

Evaluation

Find out if children can think of other reoccurring cycles, (day/night, seasons, days of the week). Have children find other dead flowers in their yards or at school and open them up to look for the seeds.

Lesson four: The marigold plant

Objective

For children to develop an awareness that living things have many parts to them and that each "part" is important to the "whole."

Materials needed

Marigolds with leaves, buds, flowers, and stems; Styrofoam tray labeled for flower parts (see Fig. 2-4).

Procedure

1 Give each child or group of children a flower stalk with leaves and buds and a Styrofoam tray (labeled with plant parts).

2 Examine the parts of a marigold plant (or other kind of plant).

Does it have leaves? (Yes.)

Who can show me a leaf? (Have child show and then tear a leaf off for the Styrofoam tray. Point to the stem. Break one off and add it to the labeled Styrofoam tray.)

Does anyone know what this long part underneath the flower is called? (Stem.)

3 Point to a bud. Break off and add to tray.

4 *Explain:* This is a baby flower that has not opened yet. It is called a bud. When it blossoms, it will be a flower.

5 Point to a smaller bud without a stem.

6 *Explain:* This bud is so small it is hard to see.

Which of these buds do you think will open first? (The larger one on the longer stem.)

Why? (The larger bud has a longer stem and the petals look larger.)

What part of the plant is missing from this plant? (The roots.)

Why is that part important to the plant?

7 *Explain:* The roots grow under the ground. If the plant had roots, and the roots were in the ground, it would still be growing.

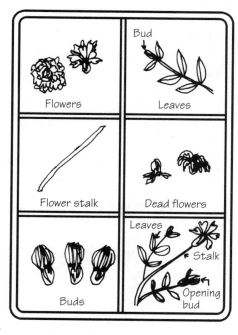 

2-4 *Dissecting a flower.*

Styrofoam lunch tray or cookie sheet

8 Finish adding appropriate parts of the marigold plant to the labeled Styrofoam tray. Discuss how each part of the plant is important to it.

9 Try to elicit from the children what they think the various parts of the plant do and why each part is important to the working system of the plant. Ask questions to find out what they know.

10 *Explain:* The leaves help make food for the plant, the stem helps the plant stand tall, the bud helps protect the baby flower until it is ready to bloom, the dried-out old flower contains a seed pod that holds new seeds to make new plants and food for animals. The roots help anchor the plant and help the plant get water.

Conclusion

Display several small potted flowering plants or take a walk outside to locate flowering plants. Have children name and point to: the stem, buds, leaves, and flower of the plant they look at.

Vocabulary

Marigold plant, bud(s), stem(s), flower parts, leaf, large, small, dried, roots.

Evaluation

If children are young and not very verbal, see if they can point to the parts of the plant as you name them. If the children are older and have better verbal ability, see if they can name the parts of the plant as you point to them, and/or see if they can find a very tiny bud hidden in the leaves.

Lesson five: Bubbles

2-5 Bubble making.

Objectives

For children to develop an awareness of how they can control the size of a bubble.

Materials

For indoor bubble making (for each child or group of children): a small container to contain the soapy solution (see recipe), Styrofoam cups, drinking straws, brownie baking pan, table, and goggles.

For outside bubble making (for each child or group of children): empty berry baskets, strainers, empty frozen juice cans made of cardboard with top and bottom removed, hose washers, plastic 6-pack holders, string, some sponges for easier clean up, goggles.

Table 2-1
Recipe for making a soapy solution

1 You will need: *Joy or *Dawn liquid detergent, water, a clean empty bucket, a measuring cup.

2 Mix one cup of liquid detergent with 8 cups of cold water.

3 Optional, add three tablespoons of glycerine. (Glycerine can be purchased at a local pharmacy. Glycerine makes bubbles last longer, so that they will not evaporate as quickly.)

4 Stir up the solution, but not too much. Avoid creating a froth on top. If one develops, skim it off the top.

5 For best results, make the bubble solution the night before you plan to use it to allow the ingredients to stabilize.

Note: Bubbles will last longer on humid days.

* John Cassidy, author of *The Unbelievable Bubble Book* has stated in his book that for the purpose of bubble making, these two brands do seem to work better than the less expensive brands.

Procedure

1 Show children the goggles. Discuss why they will need to be wearing them.

2 *Explain:* Sometimes people need to protect parts of their body from possible harm. You might want to discuss other items that people wear for safety: safety belts in cars, hard hats, fireman's protective garb, chin guards, teeth guards, etc.

Have children put on their goggles. Be sure all children that are investigating bubbles are wearing goggles. When large bubbles burst, particles of the bubbles often hit the eye, which causes a burning sensation and is extremely uncomfortable to little children. It frightens them when their eyes feel like they are burning.

3 Tell children to scoop up some bubble solution into their cup and to use their drinking straw to blow into the bubble mixture.

 Bubble solution is poisonous. Warn the children not to suck up the solution, but to blow out. The solution will taste pretty awful if it gets into their mouth. However, if they do not swallow the solution, it will not harm them.

4 Discuss what happens. See who can blow the biggest mound of bubbles.

What happens to the bubbles when they pile up high? (They pour over the side of the cup onto the table.)

What color is your bubble? (Clear with a swirling rainbow.)

5 Instruct children to pierce a Styrofoam cup with a pencil to make a hole. Then stick a drinking straw into the cup to create a bubble pipe. Dip the pipe into the solution so that the rim of the cup has a film over it. Gently blow through the straw. Observe how much larger a bubble can be made.

6 Pour some soapy solution into a baking pan. Dip some of the listed indoor materials into the solution one at a time. Have children experience the different materials by blowing through them.

What is inside a bubble? (Air.)

What happens when you blow through these materials? (You stretch the soapy solution and fill the solution with air to create a bubble.)

Why do the bubbles burst? (The soapy film dries out or evaporates.)

How can you pet or touch a bubble so it will not pop? (Wet your hand in the bubble solution before you touch the bubble.)

Can you blow a bubble inside of a bubble? (Pierce a bubble with a drinking straw and blow inside the bubble.)

Can you make a small bubble bigger?

Can you blow a bubble through your hands or between your closed index finger and thumb?

What are other things you can use to blow bubbles?

What does a bubble blowing device need to have? (A hole to blow through, or for wind to blow through.)

Conclusion

How can you make gigantic bubbles? Listen to their suggestions. Go outside to try out their ideas. If they do not suggest using two straws and a string to create a bubble frame, then show them how to create a collapsible bubble blowing frame and demonstrate it for them outside. (Zubrowski, 1979.)

Vocabulary

Bubble, solution, air, wind, evaporate, poisonous, film, air stream, collapsible frame.

Evaluation

Ask children to explain to you the kind of devices they need to use to create large or small bubbles.

How is the size of a bubble controlled? (By a steady stream of air.)

Lesson six: What are models?

Objective

For children to develop an awareness of models.

Materials needed

Rubber frog, toy model car or truck, picture of a flower, real flower, silk flower.

Procedure

1 *Explain:* Sometimes scientists use models to look at or study things. Sometimes real objects are too big to bring to class, or too small to see. So big things are sometimes made to look small and sometimes small things are made to look big.

2 Display a model toy car or truck, rubber frog, and a picture of a flower.

3 Hold up the toy truck.

Is this a real truck that we could ride in? (No.)

4 *Explain:* This is a model of a nonliving thing. We can count the windows, the tires, and the doors.

Do real trucks have four windows too? (It depends on the truck, since trucks vary.)

5 *Explain:* Some models are built exactly like the real thing. Some models are not very real looking.

6 Hold up the rubber frog.

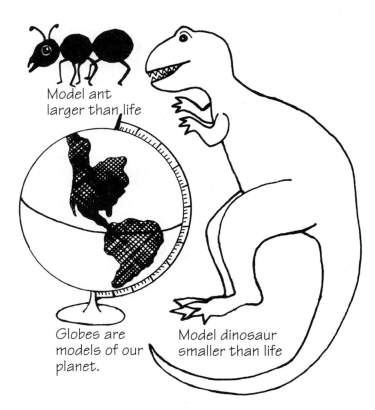

Model ant
larger than life

Globes are
models of our
planet.

Model dinosaur
smaller than life

2-6 *Models can be larger or smaller than life size.*

Is this frog real? (Yes, it is a real* model of a frog.)

Is this frog alive? (No, it is the model of something that is alive.)

7 *Explain:* The rubber frog is a model of a living thing.

8 Hold up a picture of a flower.

Is this flower real? (Yes, it is real, but it is a picture of a flower.)

9 *Explain:* The picture is real. The flower in the picture is a model. The picture is a model of a real living thing.

Conclusion

Have children draw a model of their favorite toy, their room, their house, their car, their family. Ask children to explain why we can't have a real dinosaur visit our classroom or house and how a model helps us to understand better what a dinosaur might have looked like.

Vocabulary

Model(s), exactly, compare, different, alike, real.

Evaluation

Find out if children can point to a picture or a model of "something" and then name what "it" is a model of. Have children ex-

* Real in this context means not make-believe—something tangible that we can touch and see.

plain whether the model is: the exact size, smaller or bigger than the "real" thing? Find out if the children can find something that is not a model but is "real," like a pair of scissors or a crayon.

Lesson seven: Sorting objects into sets

Objectives

For children to become aware:

• Of how objects can be arranged in an orderly way.

• Of what it means to sort or classify objects and models into groups by a common attribute or property.

Materials needed

About 15 assorted buttons, about 5 pencils of different lengths, some coins, 4 models of people, 4 models of cars, 6 fat crayons in assorted colors and lengths, 6 rocks and pebbles, 6 thin crayons in colors that match the fat crayons.

Procedure

1 Give each child or group of children a small box with assorted materials.

2 Ask them to spill out the assorted materials onto the floor.

3 *Explain* to the children that there are sets of things in the big, messy pile, but it is hard to make sense of what is in

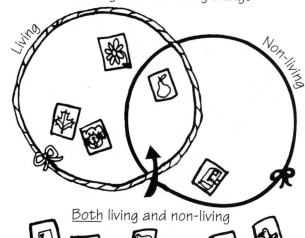

Use yarn circles to make sets and
intersecting sets with picture cards
of living and non-living things

2-7 *Sorting picture cards.*

the pile because everything is mixed together.

4 Ask the children if they can find groups of "things" in the big pile that look alike and to name those "things." (Pencils, buttons, crayons, coins, toy cars, toy people, rocks, etc.)

5 Ask the children to make a pile or sort each group of "things" they find. (There will be a set of pencils, a set of crayons, a set of rocks, etc.)

How many ways can a set be organized? (Sets can be organized many different ways, as long as the objects in the set have at least one attribute or property in common.)

6 After the big messy pile is sorted into several sets of "things" that look alike, ask the children if they can think of ways to arrange each set in an orderly way so that each set can be observed more closely. For example, pencils can be arranged from largest to shortest. Fat crayons can be color-matched to thin crayons. Toy cars can be lined up so that all the headlights are facing in the same direction and so they all have their wheels on the floor. The pebbles can be separated from the rocks, etc.

7 Discuss with children how sorting and order help us observe and find "things" more easily. Ask them to think about how food is organized into an order at the grocery store, books in a library, furniture in a house, clothes in dresser drawers.

8 Discuss the human-made order of material things in general and why order is helpful for finding "things" quickly.

Conclusion

Have the children sort a deck of playing cards into groups and subgroups. For example: reds and blacks, pictures and numbers, or matching sets of numbers or pictures into sets of four or into suits.

Vocabulary

Order, mess, arrange, separate, alike, different, match, "line-up," longest, shortest, rough, smooth, organize, sort, group, set.

Evaluation

Find out if children can arrange a messy pile of assorted "things" into several sets of objects that have something in common. If not, ask them if they see a way that the sets of objects can be arranged in an order:

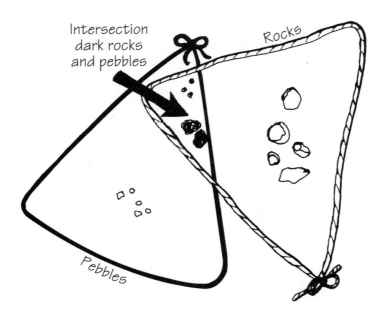

Intersection
dark rocks
and pebbles

Rocks

Pebbles

2-8 Sets of rocks and pebbles.

by size, color, texture, and/or the same directional orientation.

Lesson eight: Creating sets and intersecting sets

Objective

For children to develop an awareness that objects can be classified and grouped.

A. Sets of rocks and pebbles

Objective

For each child or group of children: rocks, pebbles, yarn circles.

Procedure

1 *Explain:* We can place things that are alike into a group. When we put things together into groups that are alike. We can observe them more closely and look for things that make the things that look alike look different from each other.

2 Have children look at their rocks and pebbles.

Do all of these rocks look alike? (No.)

How are they different? (Some are round and smooth, some are rough and sharp, some are very small, some are darker than others.)

Are they all rocks? (Yes.)

Which ones can be called pebbles? (The round smooth ones.)

Are all the pebbles rocks? (Yes.)

Are all rocks pebbles? (No.)

Why not? Elicit from children what the differences are between rocks and pebbles.

3 *Explain:* Pebbles are a special kind of rock. They are rocks that have been worn down by water or by rubbing to become smooth. Let's see if we can sort the pebbles from the rocks. We can place all of the pebbles into this yarn circle. We can place all of the rocks that are not pebbles into this other yarn circle.

Is there anything about the rocks and pebbles that makes them look alike? (Some of the rocks and some of the pebbles are dark.)

Can we form an intersection to put all of the darker-colored rocks and pebbles together? (Yes.)

Are all of the darker rocks the same color? (Probably not. Some might be tinted yellow or brown or red; some might be striped or spotted. If you look closely enough, you will be able to see differences.)

4 Ask the children to suggest other ways to sort the rocks into groups or sets. (Possible ways: large from small, broken from whole, speckled and striped from solids.)

Conclusion

Find out if children can group the rocks and pebbles and then have other children in your class guess how the rocks and pebbles were grouped.

Vocabulary

Rock, pebble, smooth, rough, round, sharp, light(er), dark(er), worn, striped, spotted, alike, different, broken, whole, group(s), attribute.

Evaluation

With a younger child, see if he/she can form a group of rocks and a group of pebbles. With an older child, see if he/she can form those groups plus an intersection of rocks and pebbles that are the same color or speckled and striped.

B. Creating sets with pictures

Materials needed

For each child or group of children: yarn circles, a deck of marked picture cards (made from an old book or children's picture dictionary that has been cut up).

Procedure

1 Ask the children the following questions:

Can you name some things that are alive in our classroom?

Can you name some things that are not alive in our classroom?

2 *Explain:* Scientists have divided the world into two large groups. One group is made up of all the things in the world that are alive, were once alive . . . all the plants and animals. The other group of things is made up of all the things in the world that are not or were never alive, like rocks and mountains.

3 Place two yarn loops into the shape of a circle. The loops should be different colors. Place one of the yarn circles so that it is intersecting the other circle.

4 Show the children that there are three spaces or areas that are enclosed inside the circles. Point out the space in the middle. This space is a special area called an intersection. Both of the circles overlap and meet here. You might want to compare this meaning of intersection with a street intersection—the area in the middle of all the crosswalks where the streets join and blend together.

5 Hold up a deck of adult-made, marked picture cards that have symbols or a color code depicting pictures as being living, nonliving, or both on their nonpicture side.

Are these cards alive? (No, they are nonliving.)

6 *Explain:* Each card has a picture on it. The picture is a model of something

real. It is a model of something living, nonliving, or both. For example:

Living = A tree, flower, person, animal

Nonliving = House, car, furniture

Both = A house with a yard and flowers; a person wearing clothes

7 Show the children each picture and ask:

Is it a model of something living or nonliving?

Does the model (picture) contain some objects that are alive and some objects that are not alive?

Where should we place pictures that show some objects that are alive and some objects that are not alive? (In the intersection space.)

8 After the children have sorted the cards, see if they can describe why and how the symbol or color code helps you to know if you separated the cards the way they have been marked.

9 *Explain* that the code is there to help you in case you do not feel sure of where to place a picture card. You can peek on the back. It is better to try to think first and then to look, or to wait until the end and to check all of the picture cards in the sets together.

Conclusion

Have children make and mark a set of their own cards from magazine pictures or from old workbooks to show pictures that represent both living things and nonliving things.

Vocabulary

Living, nonliving, both, group, divided, intersection, space, model, code, set.

Evaluation

With a younger child, find out if the child can sort out the deck of cards into "living" and "nonliving" sets. With an older child, see if he/she can sort the deck of cards out and form an intersection of sets.

Selected resource books for adults and older children

Cassidy, John. *The Unbelievable Bubble Book.* Palo Alto, CA: Klutz Press, 1987.

Preuss, Paul, editor. *Bubbles.* San Francisco: The Exploratorium, 1986.

Zubrowski, Bernie. *Bubbles: A Children's Museum Activity Book.* Boston: Little Brown and Company, 1979.

Selected literature connections for younger children

Steig, William. *Sylvester and the Magic Pebble*. New York: Simon & Schuster, 1988. (Good introduction for classifying and sorting a collection.)

Young, Ed. *Seven Blind Mice*. New York: Scholastic Books, 1993. A beautifully illustrated children's story about the importance of seeing the whole before making conclusions about the parts. Seven blind mice observe different parts of an elephant, and each mouse comes to a different conclusion about what the elephant is.

3
The five senses

Objective

To help children develop a heightened awareness of their five senses and to improve their observation skills.

General background information for parents and teachers

As adults, we are quite familiar with our ability to see, hear, smell, taste, and touch. We often take these abilities and skills for granted. We have learned how to integrate the knowledge and information gained from our senses. However, most children and many adults do not fully appreciate all of the information available to them through thoughtful and systematic use of their senses. If we use our senses fully and perceive all we can from them, they will communicate to us in a way that words do not.

If our senses are not fully developed, we can train ourselves and our children to become more observant. When we slow down from our usual pace and when we are patient about what we are observing, we begin to notice and observe "happenings" we were not aware of before. For example, if we play ball with our children in the park or jog with them along a path, we are absorbed in the physical activity of moving our body. We tend to notice our surroundings on a superficial level. However, when we walk slowly in the same park or on the same path with the purpose of observing, we begin to sense more "happenings." If we choose to stop and stay very still, we can use all of our senses. We can choose to concentrate on one sense at a time, or on many at once. Often our senses do not get used unless we concentrate on using them. If we are very still when we are outside, we can hear things that we cannot hear when we are moving. If we stop to touch "things," we can feel textures that we might not have been able to sense physically unless we stopped to touch the "things." We can smell aromas on our hands of objects we have touched or rubbed. We can even taste objects and spit out those things that might taste bitter.

Becoming fully aware of our five senses and the subtle differences that our senses can communicate to us helps us to develop the techniques of observing, comparing, matching, identifying, sorting, classifying, sequencing, and measuring. The development of these skills provides the framework for enjoying and understanding scientific phenomena as well as enriching readiness activities in reading and math.

When children become more aware of these senses, they often enjoy hypothesizing or predicting, and testing their ideas. It gives them reasons for wanting to communicate and to investigate things they are curious about. Children acquire a feeling of mastery over their world when they are allowed and encouraged to study, observe, and investigate materials that are part of their everyday life.

The child's five senses can be stimulated by familiar items. Young children absorb experiences through their bodies. They are extremely egocentric. Experiences that can be felt by them or that can be related to their own bodies are experiences they internalize and remember. For example, the word "hot" has meaning when one is burned. If a child is burned, he/she will avoid things that are called "hot." "Hot" will become an abstract idea that he/she will understand without continuing to need the "hands-on" experience of being burned.

3-2 Hot.

Young children learn through such experiences. The senses can be used as tools for enhancing these learning experiences. Not only will children be learning about their five senses, but their heightened awareness of their senses will help them become more aware of the world around them.

It is easy to recall and name all of our sense organs. All of them are located on our face: eyes see; ears hear; nose smells; tongue tastes; and skin surfaces sense touch. Our face is crucial to our identity because it houses all these senses, and because it contains the features by which other people know us.

Our hands serve us as a second set of eyes and ears. Our fingers are very sensitive to touch. If our eyes are closed, our fingers can become our "eyes." If we cannot hear, our fingers are able to sense sound vibrations. They can be trained to pick up vibrations caused by sound waves. Most of us do not need to train our fingers to read braille or to "hear" throats vibrate, but we are all capable of training and developing our fingers to become highly sensitive to the sensations felt by touch.

The list of activities in Table 3-1 is only a partial list. It has been written to entice you into thinking of your own activities. Our senses are constantly bombarded by stimuli. The important idea is to become more aware of what our senses can do for us, and to develop our senses more fully so that we can all enjoy our surroundings and our lives to their fullest. *Note:* As you do these activities with your children, try to encourage them to keep a science journal of their observations and their thoughts.

Table 3-1 Useful sense words

Sight

dazzle	dull	bright
dingy	sparkle	wavy
shiny	knotted	gnarled
transparent	opaque	clear
cloudy	dark	narrow
shady	crooked	wrinkled
glowing	flashing	

Sound

crunch	whisper	shriek
crash	fizz	snap
boom	singing	ping
splash	squeak	squeal
gasp	rattle	drip
creaking	buzz	chirp
croak		

Smell

smoky	damp	acrid
sour	sweet	musty
woodsy	grassy	fresh
antiseptic	pungent	decaying
sweaty	moldy	spicy

Taste

crunchy	sweet	fresh
hearty	rich	tasty
sour	salty	bitter
spiced	cool	fizzy
peppy	creamy	juicy
savory		

Touch

sticky	silken	soft/hard
firm	cool/cold	freezing
shivery	slimy	furry
crisp	refreshing	parched
bumpy	tickle	rough
prickly	wet/dry	jagged
sharp	crisp	crunchy
juicy	smooth	heavy
light	warm/hot	scalding

Activities and procedures

I. Sound

1. Locate a ringing bell

Material

A small brass bell.

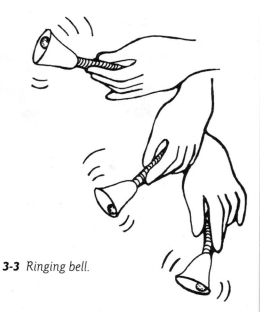

3-3 *Ringing bell.*

Procedure

Have a child sitting in a chair close his/her eyes and guess which direction the sound came from: up, down, behind, in front of, to the left, right, or middle. *Note:* This activity helps reinforce positional and spatial terms.

Going further

• Cover one ear.

Can you still tell the position or direction from which a sound is coming? (Probably not.)

• *Explain:* We usually need two ears to receive clues to tell us from which direction a sound is coming.

 Margaret Kenda in *Science Wizardry for Kids*, gave a wonderful explanation for this phenomenon as follows:

With two ears, you get a clue to the direction a sound comes when the sound vibration hits one ear a split second before it hits the other ear. And you get another clue about direction when the sound is very slightly louder in one ear than in the other. (pg. 302)

2. Guessing objects by the sounds they make

Materials

Various objects, i.e., coins, comb, ruler, rubber band, tinfoil.

Procedure

Parent or teacher shows child various objects. Child closes his/her eyes. Parent or teacher drops one of the objects. Child tries to guess which object was dropped.

The five senses

Going further

- Save empty film canisters. Put different materials or objects in each closed container (rice, sand, beans, cotton, paper clips, marbles, etc.). Have children predict what might be in the closed containers without letting them know or see the possibilities.

3. Tape-recorded sounds

3-4 *Tape-recorded sounds.*

Material

A tape recorder.

Procedure 1

Tape-record individual children's voices and familiar adult voices. See if the children can recognize each others' voices as well as their own voices.

Procedure 2

Tape-record sounds of familiar "things." For example: garbage truck, fire engine, dishwasher filling up, dog barking, telephone ringing, bird chirping, ball bouncing, airplane overhead, ice-cream truck, cricket chirping, door slamming, baby crying. Have child try to identify the sounds heard, and to decide whether the sound is made by something that is alive, or something that is not alive but mechanical or human-made.

Going further

- Discuss with children what the last thing was that they heard before they went to sleep last night, or what was the first thing they heard when they woke up this morning.

What kinds of sounds were they? (Soft, harsh, mechanical, pleasant.)

Fine points to discuss

How are natural sounds different from mechanical sounds?

What are the qualities that make them different?

What kinds of sounds appear to last longer, and to be more monotonous? (Sounds with little variety to them.)

When do sounds become monotonous and boring? (When we can no longer "hear" them because they blend into everything else. We often do not hear traffic on a busy street, or a machine that is humming, or the motor in a car, because the sound is constant.)

What are the sounds we cannot hear? (Quiet "happenings" in nature. See Fig. 3-5.)

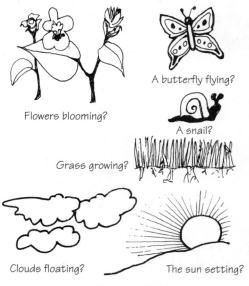

3-5 *Can you hear these things?*

Does the rainbow make a sound?

Does the sunrise make a sound?

Do butterflies make noise when they flutter?

Can we hear a bud opening up to blossom?

Can we hear clouds moving in the sky?

Can we hear an ant walk?

Why do animals make sounds? (To communicate.)

What do animal sounds communicate to us? (Hunger, fear, happiness, hurt, pain, warning.)

Why do cats purr?

Why do babies cry?

Why do dogs growl?

Why does a rattlesnake rattle its tail?

Do humming birds hum? (No, their fast vibrating wings create a humming sound.)

What are other animal sounds?

What does laughter mean?

What does a scream mean?

How can sounds be a valuable source of information about our environment?

What are some safety sounds that let us know we need to pay attention? (Police car, car horn, elevator buzzer, electric door closing on a train, school fire alarm, ambulance.)

What are some of the things you can hear before you see them? (Mosquitoes, fire engines, cars, child screaming, jet.)

Questions for older children to think about

Why do elephants have such large ears? (Probably to help keep them cool, and to swat away flies.)

Do fish have ears? (No, but most have a lateral line along their side that receives vibrations.)

*Do snakes have ears?** (No. Their bodies can sense vibrations through the ground. They cannot hear sound waves traveling in the air.)

Do insects have ears? (No. Their antennae assist them to pick up vibrations.)

How do animals that do not have ears hear?

Note: For more activities on sound, see chapter 6, which gives a more detailed description of what sounds are and how sounds travel.

II. Sight

1. Take a closer look

Materials

A magnifying glass for each child, and/or a pocket microscope.

Pocket microscopes can be purchased at Radio Shack or from science supply houses. They need two AA batteries. They usually have a power of 40×. In order to see things through them, the object has to be touching the lens.

Procedure

1 Take the children outside, turn over a rock, or a log. Take a closer look with a

* Audrey Brainard Hands-On-Science workshop.

3-6A *A magnifying glass or pocket microscope enlarges objects.*

magnifying glass or a pocket microscope.

What do you see?

2 Use a magnifying glass or pocket microscope to observe a dead insect. Dead insects can often be found after a rain or on a window sill.

What can you see with the magnifying glass or microscope that you didn't see before? (Perhaps the veins in the wings, or the hair on the legs.)

3 Use a magnifying glass or pocket microscope to observe a bird's feather or a leaf or any other object that children bring to class or find outside. Discuss with them what they can see with the magnification that they could not see with their naked eye.

2. Find matching objects outside

Materials

Leaves, rocks, or other objects easily found outside.

Procedure

1 Collect a few leaves and rocks that are in great abundance on the ground.

2 Show the items to your children.

3 Ask them to find objects that appear the same. For example, leaves from the same kind of tree that your leaf came from; rocks that are made up of the same colors (granite, blacktop, white pebbles) as the rock or pebble you show them.

4 Have them compare what they find to what you had.

Do the objects look exactly alike? (If they look closely enough, no.)

5 *Explain:* All living things are unique. No two living things are ever exactly

alike. Only some human-made things can look exactly alike.

6 Discuss what makes the found objects look different and what makes the found objects look alike. Try to help children observe details and attributes.

Going further

Children might enjoy using a magnifying glass or pocket microscope to observe the objects for more details.

3. Depth perception

Materials

None

Procedure

1 Tell children to look at something in the distance across the room or outside.

2 Ask them to cover one eye and to look at the object again.

Do you notice anything different about what you see? (It is difficult to gauge what is in front of what. Objects lose their three dimensional quality.)

3 *Explain:* We need two eyes to see depth. When we use one eye it is hard to judge distance, and to figure out what object is in front and what object is in back. Most things appear to be on a flat surface with no depth or distance between them. When only one eye is opened, moving about helps to restore a sense of depth perception.

III. Touch

1. Barefoot touch

3-6B *Barefoot touch.*

Materials

A collection of materials such as sandpaper, cellophane, bath towel, jacks, chalkboard, chalk eraser, inflated balloon, animal cage, wet sponge, dry sponge, baseball, and paintbrush.

Procedure

Show the children the materials. Have a child remove his/her shoes and socks. Choose three items from the collection. Then have the child close his/her eyes. Let the child touch an object from the three objects chosen with his/her bare feet and then try to guess which object is being touched. Have the child describe how the object feels. Later, advance to not showing the child which three objects you will choose, as this will increase the difficulty of the activity.

2. Feeling weight

Materials

Three to five empty half-gallon milk cartons. Fill each of the cartons with a different amount of sand.

Procedure

Have the children arrange the sand-filled milk cartons in order from the lightest in weight to the heaviest while blindfolded or with their eyes closed. (See Fig. 3-7A.)

Note: This activity reinforces the need to have more than one object when comparing weights. An object cannot feel "heavier" or "lighter." In order to feel weight, we have to compare the object to something else.

3. Feeling height

Materials

Cut the top off empty half-gallon milk cartons to create three to five different heights.

Procedure

While blindfolded or with their eyes closed, have the children sort the cartons according to their height. *Note:* This activity reinforces the need to have more than one object when comparing heights. An object cannot look or feel "taller" or "shorter." In order for the object to look or feel tall or short, it has to be compared to something else.

3-7A *Feeling weight.*

4. Describing touch

Materials

Samples of assorted textured fabrics: burlap, felt, satin, velvet, lace, corduroy, and tweed. Samples of assorted household products: wax paper, butcher paper, brown paper bag, plastic grocery bag, aluminum foil, coffee filter, paper towel, toilet paper, wet sponge, dry sponge, cotton balls, and sand paper.

Procedure

Ask children to feel the assorted materials and try to describe how the assorted materials feel.

What other familiar things do the materials feel like? (For example, velvet might feel like skin.)

Which material feels the roughest? Smoothest?

Which feels the softest? Hardest?

Which material feels sticky? Heavy? Light? Sharp? Wet? Bumpy? Hot? Cold?

Going further

* Collect similar looking sets of objects like small balls or coins: penny, nickel, dime, quarter.
* Have children close their eyes and try to describe the differences in touch between each of the coins.

Which coin has a smooth, thick side?

Which coin has ridges going around its edge?

5. Is touch the same all over your body?

Materials

Toothpicks.

Procedure

1 Divide children into pairs.

2 Instruct children to experiment with the toothpicks.

3 Have them touch their partner's skin with one or two toothpicks held between their fingers.

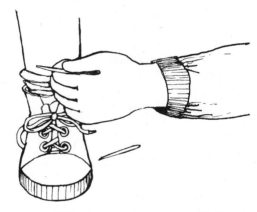

3-7B *How sensitive is your skin?*

4 Tell them to gently touch different parts of their partner's body with one or two toothpicks. See if their partner can feel whether one or two toothpicks are touching their body.

Which parts of your body are most sensitive to touch? (Tip of tongue, finger tips, and tip of nose.)

Which areas of your body are least sensitive to touch? (Back of the shoulders and legs.)

IV. Smell

1. Spices

Materials

An assortment of aromatic spices: mint, tarragon, onion, basil, parsley, thyme, marjoram, bay leaves, and garlic. Paper napkins or cheesecloth to wrap the individual crushed spices. One whole leaf of each spice left uncrushed and unwrapped.

Procedure

Children have to sniff and match the smell of the spice wrapped in cheesecloth to the smell of the unwrapped whole-leaf spice.

3-8 Smelling spices.

3-9 Mystery box.

INFORMATION "Nerve cells of the nose recognize four odors:

1 Burnt (toast, fire).
2 Rancid (moldy bread).
3 Acrid (sour like vinegar).
4 Fragrant (sweet).

A continual exposure to one odor causes nerve cells to become insensitive to that odor." (Gega, pg. 433)

2. Mystery box

Materials

Make a "feely box" (call it a "mystery box") that you can "feel through" without peeking. Either hang a piece of cloth in front of a small open cardboard box, or cut out holes on the two sides of a small cardboard box; a slice of fruit peel; crayons in the colors of fruit.

Procedure

Hide a slice of fruit peel in the "mystery box." Have children sniff and try to identify what the odor is. (Suggestions of fruit peels to hide: lemon, orange, apple, banana, cantaloupe, watermelon.) Have the children draw a circle using the color of crayon that the fruit peel smells like:

Yellow—banana, lemon.

Red—apple, watermelon.

Orange—orange, cantaloupe.

Note: This coloring activity reinforces the names of colors and the names of common foods, and develops children's awareness of how color symbols can be used to represent ideas.

3. Smelling flowers

Materials

An assortment of fresh flowers: carnation, rose, marigold, dandelion, violet, zinnia, daisy. A flower identification guidebook, or flower and seed catalog.

Procedure

Smell all the flowers. Sort out which ones have an aroma and which ones have very little scent. Look through the flower identification guidebook. Match the real flowers to models of flowers in the book. Discuss how the model does not have the aroma that the real flower has.

Note: This activity reinforces the idea that books can be used as a reference aid for identifying specimens, and that books contain useful and interesting information.

4. Take a nature walk

Materials

Gathering a variety of leaves, rocks, tree bark, and soil.

Table 3-2
Some other observations
that can be made on a nature walk

See	Feel	Smell	Hear
clouds	soil	soil	birds singing
bird's flying	mud	pond water	animals playing
hole in a tree	sand	tree bark	voices
holes in leaves	moss	leaves	cricket chirp
holes in ground	tree bark	flowers	dog barking
insects	thorns	seeds	your footsteps
a spider web	leaves	mushroom	wind
bird nest	wind	rotting log	leaves moving
an ant hill	sun	litter	water flowing
shadows	textures/shapes	animals	machines

Procedure

Take a walk. Gather things that smell. Compare the different aromas of leaves, tree bark, and soil odors. Which things smell earthy? (See Table 3-2.)

V. Taste

1. Salt and sugar

Materials

Salt, sugar, two cups.

Procedure

Pour some sugar into one cup and some salt into another cup. Discuss with your child the difficulty of telling the difference between these two "white powders." They both look alike.

What is an easy way to tell which is which? (By tasting them.)

2. Lemon juice, vinegar, and water

Materials

Lemon juice, vinegar, water, and sugar.

Procedure

Have the child taste each liquid. Discuss how each tastes. Add sugar and water to the lemon juice.

Does the lemon juice still taste sour?

Do sugar and water change the taste of the vinegar?

3. Skull and crossbones

Materials

A poison label with a skull and crossbones, ammonia.

Procedure

Show the children the poison label. Discuss with them what it means and why we should avoid ever tasting something from a bottle with this kind of label. Let the child take a whiff of ammonia to smell how bad poison would taste. Discuss how odors often tell us when something is dangerous to swallow.

Note: It is important to emphasize with children that it is not always smart to taste unknown things because they might be dangerous to us. If we taste something unknown and it tastes awful, it is wise to spit it out and not swallow it. Sometimes things taste awful, like cod liver oil, but they are good for us. It is okay to swallow something that tastes awful if we know what it is and know that it is not poisonous.

4. How we taste

Materials

A tongue chart showing where our taste buds are located. (See Fig. 3-10.)

Procedure

Experiment by tasting foods that are bitter, sweet, salty, and sour. Experiment by touching different parts of your tongue as you taste the foods.

Do foods taste different on different parts of our tongues?

Does candy taste better on the front tip of our tongue than in the rear of our tongue near our throat?

5. Use food color

Materials

Food color, mashed potatoes, and rice.

How We Taste!

Tongues have taste buds for tasting bitter, sour, sweet and salty things.

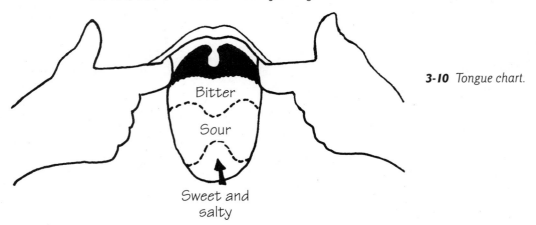

3-10 *Tongue chart.*

Procedure

Have the child taste the mashed potatoes and the rice. Then add blue food color to the rice and to the potatoes.

Does the color affect the taste of the food?

Fine points to discuss

Discuss how the color of the food we eat affects the way we think it will taste.

Can we taste the color?

Discuss how important it is to smell foods when we eat them. Smell enhances the taste of food. It is often difficult to distinguish taste from smell. Hold your nose while you taste a food.

Does the food taste as good as it does when you can smell the food as you taste it?

Going further

Taste different textured foods and describe how they feel on your tongue and what sounds they make. For example: crunchy/noisy foods—carrots, celery, crackers, pretzels; soft/quiet foods—mayonnaise, banana, cream cheese

VI. Going further with sight and touch

1. Describing attributes of sets

Materials

Attribute set. A commercially prepared attribute set can be used, or you can prepare an attribute set yourself. If you make it yourself, it should consist of at least 12 pieces for touching and sorting.

Circles: 2 large circles, 2 small circles.
Rectangles: 2 large rectangles, 2 small rectangles.
Squares: 2 large squares, 2 small squares.

One set of each of the two matching pieces should have a rough texture (sandpaper finish), and the other set of six pieces should have a smooth texture. All of the pieces in the set of 12 should be one color. Otherwise, color will become an attribute and more pieces will need to be added to the set. (If color is going to be an attribute, then each additional color set will consist of 12 additional pieces. Each set of shapes and sizes will have to be made in each additional color.)

Procedure

Children play with the 12 pieces. They describe what piece they are touching. For example:

"I am holding a large, smooth circle."

"I am holding a small, rough square."

Note: This activity helps increase a child's verbal abilities and his/her ability to clarify and distinguish.

2. Finding pieces or objects by sight or touch

Materials

Attribute set (refer to materials listed in II.1, the Describing section).

Procedure 1

Divide the 12 pieces into sets by shape, size, or texture.

Each size has a rough
texture and a smooth one

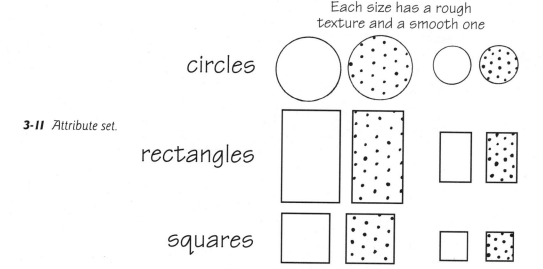

circles

3-11 Attribute set.

rectangles

squares

Procedure 2

Try the same activity blindfolded.

3. Which piece is missing?

Materials

Attribute set (refer to materials listed in II.1, the Describing section of this chapter).

Procedure

Lay out all of the pieces to the attribute set. Remove one piece from the set while the child has his/her eyes closed. Have child open his/her eyes and guess which piece of the set is missing, or feel which piece of the set is missing.

4. Mystery box

Materials

Mystery box (refer to Activity IV. 2., "Smell," in this chapter).

Procedure

Place an object inside the box. Children feel the object with their fingers and try to guess what the object is without peeking inside. Suggested items to hide in the box: a pencil, a shoelace, a ball of yarn, a sea shell, a marble, and a crayon.

5. Construction

Materials

Mystery box or "feely box" and colored wooden blocks, each block shape a different color, i.e., rectangle, green; square, red; cylinder, purple. Two of each block shape in matching colors.

Procedure

One set of blocks is inside the feely box, and the other set is outside the box. The child constructs an "arrangement" of the blocks that are outside the box in an order. Then, without peeking, the child tries to reconstruct the same arrangement of the blocks with the blocks that are inside the feely box.

3-12 "Seeing" with our hands.

Note: This activity takes a certain level of skill on the part of our fingers, since our fingers have to "see" for us. The activity can be made more difficult by adding more wooden blocks, or by trying to duplicate pictures of block formations by only looking at a "picture" of the formation and not looking at three-dimensional blocks.

VII. Fooling your senses

1. Fooling your sense of hearing*

Materials

Two 2-foot pieces of an old garden hose, or rubber tubing; two kitchen funnels.

Procedure

1 Place a funnel on each end of the garden hose. Secure with masking tape if it does not stay on.

3-13 *Fooling your sense of hearing.*

2 Have a child place the end of a hose in each of his/her ears.

3 Twist the hose around the child's body so that the opened funnel end of the hose from the left ear is near the child's right ear, and the funnel end of the hose from the right ear is near the child's left ear.

4 Tell the child with the two hoses in his/her ears to close his/her eyes. Make noises. See if the child can figure out which direction the noise comes from.

2. Fooling your sense of sight—optical illusions

A. Seeing tunnels on and in a spinning top

Materials

Several tops, marking pens, pencils, white paper circles. (The circles can be cut to be the size of the top or slightly larger.)

Procedure

1 Use one color of marking pen to create a spiral design.

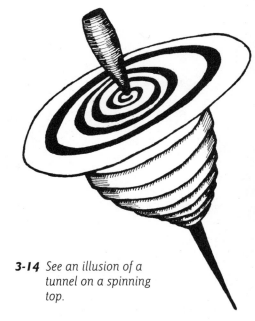

3-14 *See an illusion of a tunnel on a spinning top.*

2 Poke a hole through the center of the circle with a pencil

3 Place the spiral design on the top.

4 Observe what happens.

What happens to the spiral design when the top spins? (You will see the illusion of a tunnel.)

How does the speed of the top affect the illusion? (When the speed is very fast, you will not see a tunneling illusion.)

What happens if you change the direction of the spinning top? (When the top spins in one direction, it will look like the tunnel is pushing out at you. When the top spins in the opposite direction, it will appear as though the tunnel is taking you into it.)

Note: This phenomenon occurs because the rotation on the spinning top occurs so quickly that our eyes cannot stop the rotation. Our eyes integrate what they see. Our brains cannot process the information as quickly as the rotation of the top. Therefore, when we look at the spirals spinning or other designs that might be spinning on the spinning top, an optical illusion is created because we have fooled our brain.

Going further

Experiment by making different designs and colors on the disk and observing the illusions.

B. Seeing a floating finger tip

Materials

None.

* Adapted from Gega, page 295.

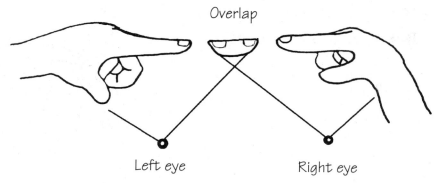

3-15 *Keep both of your eyes open and focus on a far point.*

Procedure

Instruct children to:

1 Touch your index fingers together.
2 Stretch your arms out in front of you with your index fingers still touching at eye level.
3 Keep both eyes opened.
4 Look straight ahead and focus on a far point.
5 Slowly bring your touching index fingers closer in toward the bridge of your nose.

What do you see? (It will appear that you grew a sausage between your index finger tips.)

If you focus both of your eyes on to your "touching" index fingers instead of on a far away object, what do you see? (Two fingers and no "sausage" because you are only able to perceive depth when both of your eyes are opened.)

ⓘ
INFORMATION This activity is written about in many science activity books. However, Tik L. Liem, in his book, *Invitation to Science Inquiry,* explains the reason for our eyes perceiving this strange vision of a "floating sausage" in understandable terms.

"Even though the eyes are focused on a far point, we still see objects that are closer to the eyes . . .. This is the reason why we see only a piece of the finger. Whatever image overlaps is seen more clearly." (pg. 441)

6 *Explain:* Optical illusions are the result of our brains following reasoning to what would appear to be a logical conclusion. The image of the two eye retinas have to correspond. Our visual system attempts to do the best it can, which is sometimes wrong.

3. Fooling your sense of touch—feeling temperature

Materials

Arrange three water basins on a table together. Fill one basin half full with warm water, another basin half full with hot water, and the third basin half full with cold water. Place the basin filled with warm water between the other two basins.

Procedure

Blindfold a child and have the child dip his/her hand into the hot, cold, and warm water. The child is to identify what the temperature of the water feels like. Take the blindfold off and place one hand in hot water and the other hand in cold water at the same time. After a minute, place both hands into the warm water. The warm water will feel cold to the hand that was in hot water and hot to the hand that was in cold water. (See Fig. 3-17.)

Note: This activity helps children understand the relative nature of temperature. Warm can feel both hot and cold. It depends on what our body temperature was before.

3-16 *An overlap occurs.*

The five senses

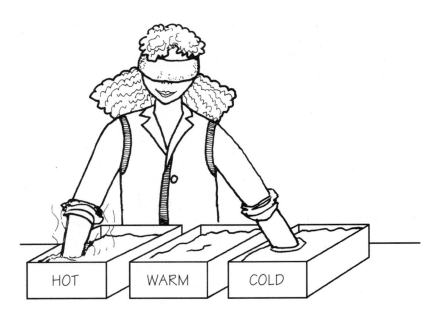

3-17 *Both hands will feel a different temperature.*

4. **Fooling your sense of taste***

Materials

Slices of: raw potato, apple, and onion.

Procedure

1 Blindfold the child who is doing the tasting.

2 Pinch his/her nose closed with a clothespin, or let him/her hold his/her own nose. Place a small slice of each food: apple, potato, and onion, one at a time, on the child's tongue. The child is to try to guess what the food is by the taste, without chewing on it.

3 *Explain:* The texture of each of the foods and the sounds it made when it was chewed would be a clue as to what the food was.

4 Let all of the children have a turn.

5 Keep a record by making a graph of how often the children were able to guess the correct food when they were not given a chance to see it or to smell it. Discuss the results.

Further resources

Dewey Decimal Classification Numbers for the human body and five senses are: 372.3, 516.22, 531.6, 541.3, 591.4, 612, and 641.1.

Selected books for children

Aliki. *My Five Senses.* New York: Harper and Row. 1989.

Ardley, Neil. *The Science Book of the Senses.* Gulliver Books (HBJ): New York. 1992.

Ball, J.A. and Hardy A.D. *What Can It Be? : Riddles About Our Senses.* Morristown, NJ: Silver Burdett, 1989.

Brandt, Keith. *My Five Senses.* Mahwah, NJ: Troll Associates, 1985. (K–3).

Brenner, Barbara, *Bodies.* New York: Dutton, 1973. (Photographs that tell a story. Shows how our body is like a machine.)

Catherall, Ed. *Touch.* Wayland Publishers Limited, East Sussex, England. 1982. (Suggested investigative activities to be done with the sense of touch.)

Davis, Kay and Oilfield, Wendy. *My Balloon: Simple Science.* New York: Doubleday, 1990. (Beautiful color photos make this an easy book for young children to use on their own.)

Evans, David and Williams, Claudette. *Let's Explore Science: Make It Change.* New York: Dorling Kindersley, 1992.

Evans, David and Williams, Claudette. *Let's Explore Science: Make It Go.* New York: Dorling Kindersley, 1992.

Evans, David and Williams, Claudette. *Let's Explore Science: Me and My Body.* Dorling Kindersley, New York. 1992.

Evans, David and Williams, Claudette. *Let's Explore Science: Make It Balance.* Dorling Kindersley, New York. 1992.

Hoban, Tana. *Circles, Triangles and Squares.* New York: Macmillan, 1974.

* Adapted from Vicki Cobb, pg. 45, *How to Really Fool Yourself.*

(Black-and-white photographs of a city environment. The photos emphasize the shapes of things. There are no words, just photos. Good for a discussion about shapes we see around us and for the development of observation skills.)

Hoban, Tana. *Is It Larger? Is It Smaller?* New York: Greenwillow, 1985.

Hoban, Tana. *Look! Look! Look!* New York: Greenwillow, 1985.

Hulme, Joy. *Sea Squares.* Hyperion. 1991. (Beautifully illustrated underwater scenes. Helps give meaning to the concept of square numbers.)

Marzollo, Jean. *I Spy a Book of Picture Riddles.* New York: Scholastic, 1992.

Ogle, Lucille, and Tina Thoburn. *The Golden Picture Dictionary.* Racine, WI: Western Publishing, Golden Books, 1989. (A good preschool and kindergarten book. The book helps develop vocabulary and sight words.)

Orii, Eiji. *Simple Science Experiments with Optical Illusions.* Milwaukee: Garth Stevens Children's Books, 1989.

Ruis, M., Parramon, J. and Puig, J. *The Five Senses Series: Sight, Smell; Taste; Touch; Hearing.* Woodbury, N.Y.: Barron's, 1985.

Waring, Jane Main. *My Feather: Simple Science.* New York: Doubleday, 1990. (Beautiful color photos make this an easy book for young children to use on their own.)

Wilson, April. Look! *The Ultimate Spot the Difference Book.* New York: Trumpet Club, 1990.

Resource books for more ideas

Brown, Robert J. *333 Science Tricks and Experiments.* TAB Books, 1984. (See chapter 5, Biology and Psychology.)

Brown, Sam Ed, *One, Two, Buckle My Shoe: Math Activities for Young Children.* Mt. Rainier, Maryland: Gryphon House, 1982. (Presents ideas for pre-school–Kindergarten.)

Cobb, Vicki. *How to Really Fool Yourself: Illusions for All Your Senses.* NY: Lipincott, 1981.

Cobb, Vicki. *Science Experiences You Can Eat.* New York: Lippincott, 1972.

(Describes cooking experiences to develop the senses.)

Discover the World of Science. Special Issue. "The Mystery of Sense: How We Manage to Touch, See, Hear, Smell and Taste the World". June, 1993, Vol. 14, number 6.

Forte, Imogene, and Marjorie Frank. *Paddles and Wings and Grapevine Swings.* Nashville, Tennessee: Incentive Publications, 1982. (Things to do with nature's treasures.)

Frank, Marjorie. *I Can Make a Rainbow.* Nashville, Tennessee: Incentive Publications, 1976. (Describes art activities that help develop the senses.)

Furth, Hans G., and Harry Wach. *Thinking Goes to School: Piaget's Theory in Practice.* New York: Oxford University Press, 1974. (Describes thinking activities to make us more aware of our senses.)

Gega, Peter. *Science in Elementary Education.* 6th ed., New York: Macmillan, 1990. (See chapter 16, The Nervous System.)

Goodwin, M.T. and Pollen, G. *Creative Food Experiences for Children.* Washington, DC: Center for Science in the Public Interest, 1980.

Grady, Denise. "The Vision Thing: Mainly in the Brain." Discover the World of Science, June, 1993, Vol. 14, number 6, pg. 56–66. (Helps explain how the brain processes information obtained from our eyes.)

Hibner, Liz and Dixie Cromwell. *Explore and Create.* Livonia, Michigan: Partner Press, 1979. [Distributed by Gryphon House, Mt. Rainier, Maryland.] (Describes various activities which develop the senses.)

Hoover, Rosalie and Barbara Murphy. *Learning About Our Five Senses.* Carthage, IL: Good Apple, 1981. (Songs, fingerplays, and games for developing awareness of the five senses.)

Kenda, Margaret and Phyllis S. Williams. *Science Wizardry for Kids: Safe Scientific Experiments Kids Can Perform.* Hauppauge, N.Y.: Barrons Educational Series, 1992. (This book is full of great innovative ideas and new ways to do familiar activities.)

Knapp, Clifford, "Exploring the Outdoors with Young People," Science and Children, October, 1979.

Liem, Tik L. *Invitation to Science Inquiry. 2nd ed.* Chino Hills, CA: Science Inquiry Enterprises, 1987.

Ontario Science Center. *Foodworks— Over 100 Science Activities and Fascinating Facts that Explore the Magic of Food.* Reading, MA: Addison-Wesley, 1987.

Rasmussen, Greta. *Discover.* Stanwood, WA: Tin Man Press, 1987. (Encourages creative thinking skills, Grades K–6.)

Rasmussen, Greta. *Nifty Fifty.* Stanwood, Washington: Tin Man Press, 1987. (A book of creative questions about familiar topics; possible answers are also provided. Grades K–6.)

Williams, R.B., Rockwell, Robert E. and Sherwood, Elizabeth A. *Everybody Has a Body.* Mt. Ranier, MD: Gryphon House, 1992.

Williams, R.B., Rockwell, Robert E. and Sherwood, Elizabeth A. *Hug A Tree, and Other Things to do Outdoors with Young Children.* Gryphon House, 1986.

Williams, R.B., Rockwell, Robert E. and Sherwood, Elizabeth A. *More Mudpies to Magnets: Science for Young Children.* Gryphon House, 1990.

Warren, Jean. *Learning Games.* Palo Alto, California: Monday Morning Books, 1983. (Describes activities to reinforce sorting, observing, and counting. Grades K–2.)

Selected literature connection for younger children

Carlson, Nancy. *Harriet's Halloween Candy.* New York: Puffin Books, 1984. (A story about classification.)

Community enrichment activities

Post office For experiencing sorting and classifying the mail, listening to sounds of the mailroom.

Car wash For observing the sequence of events that occur during a car wash.

Grocery store For observing the orderly arrangement of categories of food and nonfood items. All five senses can be used at the grocery store, especially in the produce section.

Bakery For observing odors and tasting samples. Seeing the sequential process of baking take place.

Florist For observing variety and colors of flowers, plants, and their scents.

Library For observiing how books are classified.

Circus For observing the sights and sounds and smells.

4

Magnetism

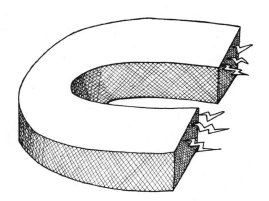

Objectives

The objectives of this chapter are for children to become aware of the following:

- That some magnets are made by humans and others are found in nature.
- How magnets behave toward each other and toward materials that are sensitive to magnetic force.
- That the strength of magnets varies.
- That magnets have invisible lines of force.
- That magnets have an invisible force field.
- That some metal materials can become temporary magnets.
- How magnets can be made.
- The laws of magnetism: Like poles repel; unlike poles attract.
- How magnets behave toward each other and toward materials that are sensitive to magnetic force.

General background information for parents and teachers

Magnetism The study of magnets and their effects.

Magnetic field The area around a magnet where a force can be detected.

Loadstone It is also spelled lodestone. It is a black rock that has magnetic properties. It is made from a mineral known as magnetite.

 (The mineral form of black oxide, $F_{e3}O_4$.) It is a natural magnet, found in nature. Loadstones made early sailing easier. They were used in compasses. Sailors no longer had to rely on the stars and the sun for navigating the seas.

Poles The ends of a magnet, where the magnetism is strongest.

North and south poles The poles are named for the direction a magnet would point if it were allowed to hang freely suspended from a string.

Repel This means to push away from; "like" poles repel.

Attract This means to pull together; "unlike" poles attract.

Permanent magnets Magnets that are made by humans. Magnets are made from steel or mixtures of iron, nickel, and cobalt.

Temporary magnets Magnets that do not keep their magnetic force. They have magnetic force only when they are in a strong magnetic field—for example, when a piece of metal such as a paper clip or a nail acts as a magnet to another piece of metal. The nail or paper clip will stay magnetic only as long as a permanent magnet is near it.

 (The magnetism is induced.)

Kinds of magnets and their poles

Bar magnets have poles at each end. Horseshoe magnets are really bar magnets that have been bent. Circular magnets have their poles on the inside and outside perimeter of the circle.

 Some circular magnets have a pole on either face. This is also sometimes true for other shapes.

Strong This is a relative term in relation to the ability of the magnet to lift or pull, attract, or repel.

Weak See previous explanation for strong. It refers to the strength of the magnet.

Iron A mineral that is affected by magnetism.

 What causes magnetism? Magnetism can be caused by electric charges that are moving. The electric charge is a constant part of the magnet. Electric current produces a magnetic field.

Iron molecules Not all molecules in an iron nail are lined up. They are randomly arranged. We can magnetize a nail by stroking it many times in one direction with a strong magnet. The stroking forces the randomly arranged iron molecules to align themselves in one direction.

Magnets that are made by humans can lose their magnetism. The atoms or crystallites of iron molecules can become unaligned and go back to a random pattern. This can happen when a magnet is dropped, heated, or hit hard with a hammer. Therefore, it is extremely important to handle magnets with care; keep them away from heat, and do not drop them. If they are treated poorly, they will lose some of their magnetic properties.

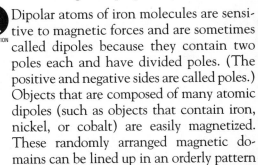 Dipolar atoms of iron molecules are sensitive to magnetic forces and are sometimes called dipoles because they contain two poles each and have divided poles. (The positive and negative sides are called poles.) Objects that are composed of many atomic dipoles (such as objects that contain iron, nickel, or cobalt) are easily magnetized. These randomly arranged magnetic domains can be lined up in an orderly pattern by the presence of a strong magnetic field.

Making magnets If the atomic dipoles all line up in the object, it becomes magnetized. The object becomes demagnetized if the atomic dipoles become unaligned.

Permanent magnets Atomic dipoles in very hard materials like steel are hard to move. They are "sticky;" to line them up, a strong magnetic field is needed. However, they will continue to stay aligned even when the magnetic field is not present.

Temporary magnets Atomic dipoles in softer materials are easier to move. They are "slippery" and can be aligned temporarily by a weak magnetic field.

 Magnetic audio tape A tape that is used to record sounds. The tape is coated with a magnetic emulsion that contains microscopic magnetic particles.

Nail before stroking
Iron atoms unaligned and arranged in random order

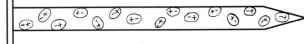

Nail after stroking
Iron atoms arranged in same direction in orderly pattern

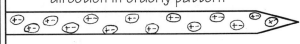

4-2 Nail before stroking; nail after stroking.

Note: As you do these activities with your children, try to encourage them to keep a science journal of their observations and their thoughts.

Activities and procedures

I. Natural and man-made magnets

I. Mystery rock

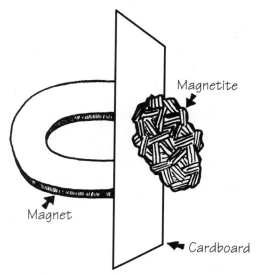

4-3 Magnet and magnetite rock.

Materials

Magnetite/loadstone,* a strong magnet, cardboard.

Procedure

1 Place a magnet on one side of the cardboard and the loadstone rock on the other side so that the magnet can be seen but the rock cannot be seen.
2 What is holding up the magnet?
3 Have them guess. They will probably say another magnet. Then show them what is on the other side. (They will be surprised to see that it is a magnetic rock.)
4 *Explain:* This rock is special. It is called a loadstone. It is made out of a mineral called magnetite. Magnetite has iron ore in it. Iron ore has magnetic properties and can attract things that have iron in them.

* Magnetite/loadstone can be purchased at a rock store, or from a science supply store or natural history museum.

2. Detecting magnetite

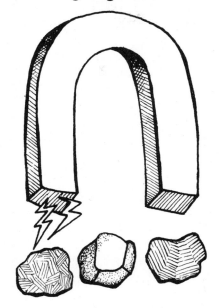

4-4 Detecting magnetite.

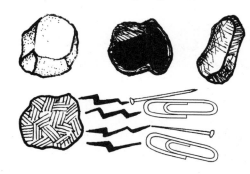

4-5 Comparing pieces of rocks and magnetite for magnetic strength.

Materials

Magnetite; assorted small rocks that are black, white, and brown; a strong magnet.

Procedure

1 Display a loadstone and assorted small rocks that are black, white, and brown.
2 Have a child approach the rocks with a strong magnet and try to guess which rock is the loadstone before the magnet approaches it.
3 Have the children observe how the loadstone "rocks" back and forth when the magnet approaches it.

3. Testing magnetite's strength

Materials

Two or three pieces of magnetite and assorted rocks, a box of paper clips.

Procedure

1 Place the paper clips in a bowl or on the floor. Approach with the assorted rocks and the magnetite. Test to see if each piece of magnetite picks up the same number of paper clips, or if one piece of magnetite is stronger than the other.

2 Have children experiment to find out which picks up the most paper clips.

Fine points to discuss

How can we tell when a magnet is strong? (By seeing how much it can pick up.)

Do size and shape affect the strength of a piece of magnetite? (No.)

Can magnetic force go through things? (Yes.)

How do we know? (Because we can observe that it does. Remind the children of the magnetic force of the magnet and the magnetite going through the cardboard from the first activity.)

4. Comparing the strength of a human-made and a natural magnet

Materials

Magnetite, bar magnet, paper clips.

Procedure

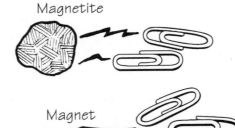

4-6 *Comparing magnetic strength of a magnet and magnetite.*

1 Hold up a human-made bar magnet. Tell the children it is a human-made magnet. Hold up a piece of magnetite and tell the children it is a natural magnet found in nature.

2 Have children experiment to see if the magnetite can lift up the bar magnet. (Find out which kind of magnet picks up more paper clips.)

Fine points to discuss

How can we tell a natural magnet from a human-made magnet? (Natural magnets look like black rocks. Human-made magnets have a definite shape.)

Is there a difference in their strengths? (Yes.)

II. Magnetic force

1. Fishing for magnetically sensitive materials

Materials

Plastic basin, "fishing bowl" filled with assorted things* in the center, a "yes" tray and a "no" tray, a magnetic "fishing pole" (a wood dowel attached to a piece of yarn tied to a magnet).

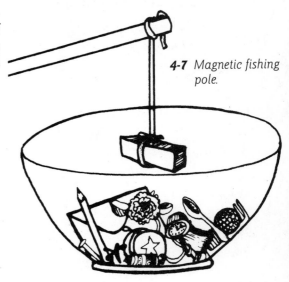

4-7 *Magnetic fishing pole.*

Procedure

1 Let's find out which things a magnet attracts or pulls. We will use this magnetic "fishing pole" to test the objects. Have the children sort the things that have been tested and put them into the "yes" or the "no" tray.

2 Discuss which things will go into the "yes" tray and which things will go into the "no" tray. Have the children guess before you bring the magnet to it. See if they guessed right.

Fine points to discuss

Does a magnet pick up all things that are made of metal? (No, only metals that contain iron.)

* "Assorted things:" sponge, nail, key, paper clips, butter container, toy cars, aluminum foil, pill container, pen, pencil, paper, shoelaces, bottle cap, coins, belt buckles, zippers, etc.

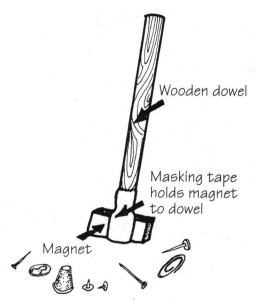

4-8 *Magnet on a stick.*

What other things in the room might attract a magnet? (Discuss and then have the children find out by going on a magnet hunt around the classroom with a magnet on a stick to find out what the magnet is attracted to.)

2. Jumping paper clip

Materials

Paper clips, bar magnet.

Procedure

1 Place a paper clip on a table. Have a child slide a magnet toward it to find out what happens to the paper clip. (It jumps toward the magnet.)

2 Have a child hold a paper clip in his or her palm. Approach the paper clip with a magnet to find out what happens to the paper clip. (It goes up.)

Fine points to discuss

Can we feel magnetism? (No.)

Can we feel its force? (Yes.)

Can we see magnetism? (We can see its effects.)

What is a magnetic force? (A push or a pull.)

3. Moving paper clip

Materials

Paper clips, magnet, paper.

Procedure

Demonstrate magnetic force by pulling and pushing a paper clip across a paper with a magnet held underneath the paper and the clip on top of the paper.

4. Feeling a magnet

Materials

Magnet.

Procedure

1 Place a magnet on a child's face or other body part.

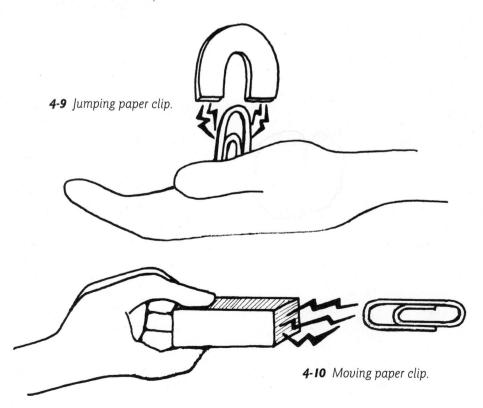

4-9 *Jumping paper clip.*

4-10 *Moving paper clip.*

2 Can you feel the magnetism when the magnet touches your skin?

3 Discuss how they can feel the magnet, but not the magnetism.

5. Feeling magnetic force

Materials
Two bar magnets.

Procedure

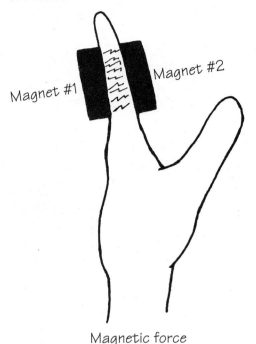

Magnet #1   Magnet #2

Magnetic force

4-11 Magnetic force can go through a hand.

1 Have a child hold his/her hand open, palm up. Place one bar magnet on the child's fingers and another bar magnet on the back of his/her fingers (immediately below the first magnet). See if the magnets will stay in place. (They will.) What will happen if you hold your hand vertically? Will the magnets still stay in place?

2 Discuss how a magnetic force is going through the child's hand. (The child cannot feel the magnet penetrate, but he/she can feel its force.)

6. Make a nail feel wavy

Materials
Two bar magnets, a large nail.

Procedure
Have a child hold part of a strong magnet in one hand and a nail or another strong magnet in the other hand. Then bring one magnet close to the other magnet or the large nail. When the magnet is close

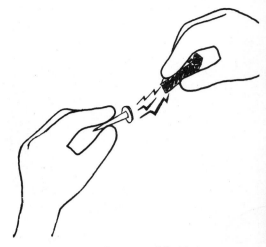

4-12 Making a nail feel "wavy.

enough to the other magnet or to the nail, the child will be able to feel a push or a pull of the force in his or her hands. It will feel "wavy," as the two approach each other.

7. Lifting a piece of paper with a magnet

Materials
Paper clip, paper, magnet.

Procedure

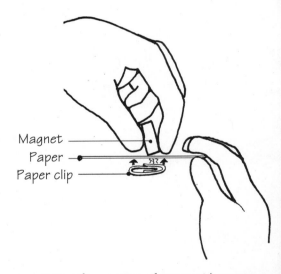

Magnet
Paper
Paper clip

4-13 Lifting a piece of paper with a magnet.

1 Cover a paper clip with a piece of paper. Have a child slide a magnet on top of the paper (above the paper clip) and lift the magnet up. (The paper will lift up.)

2 Discuss why the paper can be lifted by the magnet.

What happens when the magnet is placed above the paper clip when a piece of paper is between it and the paper clip? (A magnetic force penetrates [goes through] the paper.)

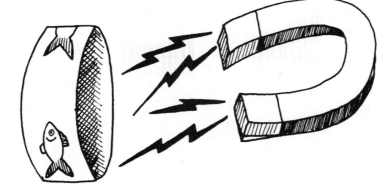

4-14 *Tin can rolls.*

4-15 *Circle game.*

Can the magnet lift the paper without the paper clip under it? (No, the paper itself is not magnetic.)

8. Make a tin can roll

Materials

Empty tuna fish can, strong magnet.

Procedure

Have a child approach a can with a magnet. Ask the child to make the can roll forward or backward by holding and keeping the magnet too far away from the can to allow the magnet to attach itself to the can, but close enough to make the can roll.

9. Play a circle game called "Let's Pretend!"

Materials

Long piece of yarn and assorted materials: bottle caps, keys, pencils, crayon, paper clip, rubber bands, etc. Place the assorted materials in the center of the yarn circle.

Procedure

1 Play "Let's Pretend"* (circle game). Adult and children sit cross-legged in a circle.

2 To play: One child chooses one object from the assortment. Adult says, "Let's pretend that I am a strong magnet. What are you, David?" David replies,

* Game adapted from Jean Harlan, *Science Experiences for the Early Childhood Years*, 5th Edition. Macmillan, 1992.

"I am a nail." Adult says, "Then we'll stick together." Adult will hold David's hand. David says to next child, "I am a magnetized nail. What are you?" If Jenny says she's a rubber band, then David continues to ask other children what they are until he finds someone to stick to. Game continues until the adult ends the game by saying, "I am a person again, you're children."

III. Magnetic strength

1. Testing magnets

Materials

Paper clips, nails, bolts, different sized magnets.

Procedure

Display the materials and a variety of magnets in different shapes and sizes. Proceed by letting children find out which magnet has the most pulling power.

Fine points to discuss

- Some magnets are stronger than others. Magnets stay stronger with a keeper. A "keeper" is a bar that goes across the ends of a horseshoe magnet. Magnets need to be put away in pairs to stay strong. One magnet helps keep the other magnet strong.
- We can find out how strong a magnet is by testing it and finding out which magnet can lift up the most things at the same time.

2. Observing magnetic force and strength

Materials

Strong magnet, paper clips, plastic tub-shaped container with lid.

Procedure

1 Fill a plastic tub-shaped container with paper clips and cover with fitted plastic lid. Have a child experiment to see if the magnet can lift the plastic container.

2 Discuss why the plastic container can be lifted. (It can be lifted because magnetic force goes through the plastic.)

3. Taking away a magnet

Materials

Strong magnet, paper clips, plastic tub-shaped container with lid.

Procedure

1 Ask the child to remove the lid to the plastic container and to remove the magnet.

2 What will happen to the paper clips and why?

3 Discuss why the paper clips fell. (They fell because the magnetic force was taken away.)

4. Magnetic sweeper

Materials

Strong magnet, lots of paper clips.

Procedure

1 Have the children spill all the paper clips on the floor.

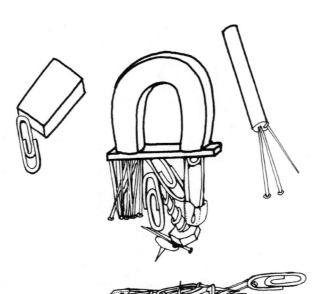

4-16 *Observing magnetic force and strength.*

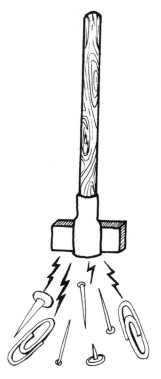

4-17 Magnetic sweeper.

2 Ask the children what is the easiest way to pick up the paper clips.

3 Demonstrate how you can use the magnet to pick up all the paper clips. The magnet will act like a "sweeper."

How could a magnetic sweeper help you? (It can be used for picking up metal objects like: pins, thumb tacks, or paper clips, that have spilt by accident.)

5. Experimenting with magnetic strength

Materials

Different-sized magnets, paper clips, nails and bolts.

Procedure

Let the children experiment with different-sized magnets to find out which one picks up the most, or how long a paper clip chain can be made by attaching them by magnetic force. Have the children test the magnets to find out which magnet picks up the most nails and bolts.

IV. Lines of force

Seeing lines of force

Materials

Plastic see-through envelope, iron filings, assorted magnets. (See Fig. 4-19.)

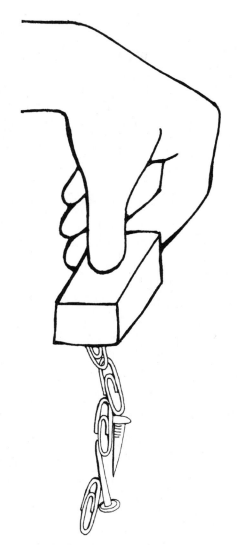

4-18A Testing magnetic strength.

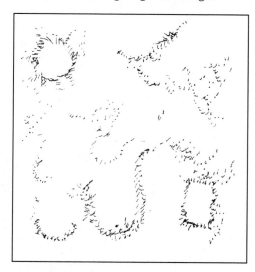

4-18B Iron filings should be kept in a plastic see-through envelope.

Procedure

1 *Explain* to children that the plastic see-through envelope contains iron filings. Iron filings come from iron when it has

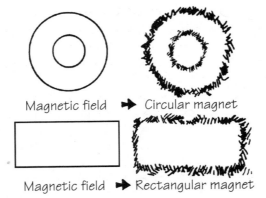

Magnetic field ➡ Circular magnet

Magnetic field ➡ Rectangular magnet

4-19 *Seeing lines of force.*

been sawed. It is iron dust (as sawdust is to wood). Iron filings are very small pieces of iron. They are inside the sealed envelope. You can see them and not breathe the dust into your lungs. The iron dust is not good for your body. The iron filings must stay inside the sealed envelope. The envelope has been taped closed for safety.

 Place a magnet on a flat surface (floor or table) underneath the see-through envelope. Tap your finger gently on the envelope. Magnetic force lines should appear. Iron filings show you a picture of the area around a magnet where its force can be felt. This area around a magnet is called its *magnetic field*. The lines formed around the magnet are called *lines of force*.

What shape will the force lines be that surround a circular magnet? (A circle.)

What shape will the force lines be that surround a rectangular magnet? (A rectangular shape that looks like an ellipse or "squared" circle.)

V. Magnetic field

Demonstrating a magnet's magnetic field

Materials

Paper clip strung to a berry basket; book; paper; magnet; rocks to weigh down the berry basket.

Procedure

1 *Explain* to children that lines of magnetic force from a magnetic field can go through the air.

2 Demonstrate with a paper clip whose wire has been strung with a string tied to a weighted object like an empty berry basket.

Berry basket

4-20 *Observing the effect of a magnetic field.*

3 Approach the paper clip with the magnet. Try not to touch the paper clip with the magnet. Instead, wait for the clip to point vertically on the thread because of its attraction caused by lines of force in the magnetic field.

4 While the paper clip is in a vertical position held up by magnetic force, have children test to see if the magnetic field goes through their hands, a thin book, a piece of paper, etc. Have children place the item being tested between the magnet and suspended paper clip.

Fine points to discuss

What makes the paper clip fall? (If the magnet moves too far away from the paper clip, the lines of force from the magnet cannot reach the paper clip. Strong magnets have longer lines of force than weak magnets do.)

Why does the paper clip stay in the air? (Magnetic force from the magnet holds the paper clip up.)

How far away can the magnet move and still hold up the paper clip? (It can move a little, but not a lot. If the magnet moves too far away, the lines of force become too weak to act on the paper clip.)

Going further: Measuring a magnet's magnetic field Place a paper clip on a piece of lined notebook paper. Put a mark on the paper where the paper clip is.

Slowly move a magnet toward the paper clip. Observe the paper clip move toward the magnet. Count how many lines of notebook paper the paper clip moves to reach the magnet. Record and compare different magnets and their pull on the same piece of notebook paper.

VI. Temporary magnets

Making a temporary magnet

Materials

Strong magnet, nail, paper clip, hammer.

Procedure

1 Demonstrate how to make a temporary magnet. Use a strong magnet, a nail, and paper clip.

2 Allow the nail to hit a hard cement floor so it will not be a magnet. Then try to pick up a paper clip with the nail. The nail cannot pick up a paper clip because it is not a magnet.

3 Then ask the children if they think they can make the nail into a magnet. Wait for their response. Then attach the nail head or point to the magnet. Pick up the paper clip.

4 Discuss why the paper clip can be lifted. (It is in the magnetic field of the nail, which has become a temporary magnet.)

5 Remove the magnet from the nail. Observe what happens.

6 Discuss why the paper clips are still attracted and attached to the nail.

7 Hit the nail with a hammer or let it fall onto a hard floor.

Will it still be a magnet? (It might be, but it will lose some of its magnetic force. It will not be as strong as it was.)

Fine points to discuss

- Magnets lose much of their magnetism if they are treated roughly. (Their molecules get all shook up and out of line.)

- Demonstrate with paper clips how molecules are lined up. (Arrange several paper clips in a line. Hit the paper clips with a hammer and observe how they bounce around and jump out of the straight-line arrangement. The same thing happens to the insides of magnets when they are dropped.)

VII. Making a magnet

1. Making a permanent magnet

Materials

Bar magnet, stainless steel needle.

Procedure

Have children stroke a stainless steel needle in one direction about 200 times with a strong bar magnet. It will become a magnet. Have the children bring the needle next to a paper clip to test it. If the paper clip reacts, then you will know that the needle has become a magnet.

2. Making a floating magnet

Materials

Magnetized stainless steel needle, sliced wine-bottle cork, bowl filled with water.

Procedure

Have a child place the magnetized stainless steel needle on a sliced piece of wine-bottle cork. Then float the cork with the needle on it in water. Have children observe what happens to the needle. It will tend to stabilize in one direction. If you spin it, it will continue to point in the same position over and over again when it stops.

4-21 *Make a floating magnet.*

Note: Beakman's World (a Television series) featured a wonderful activity, which was as follows:

1 Fill a baking dish with water.
2 Make a small tinfoil boat that floats on the water.
3 Magnetize a needle.
4 Lace the magnetized needle through the tinfoil.

Does the needle behave the same way as the needle on the cork did?

What will happen to the "needle boat" if you take another magnet and hold it over the "needle boat?"

Is it possible to "steer" the needle boat by "magnetic remote control?"

VIII. Laws of magnetism

I. Experimenting with a pair of marked magnets

Materials

Two marked magnets (each magnet has a red spot on one side and a blue spot on the other side).

Procedure

1 Have a child bring the two marked magnets near each other and observe what happens. (If the two red spots touch, they push away. If the two blue spots touch, they push away.)
2 Discuss what can be done to make the magnets attract each other. Wait for the children to respond. Then try to put a red side together with a blue side.

2. Repelling a magnet

Materials

Two marked magnets (each magnet has a red spot on one side and a blue spot on the other side).

Procedure

1 Ask the following questions:

Can one magnet push another magnet away?

How can this be done?

2 Wait to see if children can figure this out; if not, help guide them to discovering. Have children discover that when two red sides or two blue sides are placed together, one will repel the other and produce a push reaction.

3. Making a magnet do somersaults

Materials

Two marked magnets (each magnet has a red spot on one side and a blue spot on the other side).

Procedure

1 Ask the following questions:

Can you make your magnets do somersaults?

How could that be done?

2 Wait to see if children can figure out how to do it. If they cannot, show them how: Place one magnet in your open palm and the other on the back of your hand. Hold your open palm parallel to the floor. Now turn the bottom magnet over. The top magnet will flip over too.

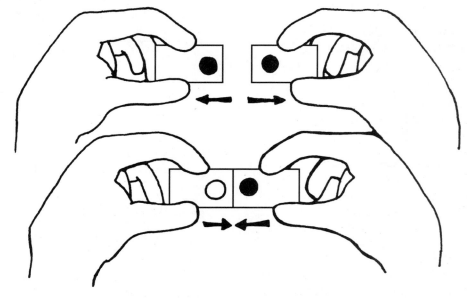

4-22 Experimenting with attracting and repelling.

4. Magnetic somersaults on a tray

Materials

Place one magnet on top of the tray;

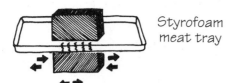

Styrofoam meat tray

place the other magnet under the tray.

4-23 Magnetic "somersaults."

A Styrofoam tray or cafeteria tray, two marked magnets (each magnet has a red spot on one side and a blue spot on the other side).

Procedure

Place one magnet on a Styrofoam tray. Hold another magnet on the bottom of the Styrofoam tray. Have the children make it do somersaults, or pull it across the tray. The repel force causes somersaults to happen; attract force causes the pull to take place. (See Fig. 4-23.)

Fine points to discuss

Explain: The laws of magnetism (likes repel; unlikes attract).

What does repel mean? (Push away.)

What does attract mean? (Pull together.)

When one magnet pushes another magnet, is that an attraction force or a repulsion force? (A repulsion force.)

What "colors" have to come together to create an attraction force? (Red and blue.)

What "colors" have to come together to create a repulsion force? (Red, red or blue, blue.)

5. Repelling and attracting magnets on a wooden dowel

Materials

Four marked magnets with holes in their centers, a thin wooden dowel that fits through the holes in the magnets.

Procedure

1 Demonstrate floating magnets (magnets with holes in their centers). Using a thin wooden dowel, show how the magnets appear to float up and down the stick. Place the magnets together so "unlike" colors touch. They will all connect. Now place the magnets so "like" colors touch. They will repel each other and appear to be floating up and down the dowel.

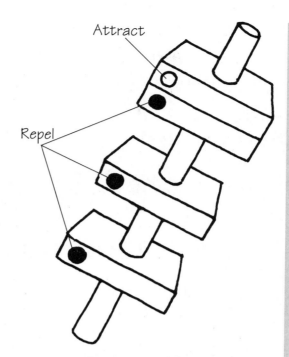

4-24 Repelling and attracting magnets on a wooden dowel.

These floating magnets have a pole on each face (side).

2 After the demonstration, let the children experiment making magnets float on a dowel or a thin plastic drinking straw.

Fine points to discuss

• The magnets appear to be floating as you move the bottom magnet up and down the dowel because they are repelling each other. The magnetic force is causing a push. (Likes repel and opposites attract.)

6. Demonstrating attract and repel through body language

Materials

None.

Procedure

1 Clasp hands together to show attraction.

2 Separate hands to show repulsion.

3 Have children think of other body language to demonstrate attract and repel with each other.

IX. Magnetic toys

1. Magnetic animal pairs

Materials

Magnetic toy frogs or turtles, or other novelty magnetic toy set.

4-25 Magnetic puppets.

Use thumb tacks or paper clips on puppet feet bottoms

Procedure

Demonstrate frog magnets. (One frog can make the other frog spin.) Then let children experiment with them.

Fine points to discuss

- Attract means to stick together; repel means to push away.
- Discuss why the frogs can make each other spin.

2. Magnet puppets

Materials

Magnetic puppets (with paper clip feet), shoe-box puppet stage,* two magnets, thumbtacks.

Procedure

1 Demonstrate magnetic puppets and shoe-box puppet stage with two magnets.

How do the puppets move? (The puppets have thumbtacks or paper clips on their feet. A magnet is moving underneath them in the box. The magnet makes them move. The thumbtacks or paper clips are attracted to the magnet. The two magnets repel and attract each other, which also causes the puppets to come together and /or to separate.)

2 Let children experiment with the magnetic puppets and/or design their own magnetic puppets. (See Fig. 4-25.)

3. Paint with magnets

(Adapted from: *Wonderscience* by Wendy and Kim Nichols.)

* Adapted from Rose Wyler.

Materials

For each child or group of children: metal washers, cafeteria tray, poster paint, a 12-inch-by-18-inch piece of paper, magnet.

Procedure

1 Place the 12-inch-by-18-inch piece of paper on the cafeteria tray.
2 Spill a small glob of paint onto the paper.
3 Place the washer into the paint. Pull the washer around the paper with the magnet from underneath the tray.

Why is the washer moving? (Magnetic strength pulls the washer through the paint.)

4 A variation on this idea is to use a maze from a coloring book instead of paint. Place a magnet, or a paper clip on top of the maze. Put the maze on a cafeteria tray. Put a magnet underneath the maze, and pull the magnet or the paper clip around the maze. *Note:* If you use a magnet on top of the maze it will be repelled unless it is pulled from the end of the magnet that attracts the other magnet.

X. Magnetic poles

1. Compass

Materials

Compass, marked loadstone on a string.

Procedure

1 Show children a compass.
2 *Explain* that the needle in the middle is a little magnet. When it stops spinning, it always points in a north/south direction. In the olden

days, sailors used the sun and stars to navigate, using a loadstone for a compass. They hung the loadstone by a string and used the stone to help lead them toward their destination. If they knew where north was, it was easy to determine east and west.

3 Let children experiment with the compass. Tell them to spin it and to observe where it points when it stops.

4 Hang a marked loadstone on a string. Spin it. See where it points when it stops spinning.

2. A floating compass

Materials
See Activity VII, Procedure 2.

Procedure
Let the needle float. Place a compass near it. When the needle stops, have the children compare the direction the compass needle points with the direction the floating needle points.

Will Beakman's "magnetic needle boat" behave the same way?

Why or why not?

Fine point to discuss
How can you tell if the needle has been magnetized? (If it has been, then it should be able to make the needle on the compass spin.)

3. Finding a magnet's poles

Materials
Strong magnet, paper clips.

Procedure
The ends of a magnet are called its poles. Like poles repel and unlike poles attract, just like the colors that marked the magnets. Magnets are strongest at their poles.

1 Ask the following questions:

How can we prove this with paper clips?

Where will most of the paper clips stick?

2 Have children experiment to find out. (Most of the paper clips will stick on the ends of the magnet.)

Further resources
Dewey Decimal Classification Number for magnetism is: 527.2, 621.31

Selected books for children

Adler, David. *Amazing Magnets.* Mahwah, NJ: Troll, 1983. (For older children.)

Brown, Bob. *Science For You: 112 Illustrated Experiments.* TAB Books, 1988. (For children who can read, see chapter 1—Experiments with Electricity and Magnetism.)

Catherall, Ed. *Exploring Magnets.* Milwaukee: Raintree, 1990. (Good color sketches on what magnets can do.) Gr. 4–8.

Challand, Helen. *Experiments With Magnets.* Chicago: Children's Press, 1986. (Gr. K–3.)

Fitzpatrick, Julie. *Magnets.* Morristown, NJ: Silver Burdett, 1987.

Freeman, Mae. *The Real Book of Magnets.* New York: Scholastic, 1970. (Gr. K-3.)

Kirkpatrick, Rena K. *Look at Magnets.* Milwaukee, Wisconsin: Raintree, 1985. (Gr. 2–4.)

Santrey, Laurence. *Magnets.* Mahwah, NJ: Troll, 1985.

Selected resource books for adults and older children

Activities Integrating Math and Science (AIMS), Mostly Magnets. Fresno, CA: AIM'S Educational Foundation, P.O. Box 8120, Fresno, CA 93747-8120.

Beakman's World, A Universal Press Syndicated television program, distributed by Columbia Pictures, produced by John Ford for the Learning Channel, P.O. Box 30087, Kansas City, Missouri 64112. (Clever, cuteand comical weekly

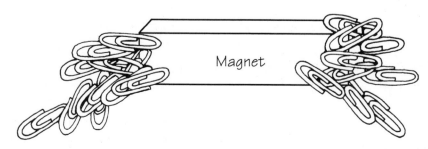

4-26 *Finding a magnet's poles.*

Magnet

television program for children. Focuses on different science concepts.)

Brown, Robert J. *333 More Science Tricks and Experiments*. TAB Books. 1984. (See Chapter 8, Electricity and Magnetism.)

Challoner, Jack. *My First Batteries and Magnet Book: A Life-Size Guide to Electricity and Magnetism*. New York: Dorling Kindersley, 1992. (Fun magnetic and electrical toy projects to make using arts and crafts with your child or children. Good way to spend a rainy day.)

Gega, Peter C. *Elementary Science Education, 6th ed.* New York: Macmillan, 1990. (See chapter 11—Magnetic Interactions.)

Harlan, Jean. *Science Experiences for the Early Childhood Years, 5th ed.* New York: Macmillan, 1992. (An excellent science resource book to use with younger children.)

Jennings, Terry. *Magnets*. New York: Glouster, 1990. (Good for older children that can read.)

Nichols, Wendy and Kim. *Wonderscience*. Palo Alto, CA: Learning Expo, 1990. (See chapter 1, Forces and movement.)

Taylor, Barbara. *More Power to You: The Science of Batteries and Magnets*. New York: Random House, 1992. (Electric Circuits/Experiments/Magnetism.)

Whyman, Kathryn. *Electricity and Magnetism*. Gloucester, 1986. (Good for older children that know how to read.)

Wood, Robert W. *Physics for Kids: 49 Easy Experiments with Electricity and Magnetism*. TAB Books, 1990. (For children who know how to read and want to do more activities with magnets and electricity.)

Wyler, Rose. *Magic Secrets*. New York: Harper Children, 1991. (Gr. K–3.)

General community enrichment activities

Junk yard (with big electromagnet) Have children observe the electromagnetic crane in action.

Go on a magnetic hunt around a building Observe how and where magnets are used.

Take apart a motor (Find a magnet inside.)

5

Static electricity

Objectives

The objectives of this chapter are for children to become aware of the following:

- Static electricity's presence.
- That static electricity can be produced on a dry day by the action of friction.
- That static electricity can be collected, but it is hard to hold on to.
- The meaning of force.
- How small "small" can be.
- That models help us understand the atom.
- That water reduces or eliminates static electricity.
- The nature of static electricity.

General background information for parents and teachers

Static electricity Static electricity is an accumulation of electric charges on an insulated body. It is an electric discharge resulting from such an accumulation. When it is around, it creates a cracking noise and/or a shock from the electric charges.

Static electricity can be obtained by vigorously rubbing two different dry materials together. Friction from rubbing and close contact causes electrons to transfer from one dry material to another. Static electricity usually cannot harm anyone. It is not powerful like current electricity. It is okay and safe to play with, but it is not safe to play with current electricity (unless the voltage is low, as with 6-volt batteries).

Static electricity is free electrons and atoms that are missing electrons. In a material that is a poor conductor, the free electrons are unable to move to where an atom without an electron exists, so the charges remain in the material. That is, electrons can be grouped in one place (in one of two materials rubbed together) and the atoms without electrons in another place (the other material).

Note: Lightning is the result of static electricity discharging. Lightning can be quite harmful. There are also machines that generate static electricity. These machines can give quite a jolt.

Current electricity Current electricity refers to electricity that flows, like the current in a stream or river. When the current is turned on, it is constantly in motion.

Static Comes from a Greek word that means standing. Static electricity is usually at rest. It can be found on the surfaces of most materials. When the weather is dry, static electricity can be temporarily collected. *Note*: When you rub dry, freshly shampooed hair, it creates static better than does oily hair.

Electricity A term referring to the movement of electrons (including electrons that are in the wrong place as in static electricity).

Atoms Everything is made up of atoms. Atoms are microscopically minuscule units of matter. They are the smallest divisible pieces of matter that still retain their elemental properties. (An atom of iron is the smallest particle that is still iron.) Although we are unable to see atoms, scientists have developed an understanding of atoms through experimentation. We know they exist.

Theoretical models of the atom have been proposed over the years, and these models have certain properties. Scientists have tested actual materials to prove or disprove how good a model is.

It is theorized that:

a Atoms are made up of tiny electrically charged and non-electrically charged particles.

b The nuclei of atoms are made up of protons and neutrons. Protons are positively charged. Neutrons are neutral.

c Electrons are negatively charged and orbit around the positively charged nucleus.

d The positive protons in the nucleus cancel out the orbiting negative electrons. Nuclear forces hold atoms together.

e The protons and neutrons in the nucleus are "heavy" and stay together as a tight-knit group in the center of the atom.

f The electrons of the atom are much "lighter" in weight than the nucleus. Electrons travel alone and far away from each other in separate orbits (as the planets do around the sun). The paths of the individual electrons do not meet because their like negative charges repel one another.

Nuclear forces Nuclear forces appear to hold atoms together. They are extremely powerful and are still not well understood by scientists. The electrical forces of all the protons tend to blow the atom apart because electrical forces repel each other. There must exist a more powerful force at close distances that holds the nucleus together. When scientists study atoms with atom smashers, they are studying what holds atoms together.

Electrons Electrons are very tiny particles that orbit around the nucleus of atoms. Electrons carry negative electric charges.

Electric charges Can be positive or negative. If it is neutral, it is not a charge.

Electrically positive A positive charge is caused when atoms lose electrons. It has a force. A force is a push or a pull. The force makes it possible for paper to stick to a wall or for items that are electrically charged to "stick together."

Electrically negative A negative charge is caused when atoms gain electrons, or when electrons are knocked free of an atom and remain loose. Like a positive electrical charge, a negative charge also has a force that causes it to push or pull, thus causing materials to "stick together."

Electrically neutral A neutral material has an equal number of positive and negative electric charges that have canceled each other out. It does not have a force or charge.

"Free" or separated electrons "Free" or separated electrons cause static electric charges. Electrons become free and transfer to other materials when they are attracted to a material that has a stronger attraction. This transfer occurs when two different dry materials are rubbed together vigorously.

a The atoms of the two dry materials are jostled through the friction action of vigorous rubbing. The heat from friction and the collisions of electrons caused from jostling cause the outer orbiting electrons to separate from their atoms.

b One of the two materials will have temporarily lost electrons and will carry a positive charge. The other material will have temporarily gained electrons and carry a negative charge.

c Rubbing two different, dry, "electrically neutral" materials together does not produce electric current. It merely creates a temporary imbalance in the number of electrons possessed by the atoms of each material.

Use of static electricity Static electricity has no real practical use except to help young children understand simple concepts about electricity. It is easy to collect on a dry day, but hard to hold on to. Moisture shortens the time span of a charge's force. Moisture helps a charge neutralize itself. Only separated or "free" electric charges (+ or −) carry force. When an electron is no longer separated or "free" from its atom, it is neutral and carries no force. (No force equals no charge.)

Note: Do not attempt to do static activities unless the air is very dry. Creating static electricity depends upon the lack of humidity or moisture in the air. Static is easiest to create on a dry, cold winter day, when you notice your hair is "crackling."

A law of electricity As in magnetism, like electrical charges repel and unlike electrical charges attract. Positive attracts negative. Positive repels positive. Negative repels negative.

Conductors Conductors are materials that allow electric charges to pass and spread through them easily (like metal and water or moisture). Static electricity cannot accumulate and collect on things when electrons flow easily. If there is no conduction path to remove a charge, then static electricity stays at rest and separated, and static force results. (Force equals charge.)

Static electricity can be induced on a conductor by bringing an object with a charge on it near the conductor. Because opposites attract, one charge on the normally neutral conductor is attracted to the charged object, and the other charges move as far away as possible.

Insulators Insulators are materials that do not allow electric charges to pass through them easily (like rubber, glass, and plastic). Electrons cannot move easily

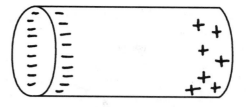

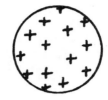

Conductor

Charged object

5-2 Charged object and conductor.

through an insulator. Insulators help keep a charge in place.

Electric wires are covered with insulation to keep the electric charge concentrated in the wires and to protect materials that the live electricity could hurt or damage. The insulation around electric wires also helps to prevent live electrical wires from touching each other and causing a short circuit.

Note: As you do these activities with your children, try to encourage them to keep a science journal of their observations and their thoughts.

Activities and procedures

I. Creating static electricity

I. Creating static electricity with balloons

Materials

Inflated balloons for each child or group of children.

Procedure

1 Have children rub the balloon against a wool sweater. It will start to sound "crackly." (Bits of dust and fiber in the air will stick to the charged balloon.)

2 Have the children place the balloon against the wall. (It will stick to the wall.)

Fine points to discuss

Why does the balloon stick to the wall? (It has an electric charge.)

What is a charge? (In science, it is not the way we pay for things. A charge is a scientific word that means something has been energized or given energy. The electric charge is caused by static electricity. The charge makes the balloon "cling" to materials like the wall, which are not charged.)

How does rubbing help us get a charge? (Rubbing creates heat, and a "closeness" between two materials that are rubbed. Rubbing causes static charges to transfer from one material to the other.)

Explain: The wall has to have an opposite charge for attraction to occur. Remember that in static, as in magnetism, opposites attract.

The charge can be induced (produced) if the wall is ever so slightly conductive. If a balloon is electrically negative and brought near an electrically positive wall, the balloon will repel negative charges and attract positive charges. These opposite charges on the wall and the balloon are what make the balloon stick to the wall.

2. Feeling heat from friction

Materials
None.

Procedure
1 Have children rub their hands together hard and fast.

How do your hands feel? (They should feel warm.)

2 *Explain*: Heat is energy. The heat is created from the friction caused by rubbing.

Fine point to discuss

Where is electricity? (Electricity is everywhere. But most materials are usually "electrically balanced" so we do not feel or see the effects of the energy. When materials are not neutral, we can feel the effects of the temporary energy. It is called static electricity.)

3. Attracting a charged balloon

Materials
For each child or group of children: inflated balloons, string.

Procedure
1 Have children tie a string to the end of a charged balloon. Tie the balloon so it will hang freely. Have a child approach the charged balloon with the palm of his or her hand opened. The balloon will be attracted to the child's hand.

2 *Explain*: Our skin is oily and somewhat conductive, so it is easy for some electrons to transfer or move. Opposite charges attract, so the balloon will stick to the palm of our hand.

Our hair is also slightly conductive and we can induce a charge that causes our hair to be attracted by a balloon. However, the individual hair strands that are attracted to the balloon will also tend to repel one another as they stand on end, or stick up and out).

3 Have a child hold his or her hand flat against the side of the balloon. The child's hand will lift the balloon up because the charge stays attracted to the child's hand and causes lift to occur when his or her hand goes up. (See Fig. 5-3.)

4. Attracting and repelling charged balloons

Materials
For each child or group of children: two inflated balloons, string.

Procedure
1 Have children cut a piece of string about two or three feet long and tie one end of the string to each balloon.

2 Hang the two balloons suspended on a hanger. (If there is no place to hang the hanger, then, if necessary, hang the hanger from a broom handle supported by two chairs, or two tables.)

3 Allow the two balloons to hang freely. Have the children observe what happens to the balloons. (If left to hang free, they will touch each other.)

4 Now charge each of the balloons by rubbing them on wool or animal fur. Have the children observe what happens to the balloons. (The balloons repel each other because they have like charges.)

5 Tell children to place their hand between the two balloons that are repelling each other. Have children observe what happens to the balloons. (The charged balloons will touch the child's hand.) (See Fig. 5-4.)

Fine points to discuss

How are electrical charges like magnets? (Electrical charges behave as magnets do; likes repel and unlikes attract.)

What do we know about charges, particles, and electrons? (Charges are caused by very tiny

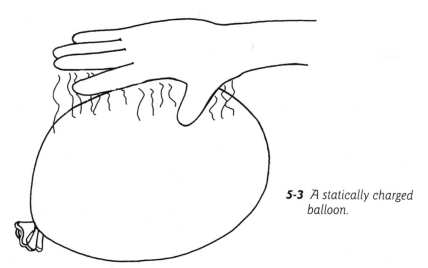

5-3 *A statically charged balloon.*

particles called electrons, which we cannot see. No one has ever seen an electron. Scientists have theories that help explain things. Sometimes scientists talk about their theories of electrons, atoms, and molecules to explain how things happen.)

5. Creating static electricity with newspaper

Materials

Newspaper, pencil.

Procedure

1 Place a half sheet of newspaper or newsprint on a flat, smooth wall. Have the children rub the sheet of newspaper or newsprint with a pencil held flat (horizontally) against the wall. Have the children observe what happens. (The paper is able to stay put on the wall. Static electricity is holding the paper on the wall.)

2 After a while, the paper will stop clinging and fall to the floor. (The paper will become electrically neutral or balanced again.) (See Fig. 5-5.)

Fine points to discuss

Why was the paper able to "stick" to the wall? (Extra electrons were collected on the paper from the pencil. A static charge was caused by extra electrons or a shortage of electrons.)

Explain: The static charge caused the paper to "stick" to the wall. When the air is dry, extra electrons can be collected on the surface of some materials that are rubbed. When we rub two materials together, some places will have an excess of electrons and others will have a shortage.

Why did the paper fall? (The extra electrons found another place where they could stay. It is difficult to hold onto extra electrons. They do not stay put.)

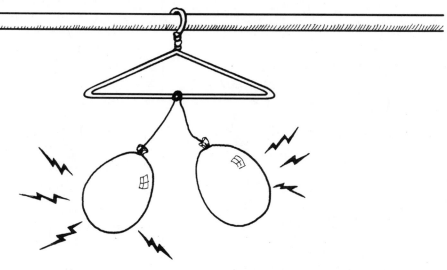

5-4 *Statically charged balloons repel each other.*

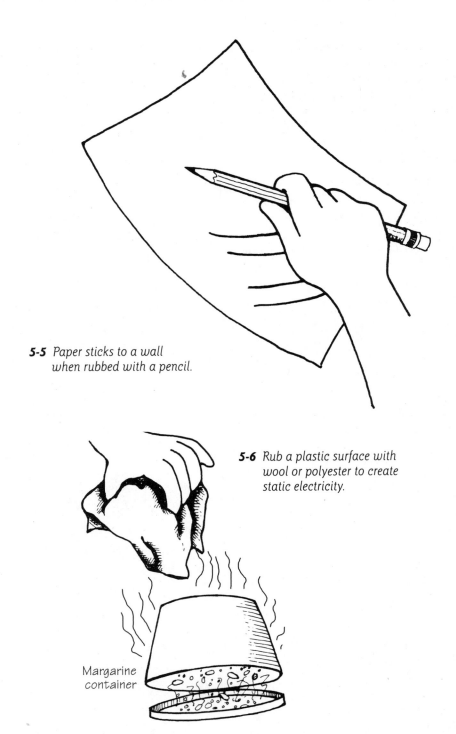

5-5 *Paper sticks to a wall when rubbed with a pencil.*

5-6 *Rub a plastic surface with wool or polyester to create static electricity.*

Margarine container

6. Creating static electricity with an empty plastic container

Materials

Empty plastic margarine container with a lid; puffed rice; salt; pepper; a piece of wool.

Procedure

1 Fill the container with about ten pieces of puffed rice, a dash of salt, and a dash of pepper.

2 Remove the lid and empty the contents (puffed rice, salt, and pepper) onto the lid. Have a child lift the empty margarine tub up and hold it about half an inch above the lid. Observe whether the empty plastic container will lift any of the particles on the lid. (It might.)

3 Place a child's hand inside a plastic container so that the child's hand is touching the bottom of the inside of the container. Have the child use his or her other hand to rub the outside bottom of the container vigorously with a piece of wool to create static electricity.

4 Again, lift the empty but charged plastic container up and hold it about half an inch above the lid with the puffed rice, salt, and pepper. Again, have the child observe what happens. (The puffed rice will be lifted up, along with some of the salt and pepper particles.)

Fine points to discuss

Why was wool rather than something else used to rub the bottom of the margarine tub in order to create a static charge? (Wool comes from lamb's fur and it contains protein. Hair and fur contain protein. Protein can create static charges, especially on dry days when the materials are rubbed against plastics. Electrons are either scraped off of the wool and are collected on the bottom of the plastic tub, or they are collected on the wool from the bottom of the plastic tub.)

• *Explain:* For a long time, natural fiber materials like wool and silk have been used to generate static electricity. In recent years, human-made fibers have come into existence. Static cling occurs in materials made by humans.

Scientists have devised chemicals to reduce the static generated by clothes made from human-made fibers. They have created things to add to washing machines and clothes dryers to help further reduce the amount of static electricity produced in clothes made from human-made fibers. *Note:* Some plastics and human-made fibers are much better than wool or silk for generating static electricity.

Why are the particles of cereal, salt, and pepper lifted? (The particles of cereal, salt, and pepper are very light in weight and are uncharged. Unlike charges are attracted to the charged piece of plastic.)

II. Understanding force

I. Make a tin can move

Materials

Empty tin can, a magnet.

Procedure

1 Place a tin can on its side. Ask the children how the tin can can be made to move.

2 Use your hand to push or pull the can.

3 *Can the can be moved without touching it?* (Yes, by blowing on it.)

5-7 *A force pushes or pulls.*

4 If the children do not respond by saying "blowing on it," then show them how it can be moved by blowing on it.

5 Ask if a magnet can make the tin can move.

6 Demonstrate how the magnet can make it move without touching the can.

7 *Explain:* Our hands, the air, the magnet, and static electricity are all forces. Forces can pull or push things.

Fine point to discuss

What does a force do? (It pushes or pulls things.)

2. Bouncing a ball

Materials

A ball.

Procedure

1 Drop a bouncing ball. Observe how high it bounces.

2 Ask the following questions:

Can we make the ball bounce up higher?

How? (By moving our hand down fast before we let go of the ball.)

Fine point to discuss

How can we control the force of the ball's bounce? (The fast movement of our hand before we let go of the ball gives energy to the ball. The extra energy adds more force to the bounce of the ball. The ball will push off the floor with more force, and the ball will bounce higher than when it is just dropped.)

(Charges can have a weak force or a strong force. A strong charge has a lot of energy.

The energy comes from the loose electrons. If the electrons stay loose, the charge stays "strong." If the electrons do not stay loose or separated from their atoms, then the static electric charge is weak and becomes neutral.)

3. Electrically charged plastic tube makes a toilet paper roll roll

Materials

For each child or group of children: a toilet paper tube, a formica desk top, a plastic container tube such as the kind that the product called Crystal Lite is packed in, fleece cloth that is made out of polyester/cotton (like the cloth from which sweat pants are made).

Procedure

1 Rub the plastic container tube with the material that is made from 50% polyester/50% cotton.

2 Slowly approach the toilet paper tube with the charged plastic container tube.

3 Observe what happens to the toilet paper tube.

Why does the toilet paper tube roll? (Electrically charged objects can exert force on each other.)

4 Experiment to see if the plastic container tube can make other objects move.

Does it make a difference whether a lid is on the plastic container tube, so that the tube is closed at both ends?

Note: This activity can be done on a semihumid day.

III. The very small

1. Breaking cereal into particles

Materials

Puffed rice, toothpicks, magnifying glass.

Procedure

Have the children take a piece of puffed rice cereal and pick it apart. Have them find out how small a piece of puffed rice can be picked apart and still be a piece or particle of puffed rice. (The piece can be extremely small.)

Fine point to discuss

How small is small? (Too small to see. Salt and pepper are very small particles. A

5-8 Crushed cereal.

piece of puffed rice is made up of many particles.)

2. Crushing salt and pepper

Materials

Salt and pepper, magnifying lens.

5-9 Salt-and-pepper dust.

Procedure

1 Have children crush or grind the salt and the pepper down. Have them find out if it can be made into salt dust and pepper dust (obviously it can). Keep the two kinds of dust separate.

2 Have the children test to find out if these small particles are still salt and pepper by tasting the dust.

3 Allow each child the chance to make his/her own salt or pepper dust and to taste it.

4 Have the children look at the tiny particles through a magnifying lens and have them observe whether or not the particles are all the same size. (They are not. They are different shapes.)

3. Jumping salt and pepper

Materials

Empty plastic container, salt dust, pepper dust, a piece of wool.

Procedure

Have a child rub an empty plastic margarine container with a piece of wool to get the container charged. Have the child bring it near the particles of salt dust and pepper dust and then observe what happens. (The particles jump onto the bottom of the tub and stay charged longer.)

Fine point to discuss

Why do the particles stay charged longer? (The particles weigh less and are more sensitive to static electric charges. They are more sensitive than the larger pieces of puffed rice were.)

Note: The dust of salt, pepper, and puffed rice is made up of very small particles. When we compare the size of these dust particles to the size of an electron particle, the particles of salt, pepper, and puffed rice dust are gigantic—as gigantic as an elephant would look if it were standing next to an ant.

4. Model of an atom made from basketballs and tennis balls

Materials

Two basketballs, two tennis balls.

Procedure

Demonstrate how electrons collide when they are jostled and brought close together through rubbing and friction. Use two large basketballs and two tennis balls as a model of an atom. The tennis balls are models of electrons orbiting around the basketballs, which are models of the nucleus. When the tennis balls collide, they bounce off away from their orbit. They are shaken loose from the atom by the collision.

Fine point to discuss

What happens to the two balls when they collide? (They bounce off in a new direction. They get shaken off their path or orbit. The same thing happens when two materials are rubbed vigorously. Electrons get shaken loose. Electrons that are separated or shaken loose cause static electricity to occur.)

INFORMATION Atoms are extremely small. So small it is difficult to even comprehend. Richard Feynman, a renowned physicist, described an atom's size in his lecture this way:

If an apple is magnified to the size of the earth, then the atoms in the apple are approximately the size of the original apple. (The Feynman Lectures on Physics, Vol.1, Ch.1, pg. 1–3)

5. Inference model*

Materials

For each child or group of children: a covered shoe box, an object such as a pencil, a marble, or a penny.

Procedure

1 Tell the child to shake the box and try to guess what is inside the box.

* This activity was adapted from Esler, page 418.

A model

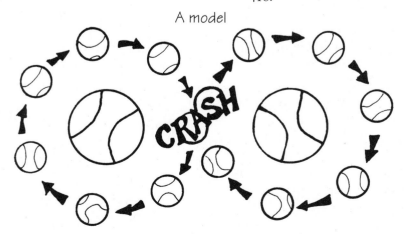

5-10 A model of the collision of orbiting electrons.

2 Record and graph what the children think might be in the box. Then open the box to see if they were able to guess what the mystery object was inside of the covered box.

3 *Explain*: Even though you cannot see what is inside the box, you can guess or make inferences about what might be inside, based on the sound you can hear.

Although no one has ever seen an atom, or an electron, scientists have been able to learn much about atoms and electrons by creating models from inferences based on observable phenomena, and by then testing the model on real materials.

IV. Lightning

1. Creating sparks with leather shoes on a rug

Materials

Children with leather-soled shoes.

Procedure

1 *Explain*: When static electricity charges are exchanged, sparks fly.

2 Have the children rub their leather-soled shoes against a carpet and then touch a metal doorknob. A shock can be felt. If the room is darkened, it is sometimes possible to see a spark.

3 *Explain*: Our bodies, which are wet inside, act as conductors. The charges generated on our shoes that are rubbed against the carpet manage to collect up our whole body. When we put our finger near a metal doorknob, it induces an opposite charge for the doorknob near our finger. The neutral doorknob has electrons that move about. Each end of the doorknob has opposite charges. The attraction of charges between our fingers and the nearby doorknob often can discharge. This discharge that we see is a minor form of lightning. That is why we see a spark.

Fine points to discuss

What causes lightning? (When clouds exchange charges, lightning is created and energy can be seen. The energy from the charge has been let loose and is in the air. Lightning is caused by huge charges of static electricity.)

Why does lightning occur during a wet storm? (Lightning occurs when a lot of moisture is present. Moisture helps carry or conduct electrons either toward each other or away from each other.

Big static charges are built up on clouds. The clouds are made of water droplets that do not touch one another. Down on the ground, the surfaces become covered with a thin film of water. This thin film of water on the ground tends not to hold any static charge.)

Why is it difficult to create static electricity on a wet day? (On a wet day, electrons flow easily. Static occurs when electrons are at rest and shake loose easily. On wet days, electrons do not separate easily. They flow through the moisture. The moisture acts as a conductor.)

2. Lightning safety tips

 Note: When talking about lightning, it is a good idea to discuss the safety tips shown in Table 5-1.

Table 5-1 **Safety tips during a lightning storm.**
1 Seek shelter indoors, but avoid touching electrical appliances or plumbing fixtures.
2 Stay away from open fields, hills, water, and trees that stand alone.
3 Cars with windows rolled up are safe places to be.

Fine points to discuss

(With older children, you might want to discuss the reasons for the safety rules shown in Table 5-1.)

V. Playing with static electricity

1. Static hair

Materials

Clean, recently washed hair; a plastic comb.

Procedure

Comb a child's hair briskly. If it is a dry day and the hair has just been washed and is not greasy and wet, static will be created. It might be necessary to comb hair for awhile to generate the static.

5-11 *Statically charged hair.*

Fine points to discuss

How can we tell that static has been created? (Hair starts to sound crackly, and is attracted to the comb. The hair appears to stand on end.)

Why is static created? (The friction of the comb rubbing against the hair causes the electrons to separate. The separated electrons are collected on the comb from the hair.

The comb has a negative charge and the hair has a positive charge. The hair has lost electrons and is positive. The comb has gained electrons and is negative.)

2. Hair raising

Materials

Hair with static electricity.

Procedure

Observe that the hair appears to stand on end when the comb is no longer near the hair.

Fine point to discuss

Why does the hair appear to stand on end when the comb is no longer near the hair? (The individual hairs, like the balloons from Activity #1, Procedure 4, are repelling each other with a like charge. The hair is attracted to the comb when the comb comes near. The comb has a different charge and attracts the hair.)

Review the point that static electricity is similar to magnetism: "likes" repel and "unlikes" attract.

3. Making paper "walk"

Materials

Tissue paper or newspaper, sewing thread, plastic drinking straw.

Procedure

1 Cut out two "people shapes" from tissue paper or newsprint.

2 Tie a piece of sewing thread to each of the paper people's heads.

3 Hang the two threads from a plastic drinking straw.

4 Keep the two paper dolls about two inches apart.

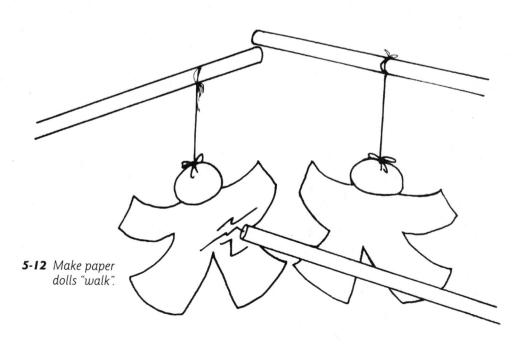

5-12 *Make paper dolls "walk".*

5 Rub another plastic straw through a child's hair. (For best results, be sure hair is squeaky clean.) Keep rubbing or stroking the child's hair with the straw until the straw is charged.

6 Have a child gently rub the "paper people dolls" with the charged straw.

7 Have a child approach the paper doll with the charged straw and observe what happens to the paper dolls. (They will move in circles.)

8 Let children experiment with making paper "walk."

Fine point to discuss

Why do the paper dolls move and turn in circles? (The charged straw carries extra electrons that carry an invisible electronic force.)

4. Static tube

Note: This activity can be done on a semi-humid day.

Materials

For each child or group of children: a clear acrylic or cellulosic packing tube* (the kind that pony tail holders are packed in at the grocery store or drug store) with two lids (so that the tube can remain closed), tiny silver candy balls (the kind used to decorate cakes and cookies**), polyester /cotton sweatpant cloth or polyester/cotton handkerchief.

Procedure

1 Place about 10 or 20 silver candy balls inside the plastic tube. Cap both ends closed.

 If you have little children, you might want to glue the caps onto the ends. The bottle of "silver decors" specifically states on the front label: "Use only as a decoration, not a candy," and the ingredients panel on the side of the bottle states: "Sold as a decoration only."

2 Rub the closed tube vigorously with the sweat cloth material.

3 Observe how the balls interact with each other.

4 Move your finger along the tube and observe what happens.

---

* Flex Tubes (clear cellulosic packing tubes) can also be ordered from Brockway-Flex Products, 445 Industrial Road, Carlstadt, N.J. 07072. Tel. #800-526-6273.

** I use the product by McCormick called cake mate Silver Decors.

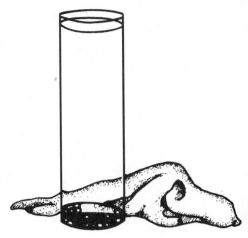

5-13 *A statically charged tube.*

Note: Audrey Brainard as well as Wendy and Kim Nichols in their book Wonderscience suggest putting tiny Styrofoam beads inside the static tube. You might want to make each kind of tube and compare how the force of static affects both materials.

Fine points to discuss*

What makes the beads/balls move?

Is there a pattern to their movement?

How can you control their movement?

What happens if you rub the tube with (or on) different materials?

What happens to the tube if you leave the tube undisturbed for awhile?

What happens to the beads/balls if you rub one end of the tube?

Can you make the beads/balls move without sticking to the tube or to each other?

How can you get rid of the static charge inside the tube?

What happens when you bring two static tubes next to each other?

Do the beads/balls behave the same way inside of other plastic containers?

Do other particles behave the same way as beads/balls inside a plastic tube?

5. Silver candy balls on grooves

Materials

Silver candy balls; a long-playing record; a large, shallow plastic container or cardboard box; a piece of 50% cotton/50% polyester sweatpant cloth.

---

* These suggested questions about tiny Styrofoam beads were acquired from Audrey Brainard's "Hands-On-Science" seminar.

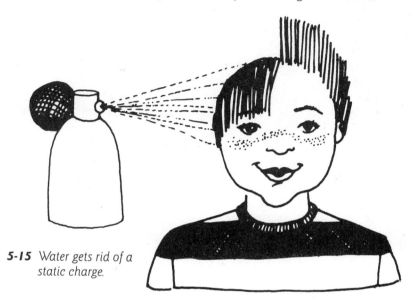

5-14 Statically charged silver candy balls on a grooved record.

5-15 Water gets rid of a static charge.

Procedure

1 Place the long-playing record inside of a shallow container so that it lies flat.
2 Charge the long-playing record by rubbing on it with the cloth.
3 Place about ten candy silver balls on the grooves of the charged, long-playing record. Observe what happens.

Note: If you use a large shallow plastic container* like the kind waiters use to clear tables at restaurants, you will be able to observe another interesting reaction of the balls when they meet on the grooves of the bottom of the container, or when they meet on the rounded edge of the sides.)

What happens to the balls when they are on grooves?

Can you predict how the balls will move?

* Large shallow plastic containers used for clearing tables in restaurants can usually be purchased at The Price Club.

What happens when two balls meet?

Why do you suppose this happens?

6. Getting rid of static

Materials

Atomizer filled with water; static charges on hair or on newspaper.

Procedure

Have a child spray the static electric charge with an atomizer. The spray of water will create a moist situation. Have children observe what happens to the static. (It will disappear.)

Fine point to discuss

Why does the static disappear? (The moisture helped the electrons flow back to an atom. The water acted as a conductor that led the way for the separated electron to find an atom that needed an electron.)

Further resources

Dewey Decimal Classification Number for electricity is: J557.

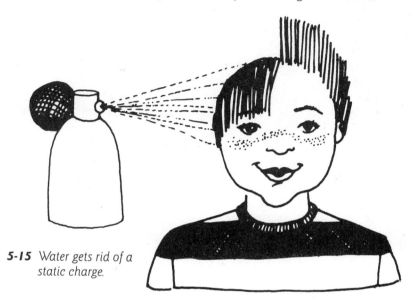

Selected books for children

Branley, Franklyn. *Flash, Crash, Rumble and Roll*. New York: Harper and Row, 1987.

Brown, Bob. *Science For You, 112 Illustrated Experiments*. TAB Books, 1988. (See page 13, "Sparks.")

Brown, Bob. *More Science For You, 112 Illustrated Experiments*. TAB Books, 1988. (See page 80, "Static and a bubble," page 81, "Muscle-power electricity.")

Resource books for adults and older children

Brown, Robert J. *333 More Science Tricks and Experiments*. TAB Books, 1984. (See chapter 8, Electricity and Magnetism.)

Feynman, Richard Philip. "The Feynman Lectures on Physics". Volume 1, Commemorative Issue. Menlo Park, CA: Addison Wesley, 1989.

Mebane, Robert C. and Thomas R. Rybolt. *Adventures with Atoms and Molecules*. Hillside, NJ: Enslow, 1987.

National Science Resource Center (NSRC). Science and Technology for Children. *Electric Circuits, Teacher's Guide: Student Activity Book*. Washington, DC: National Science Resource Center, 1992.

Selected literature connection for younger children

Schwartz, David M. *How Much is a Million?* New York: Scholastic, 1985.

General community enrichment activities

Visit a beach to observe the millions of grains of sand (to develop an awareness of how small a molecule is, and of how much space a million particles of sand would take up).

6
Sound

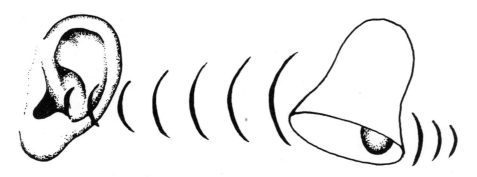

Objectives

The objectives of this chapter are for children to become aware of the following:

- That sounds are caused by vibrations.
- That many kinds of vibrations can be seen, felt, and heard.
- That an action of force or energy is needed to start a vibration.
- That a lot of force creates a loud noise, but a little bit of force creates a soft noise.
- That vibrations can make things nearby vibrate.
- That vibrations can travel through objects.
- The meaning of the terms vibrate, energy, echo, reflection, bounce, absorb, wave, pitch, and frequency.
- The relative differences between volume terms (loud and soft) and pitch terms (low and high).

- That different sizes of vibrating objects can create different frequencies and pitches when they vibrate.

General background information for parents and teachers

Sound The source of all sound is movements or vibrations. When there is no movement, there is no sound to be heard. Sound is a form of energy. Energy is needed to make a sound.

The speed of sound The speed of sound is 1,100 feet per second. Light travels faster than sound. During a lightning storm, we see the lightning before we hear the sound of the thunder.

Vibration A vibration is a back and forth motion. When vibrations stop, sound stops. Vibrations can cause other things nearby to vibrate.

Larynx The part of the human throat that houses the vocal chords.

Sound waves Sound travels in waves. Sound waves can move through things. Waves move best through solid objects like the earth, metals, and wood. Sound waves do not travel as well through a gas such as air or through spongy materials like pillows, which contain air pockets. All vibrations cause sound waves.

Measuring a wave The length of a sound wave is measured from one crest to the next, or from one trough to the next.

Crest The high part of a wave.

Trough The low part of a wave.

Cycle A complete wave from one crest to the next.

 Hertz Describes the frequency of a wave's cycle. The hertz "number" tells the number of cycles to pass by a given point in one second.

Sound absorption Materials that absorb sound waves often have air pockets. Air pockets trap sound waves. Some building materials are designed to catch and absorb sounds. (Have the children examine a piece of acoustical ceiling tile and observe the holes.)

Echoes An echo is caused by a sound wave that bounces back from an object, like a ball bouncing off a wall.

Reverberation A prolonged echo effect.

 Refraction Refraction occurs when sound waves are bent, and parts of the sound wave travel at different speeds. This happens on a windy day because the different air currents refract or bend sound waves.

Feeling sound vibrations Many sound vibrations can be seen as well as felt. Deaf people take advantage of their other senses to "hear" what their ears cannot hear.

Energy In physics, the term energy refers to the capacity to do work.

Energy transfer Energy transfer occurs when energy is released and causes other things nearby to vibrate. Once the energy is used to start a vibration, the vibration stays in motion until that energy given to start the "reaction" of vibration is dissipated.

Chain reaction A chain reaction is a self-sustaining "reaction" of energy being transferred that does not dissipate.

 Conservation of energy A law of physics that states that the input of energy is equal to the output of energy. Energy can neither be destroyed nor created. It can be changed from one form into another, but the total amount of energy in our universe is always constant. It never changes.

Kinetic energy The energy of motion.

Potential energy Stored energy, or energy of position.

Audible sound Sound vibrations that can be heard.

Inaudible sound Sound vibrations that cannot be heard because the frequency is too high or too low for our ears to be sensitive to. Dogs, dolphins, and bats can hear sounds at higher frequencies than are audible to human ears.

Ultrasonic waves Bats and dolphins can hear ultrasonic waves that are inaudible to human ears. These animals make use of echoes in conjunction with their hearing.

Frequency The rate or speed of a vibration. Frequency measures the distance and time between crests.

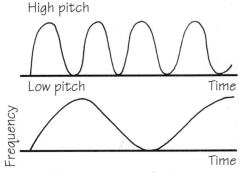

- Different number of vibrations
- Same amount of time
- Same height of wave crests (same amplitude)

6-2 Pitch corresponds to a wave's frequency.

Pitch The "highness" or "lowness" of a note on a musical scale. Pitch corresponds to frequency. On a musical scale, the low notes have a lower frequency. When vibration of low notes occurs, they sound lower, slower, and heavier, whereas the high notes on a musical scale have a higher frequency. When they vibrate, they sound faster, higher, and lighter.

Musical scale Composed of musical notes with increasing pitch at regular intervals.

Noise A combination of sound tones or notes or unrelated frequencies.

Decibel The unit of measure used to measure intensity (Brainard, NJSTA). It refers to the amount of pressure received at the eardrum from sound vibrations.

Amplify To intensify or to make something louder.

Intensity Refers to the loudness or softness of a sound. Intensity varies with the amount of energy used to produce a sound and the amount of air that it causes to vibrate. (Brainard, NJSTA.)

Amplitude The intensity and loudness of a sound. It is measured in decibels. Amplitude measures the height of a wave's crest (above the equilibrium level).

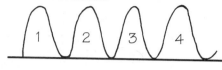

Loud soundwave

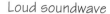

Soft soundwave

- Same number of vibrations
- Same length of time
- Different heights of wave crests (different amplitude)

6-3 The volume of a sound corresponds to its amplitude.

Volume The degree of loudness or the intensity of a sound. When we turn up the "volume," we amplify or increase the intensity of vibrations. Volume can be loud or soft.

Musical resonance The quality that increases and lengthens musical tones, resulting in an increased amplitude or loudness of sound. This resonance is caused when the sound waves from one object cause another object that is larger to vibrate. The additional sound vibrations produce a louder sound by putting a larger amount of air into motion.

The design of musical instruments that produce musical tones Musical tones are created by instruments. The tones can be modified through an understanding of the force or energy needed to make loud or soft sounds, and through an understanding of how to mechanically change or vary the frequency or speed of a vibration to control pitch. Pitch can be high or low. Intensity of volume varies with the amount of energy used to create the sound. (Brainard, NJSTA.)

Table 6-1 Things to know when designing stringed instruments

1 Loose strings vibrate at a low frequency and tight strings vibrate at a high frequency.
2 Long strings vibrate at a lower frequency than short strings.
3 Heavy strings vibrate at a lower frequency than light strings.
4 On a piano, the weight, rather than the thickness, affects lower pitches.
5 On a rubber band, the pitch goes up as the tension is increased.

Quality or timbre The characteristic of an individual musical instrument. The quality that makes a clarinet sound like a clarinet and a French horn sound like a French horn. The same pitch can be played on different instruments, but the quality of the sounds will be different. Quality depends upon the material the vibrating object is made with, as well as the size and the shape of the object (Brainard, NJSTA.)

Note: As you do these activities with your children, try to encourage them to keep a science journal of their observations and their thoughts.

Activities and procedures

I. Sounds are made when something vibrates

1. Noisy paper

Materials

A piece of notebook paper.

Procedure

1 Ask the children the following question:

Can the paper make a noise? (They will probably respond "no." Or they might suggest that it needs to be "rattled" in some way.)

2 Hold the piece of paper with two hands and shake it.

Is there a noise? (Yes.)

When does the paper make a noise? (When it is moved.)

2. Vibrating ruler

Materials

An 18-inch wooden ruler.

Procedure

1 Extend the wooden ruler over the edge of a table. Hold one end of the ruler with your hand and pluck the extended edge with your thumb. The ruler will make a sound.

What happens to the ruler when it makes a sound? (It moves.)

2 *Explain*: The ruler moves back and forth very fast. This kind of very fast movement back and forth is called a vibration.

3. Humming

Materials

None.

Procedure

1 Have the children place their fingers on their throats and say "mmmmm" in a low tone.

How does your finger feel? (Their fingers should feel "tickly.")

2 Have the children find a partner. Each child should feel the other child's throat while they each say "mmmmm" or talk to each other.

 Caution the children to hold their fingers straight and not to press hard on the other child's throat.

Is it easier to feel the vibration on their own throat or on someone else's throat? (It is easier to feel on someone else.)

Fine points to discuss

Can our fingers "hear?" (Some people who cannot hear very well, or who cannot see or hear, can "hear" what someone is saying by feeling the person's throat when the person is talking. Every sound has a different feel. Our fingers can be trained to "hear" what our ears cannot hear. Helen Keller was blind and deaf but she was able to train her fingers to "hear.")

Note: You might want to encourage children to stay with their partner and to feel and "hear" different throat sounds with their fingers so that they can understand better how sensitive their fingers are to vibrations.

Going further

If you have a cat that likes to purr, try feeling the cat's throat to feel the vibration. Be gentle when you feel the cat's throat, so as not to hurt the cat. Does it feel like your friend's throat felt when they were talking?

4. Wiggling

Materials

None.

Procedure

1 Have the children wiggle around, slap their knees and clap their hands. Then ask them to sit very still.

2 Ask the children the following questions:

When did they hear more noise?

When they moved or when they stayed still? (When they move there is more noise.)

II. We can see things vibrate

1. Vibrating rubber bands

Materials

A rubber band.

Procedure

1 Have children pluck a stretched rubber band.

2 Ask the children the following questions:

What do you see and hear? (They can see a vibration and hear a sound.)

Does the rubber band make sound when it is not vibrating? (No, it cannot.)

2. Vibrating rice

6-4 Rice vibrates or bounces on a coffee can drum when the drum is struck.

Materials

An empty coffee can with a plastic lid; some uncooked rice grains; and a spoon.

Procedure

1 Have children place a few grains of rice on top of the coffee can drum. Strike the top of the can with a spoon.

2 Observe what happens to the rice grains. (They will bounce on top of the plastic lid.)

What causes the rice to bounce?

Why can we see the rice bouncing? (We can see the rice bouncing because sometimes we can see the effects of a vibration.)

3. Noisy bell

Materials

A small metal bell with a clacker.

Procedure

1 Tell child to hold the bell by the clacker and shake it.

Why is there no sound from the bell? (The clacker is not hitting the bell and causing a vibration.)

2 Allow the clacker to hit the bell.

What do you see when you hear the bell ring? (You see the clacker strike against the metal on the bell. You hear the metal on the bell vibrate when it is struck.)

4. Tuning fork splash

6-5 Create a splash with a vibration.

Materials

A tuning fork, a pie pan filled to the top with water, newspaper.

Procedure

1 Hit the tuning fork against your palm. Place it near each child's ear so that he/she can hear that a sound is coming from the tuning fork.

2 When the fork is not making a sound, and is therefore not vibrating, place the tuning fork in the pan of water. Observe what happens to the water. (Nothing much.)

3 Hit the tuning fork against the palm of your hand so that it will vibrate. While it is vibrating, submerge a tip of the fork into the water. Observe what happens. (A splash effect should occur.)

Fine points to discuss

What causes the water to splash when the vibrating tuning fork hits the water? (The vibrations.)

How do we know the tuning fork is vibrating when it makes a sound? (We can see the vibration effect in the water. We can also see the blurry look of the prongs when they are vibrating.)

What has to happen to the tuning fork for it to make a sound? (It has to be moving.)

 Note: Never strike a tuning fork against a hard surface. The palm of your hand is always available for striking. The tuning fork will only make a sound while it is vibrating.

III. We can feel things vibrate

I. Humming straws

Materials

Drinking straws.

Procedure

1 Pass out a straw to each child. Let the children blow through the straws. Ask them to hum a note through the straw and to feel the other end of the straw with their palm. (See Fig. 6-6.)

How did your humming feel through the straw on your palm? (It should feel tickly.)

2 Have the children place a finger over the end of the straw while they are humming. Observe what happens to the sound. (The sound becomes muffled. It is not free to move outside of the tube.)

3 Have the children tap the end of the straw while humming and listen to the different rhythmic effects that can be created. (See Fig. 6-6.)

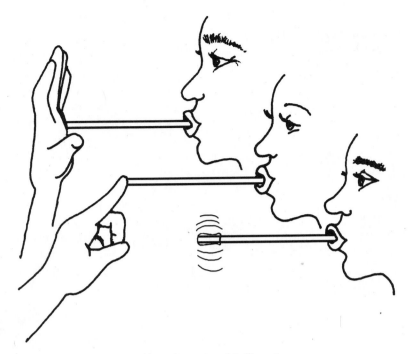

6-6 *Hum through a drinking straw.*

2. Kazoo

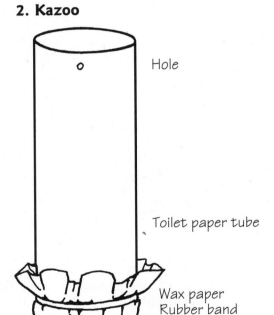

Hole

Toilet paper tube

Wax paper
Rubber band

6-7 *A homemade kazoo.*

Materials

Cardboard tube from paper towels or toilet paper; waxed paper; rubber band; sharpened pencil for poking a hole through tube.

Procedure

1 Have each child make his/her own kazoo. To make a kazoo, place a small, square piece of waxed paper on the end of the cardboard tube and secure it tightly with a rubber band. Poke a hole through the tubing with a sharp pencil.

2 Have the children hum through the kazoo and feel the end of the kazoo with their fingertips while humming. (Children will feel vibrations from their own sounds in the tube.)

3 Ask the children what happens to the kazoo sound when they cover the end of the tube with their hand or when they cover the little hole in the tube. Have them experiment to find out. (When the air hole is left open, the sound is louder; when the hand covers the end, the sound is very muffled.)

3. Feeling a radio vibrate

Materials

A radio.

Procedure

1 Turn the radio on. Turn the volume up. Have the children feel the sound vibrations from the radio's speaker.

2 Have the children feel the difference between loud and soft volume on the radio's speaker.

6-8 Make and listen to a megaphone model.

IV. Vibrations can cause other things nearby to vibrate

I. Megaphone model

Materials

Tuning fork, paper cup or Styrofoam cup.

Procedure

1 Hit the tuning fork firmly against your palm. While it is vibrating, allow the tip of one prong of the fork to lightly touch the bottom of a paper cup.

Why can the sound of the tuning fork be heard when it touches the cup? (It can be heard because the vibrations from the tuning fork cause the paper to vibrate. This creates a louder sound. More air is made to vibrate [at a larger amplitude]. The sound is intensified or amplified.)

2 Have the children experiment touching other parts of the cup. Ask if the sound is as loud when the vibrating tuning fork touches the sides or the rim of the cup as when it touched the bottom of the cup. (It is loudest when it touches the bottom of the cup. The sound coming from the cup at the bottom is amplified more because the cup is shaped somewhat like a megaphone. The sounds are able to resonate on the cup, creating an amplification and a prolongation of the sound.)

2. Going further: Make a model of a gramophone

Note: For younger children, you might want to demonstrate how a gramophone works. Older children can try to make the gramophone model themselves.

Table 6-2 To create a model gramophone
1 Stick a straight pin through the side of a Styrofoam cup to create a model of a gramophone speaker.
2 Turn on the record player with the volume turned off so that it will spin the record.
3 Place the pin going through the cup onto an old record.
4 Listen to the sound coming out of the Styrofoam speaker.

How does a gramophone work? (Vibrations from the needle moving over the grooves are carried to the pin. The vibrations travel up the pin to the cup. These vibrations are then amplified by the Styrofoam cup.)

How can we change the speed of the record's rotation? (Either place your finger on the record to slow it down or use the appropriate control on the turntable.)

How does changing the revolutions per minute (RPM) change the sound? (The faster rpm creates a higher lighter pitched sound. The slower rpm creates a lower heavier pitched sound.)

3. Tuning fork amplification

Materials

Blown-up balloon, tuning fork or comb.

Procedure

1 Lightly place the side of one prong of a vibrating tuning fork on an inflated balloon. Observe what happens.

6-9 Amplify sound on a balloon.

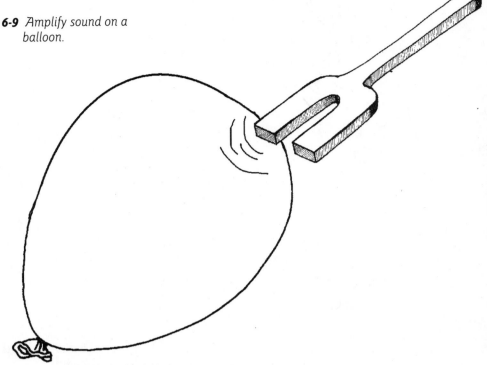

Why does the sound of the tuning fork become louder when it touches the balloon? (The vibrations from the tuning fork made the surface of the balloon vibrate. Vibrations cause other things nearby to vibrate.)

2 Repeat the same procedure with a comb vibrating on a balloon. Ask the children to use their fingers to make the teeth of the comb vibrate on the balloon's surface.

4. Waxed paper vibrations

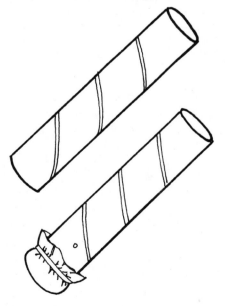

6-10 Wax paper vibrating on a kazoo makes a sound.

Materials

Toilet paper or paper towel tube, a homemade kazoo made from toilet paper or paper towel tube.

Procedure

1 Hum through the cardboard tube. Then hum through the homemade kazoo.

2 Ask the children the following question:

Why does the humming sound different in the kazoo? (It sounds different in the kazoo because the humming at the top of the tube causes the waxed paper at the end of the tube to vibrate. The added vibrations cause a different sound to occur.)

5. Paper clip vibrations

Materials

Empty coffee can with plastic lid; long, thin rubber band or string; a paper clip.

Procedure

1 Thread the paper clip with a long, thin rubber band or string.

2 Allow the threaded paper clip to dangle in front of the empty coffee can with a plastic lid lying on its side. The paper clip should be touching the surface of the plastic lid at about the center of the lid.

3 Have a child gently tap the metal end of the coffee can lying on its side. Have children observe what happens

6-11 *The paper clip bounces from vibrations when the can is struck.*

to the paper clip when the can is tapped gently and when the can is tapped harder.

Why does the paper clip jump?

Why does the paper clip jump more when the can is tapped harder? (The paper clip jumps or moves because the vibrations caused by the tapping cause other things to vibrate. The vibrations bounce around on the inside of the can and continue to vibrate, causing the paper clip to bounce or vibrate.)

V. Vibrations can be absorbed and stopped or left free to bounce

1. Holding sound

Materials

Toy xylophone, a mallet.

Procedure

1 Have a child strike the metal plates with the mallet. It should make a short, light sound.

2 Have a child strike the plates again, but this time have the child hold the mallet on the plate after striking it to create a pounding sound, rather than a light, bouncing sound.

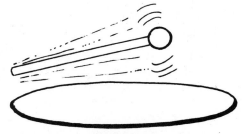

Striking a metal plate is loud!

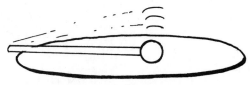

Holding the mallet on the metal plate absorbs the soundwaves making less sound!

6-12A *Freely vibrating sound and muffled sound.*

Which kind of sound is prettier or more pleasant to listen to—the bouncing mallet sound or the pounding-and-holding mallet sound?

3 *Explain:* Sound vibrations can be left free to vibrate or can be held and stopped. When the mallet stays on the metal plate after it strikes, it is holding and absorbing the vibrations, and the sound vibrations are not free to bounce.

2. Muffling sound

Materials

A jingle bell for each child or group of children.

Freely vibrating sound

Muffled sound

6-12B A closed fist around a jingle bell.

Procedure

1 Have children shake their jingle bell and listen to it.

2 Ask the children the following questions:

What do you think might happen to the sound from the jingle bell, if you cup and close your hand around the jingle bell when you shake it?

Which way does the bell sound louder and prettier to hear? (It sounds prettier to hear and louder when your hand is left open because the sound vibrations are left free to travel and bounce. When the sound is muffled inside your closed fist, it is harder to hear and does not sound as light and as long. When sounds are able to echo or bounce around after they are started and then fade away or blend with a new vibration, they are called resonant sounds.)

3. Knocking on hard and soft surfaces

Materials

Something soft like a pillow or a sweater.

Procedure

1 Have the children knock on the floor or a desk with their fists.

2 Then have children knock on the same surface, but this time have them place "something soft" between their fist and the surface.

Do both knocks sound the same? If not, why not?

What does the "something" that is soft do to the sound? (The "something" that is soft absorbs or isolates the sound vibrations. The hard surface allows sounds to bounce and echo.)

Fine points to discuss

Is it quieter to walk across a floor that has a rug than on one that does not have a rug? (It is quieter to walk across the floor that has a rug because the rug absorbs or isolates some of the sound.)

What are some other things in the room that help absorb sounds? (Draperies, ceiling tiles, soft furniture, almost anything that is soft or has a lot of holes like the ceiling tile.)

What are some of the things in the room that bounce sound off? (Most of the hard surfaces, like the walls, the uncovered floor, the desks or hard chairs.)

VI. Resonance and echoes cause amplification of sound vibrations

Amplifying a music box

Materials

A music box outside of its casing with absolutely no amplification or resonance. (A commercial product that fills the bill for this activity is the Hurdy Gurdy, found in many gift shops, especially airports, as a novelty item. It is distributed by Alfred E. Knobler and Co., Moonachie, N.J.)

Procedure

1 Hold the music box up in the air and turn the crank. It will be difficult to hear the music. The sound vibrations will be absorbed in the air and will scatter.

2 Place the music box on a hard surface like a desk, the wall, or a window. Turn the crank, and the children will hear a drastic difference in volume coming from the music box.

Why can we hear the music box better when the music box is placed on the desk, door, wall, or window but not so easily when it is held in the air? (The hard surface allows the sound vibrations to resonate and amplify themselves. The hard surface allows the music to sound more resonant or full.)
Note: The volume and the quality of the sound are directly related to the size of the surface and the kind of material from which the surface is made. Have the chil-

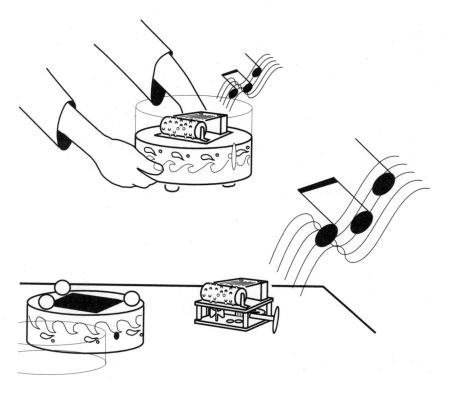

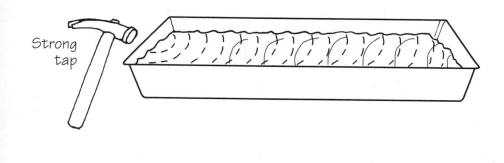

6-13 *Amplify the sound from a music box cylinder.*

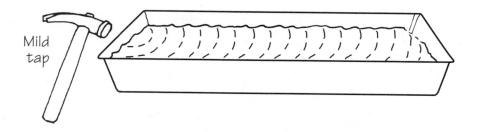

Strong tap

Mild tap

6-14 *Hammer strikes a pan of water.*

dren experiment with the music box by placing it on different kinds of surfaces like windows, a clock face, the sink, a wooden door, cinder-block walls, metal pots, plumbing pipes, an unopened tissue box, an empty tissue box.

VII. Sound vibrations travel in waves.

Making waves with water
Metal broiling pan half-filled with water; a hammer; newspaper (to absorb possible spills). (See Fig. 6-14.)

Procedure
1 Have a child gently tap the top edge of the broiling pan with a hammer. Have the children discuss their observations. (The water will vibrate from the sound vibrations. Little waves will be visible on the surface of the water. They will look like ripples.)
2 Ask the children the following questions:

Does the hammer actually hit the water?

If not, why does the water appear to be moving? (The water itself was not hit. The water is moving because the vibrations from the pan and the sound waves were started by the tapping on the pan.)

What will happen to the ripples on the water if the pan is hit very hard and fast with the hammer?

Will the waves get bigger? (The children will probably respond that the waves will get bigger and will splash. Have a child hit the pan hard several times quickly. Have the children observe what happens.)

2. Making waves with rope
Materials
A piece of rope about 12 feet long or less tied to an object about 3 feet off the ground.

Procedure
1 Hold the rope in your hand and dangle it. Have the children observe what happens to the rope. (Children will see a wave effect.)
2 Ask the children the following questions:

Will the wave look different if the rope is moving fast or slowly? Experiment and discuss what happens. (When the rope moves faster, it begins to look blurry. The rope will begin to make a whirring or "windy" sound.)

Which wave has more energy, the low, slow wave or the fast, high wave? (The fast and high wave has more energy.) The children can feel how tired their arms will become making a fast, high wave, and how much less energy they will need to make a low, slow wave with the rope.

Fine points to discuss
Do these rope waves look like other waves you have seen before? Where do you usually see waves? (At the beach.)

What kinds of waves at the beach can knock you over? (Large waves with crests.) Explain to children that a crest is the highest part of the wave.

Do all waves at the beach carry enough energy or force to knock you over? (No. Waves vary in their intensity of strength and force. Waves that are small and have a low crest are not very powerful.)

Do all waves carry energy? (Yes.)

Can large sound waves knock you over? (No, but if they are too loud for a long period of time, they can damage your eardrums. If our eardrums are damaged, we can lose some of the sensitivity that allows us to hear well. Our ears are very delicate and sensitive sense organs.)

3. Air molecules carry odors and sound
Materials
Perfume and atomizer to spray perfume.

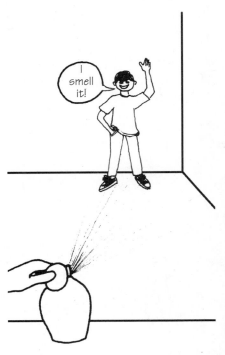

6-15 Smell the aroma of perfume molecules in the air.

Procedure

1 Ask the children the following questions:

Have you ever been able to notice that supper was ready when you were not in the kitchen?

How did your nose help you to know?

2 *Explain:* Molecules are very small things in the air. They are invisible. We cannot see them, but sometimes we can smell them. When we smell someone's cooking in another room, we are smelling molecules of the cooking odors in the air. The odors travel to our noses through molecules in the air. We cannot see molecules but we can sometimes smell them. Molecules of air also carry vibrating sound waves.

3 Spray the perfume in the air from a far corner in the room. Ask the children to raise their hands when they smell the molecules of perfume in the air.

4. Seeing wave energy transfer

Materials

A "Slinky"* (a commercial toy that looks like a giant spring made of plastic or metal).

Procedure

1 Have a child hold one end of the Slinky. Stretch the Slinky out. Hold a clump of the spring and let go of one coil. Have the children observe the bounce and the vibration that takes place up the spring and back to you. The vibration or wave will continue until it runs out of or transfers the energy that was set into motion when the coil was let loose.

2 Continue to let coils loose while a child holds one end of the stretched-out Slinky. Compare the difference in the kind of vibration or energy release that takes place when one or several coils are let loose at the same time.

* Manufactured by James Industries, Inc.

3 *Explain:* When we let go of a coil on the Slinky, we are observing a chain reaction of energy being transferred. The Slinky is an observable model to look at to better understand how a sound vibration behaves. A sound vibration is really an invisible wave that carries energy. The sound from a sound vibration continues until all of its energy has been absorbed and then it stops.

5. Molecule model of energy transfer in an oscillating or vibrating wave

Materials

Two 12- or 18-inch plastic rulers with a groove down the center; about 10 or 12 glass marbles all the same size, one marble much larger than the others; two wooden blocks; masking tape.

Procedure

1 Tape the two plastic rulers together with masking tape so that they will stay together. Emphasize the groove with the tape so that the integrity of the groove will still be apparent. Rest each end of the taped rulers on a wooden block to create a double ramp. (See Fig. 6-16.)

2 Line all of the marbles up on the ruler except for the largest one. Have a child take one marble and lift it up the "ruler ramp" to the top end of the ruler, then let go of the marble. Have the children observe what happens and discuss it with them. (If you let go of one marble, only one marble will bounce off on the chain of marbles. The energy from the moving marble will transfer to the other marbles that are in line, and the last marble will receive the energy. The last marble will then give its energy back to the chain of marbles and the first marble will bounce off. This energy transfer will continue as it did in the Slinky until all of the energy from the original marble has been absorbed.)

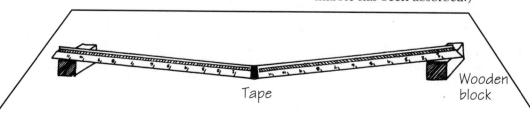

6-16 *Homemade hinged, grooved rulers.*

Tape

Wooden block

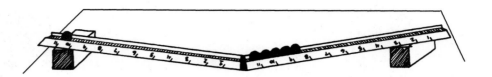

6-17 *Eight to ten marbles on homemade, hinged, grooved rulers.*

What do you think will happen if two marbles are lifted up on the ramp and then the marbles are let loose?

3 Discuss what might happen. Then find out. (This time two marbles will bounce off the end of the chain of marbles.)

4 Continue to observe what happens with two, three, four, five, and six marbles being lifted up the ramp and then being let go. Have the children make a prediction and then test it out. Discuss the results after each trial.

5 Set up all the marbles in a row on the groove of the ruler. Show the children the large marble. Ask them what will happen if you send the large marble down the ramp. Let them make predictions. Then have the children test it out and see what happens. (The large marble will make only one marble bounce off the end. The one large marble will carry more energy in it than the one smaller marble did, so the bounce at the end of the chain of marbles will be more dramatic.)

6 *Explain:* Each of the marbles is a giant model of a molecule. The marbles show what happens to a molecule of air that is carrying energy from a sound vibration. The model shows what happens when energy is transferred or moved from the first object to the next object in a line until it reaches the end of the line of objects. *Note:* This same effect can be demonstrated with dominoes standing in a line or with a deck of playing cards standing on their edges.

Fine points to discuss

How is energy transferred in a sound vibration? (One molecule of air makes another molecule of air move.)

How do vibrations of molecules affect sound? (When more molecules of air vibrate, the sound is louder.)

Where does energy come from in a sound wave? (Energy comes from movement or action. When there is no action, there is no sound.)

What is energy? (Energy is power or strength that can create an action. Energy is needed to create sound. Energy comes in many forms: heat from the sun, food we eat, gasoline for the car. Energy can be stored for future use or put into use. Energy usually involves movement or action.)

VIII. Sounds are able to travel through things

1. Floor sounds

Materials

None.

Procedure

1 Have the children place one ear directly on the floor and listen to footsteps. Do this on the playground, in the classroom, or in the house.

2 Ask the children the following question:

Do the sounds seem louder on the ground or in the air? (On the ground.)

2. Sounds through wood

Materials

A board or wooden mop handle.

Procedure

1 Demonstrate to children how to listen through a board. Place one end of the board on the ground outside and the other end of the board at your ear. (The sound travels from the ground through the wood.)

2 Have children listen to sound through wood.

3. Sounds through tubes

Materials

A wind-up toy or ticking alarm clock or a timer, a cardboard tube.

Procedure

1 Have the children listen to the ticking object on a table and then put the cardboard tube next to the ticking sound.

6-18 *Listening through a cardboard tube.*

2 Ask the children the following question:

Does the ticking sound louder through the tube? If so, why? (The vibrations sound louder through the tube because they are confined to the tube.)

4. Stethoscope

Materials

A toy stethoscope (commercial product).

Procedure

1 Have the children listen to a sound with a stethoscope in their ear and without it in their ear. Rub on the end of the stethoscope lightly with your finger. It will not sound very loud, but it will be very loud when the stethoscope is in the child's ears.

2 Discuss with children where the sound in the stethoscope goes, and why it sounds so much louder when the stethoscope picks up a sound. (The sound is confined to the tube. The sound goes directly to the listener's ear, through the air vibrating inside the tube.)

5. Whispering hose

Materials

Two funnels and a length of old hose or clear plastic tubing about 6- to 8-feet long, some masking tape to secure funnels to the ends of the hose. (See Fig. 6-19.)

Procedure

1 Make a Whispering Hose Phone. Demonstrate the hose to the children.

⚠ CAUTION *Explain:* It is only used for whispering because the sounds will be too loud for their ears if they talk in the funnels instead of whispering in them.

6-19 *Whispering and listening through a hose.*

2 Have two children use the phone. One child listens while the other child whispers. Discuss how the sound travels with the children.

6. Tin can "telephone"

Materials

Two tin cans, awl to punch holes in bottom center of cans, two plastic buttons, length of string about 12-feet long.

Procedure

1 Make a tin-can telephone. Place the button inside the can. Tie the button to the string. The button helps amplify the sound inside of the can.

2 Let the children talk through the cans. Discuss how the sound travels through the string. *Note*: The string must not sag. It needs to be pulled tight to vibrate but not too tight or it will break.

7. "Chime" from metal

Materials

A metal grill from the inside of a broiler pan; a metal kitchen fork; a metal clothes hanger; a metal washer or a nail; a pair of shoe laces or a piece of string about 3-feet long.

Procedure

1 Place the fork, hanger or the grill in the middle of the piece of string and tie the string around the metal so that each end of the string can reach the child's ears. (See Fig. 6-21.)

6-20 *Talking and listening through a string on a tin-can telephone.*

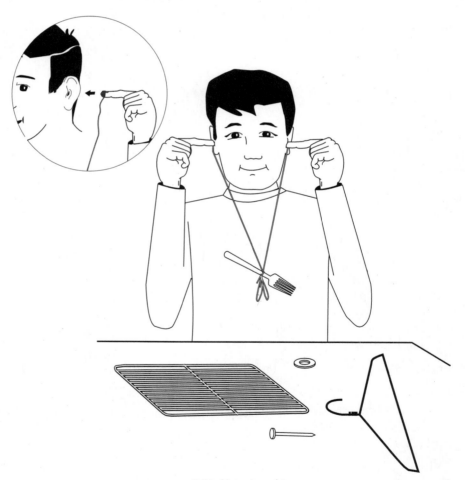

6-21 *Listening chimes.*

2 Instruct children to gently wrap the shoelace or string around their index finger's tip and to then gently stuff the string or soft part of the shoelace into their ears.

3 Have a child strike the metal with an object. (The sound will travel up the string to the child's ears.) Discuss with children how the metal sounds when it is tapped and how the sound traveled

to their ears. (The metal should sound like a pretty chime or bell.)

8. String sound

Materials

A piece of string about one foot long.

Procedure

1 Hold onto the string with both hands. Ask the children if the string can make a sound. Snap the string by pulling your hands apart quickly. Have the children observe what happens to the string.

Why does the string make a sound? (The string moved or vibrated and we could hear the movement which produced a sound.)

2 Have children experiment shaping a string.

9. Sound through pipes

Materials

A piece of metal pipe.

Procedure

1 Demonstrate to children how sound travels through a pipe. Bang on the pipe with a pebble. Place the pipe near a child's ear and bang on the pipe softly.

2 Discuss how the sound travels and why it sounds so much louder when your ear is on the pipe.

How might the sound change if you tap something soft on the pipe?

IX. Different sounds can be made with the same objects if they are different sizes

1. Sound vibrations

Materials

Sets of two or three objects that are made from the same material but are different in length, thickness, or surface area. (For example: matching metal pot lids in different sizes; clay flowerpots in different sizes; nails; cut pieces of fishing line; hollow pieces of bamboo; rubber bands of different lengths; or a set of nails, fishing lines, or rubber bands of different thicknesses; a xylophone; different-length pencils (same width); bells of different sizes; soda bottles filled with different amounts of water.)

Procedure

1 Arrange each of the sets of objects in order according to their size, smallest to largest. The size differences should be extreme and very obvious. *Note*: No need for subtle size differences here; contrasts are important. Each set of

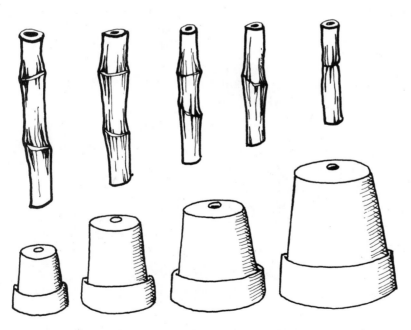

6-22 *Different sounds can be made with the same objects if they are different sizes.*

objects should contain two or three items so that the pitch differences of each set will be distinct.

2 Tap, strike, or pluck an object in a set. Then do the same to the other objects in that set. Have children observe the different sounds that are made from each of the objects in the set.

Which object makes a sound that is very deep, heavy, and low?

Which object makes a much lighter, higher, and "thinner" sound?

3 Proceed to have children experiment with each set of objects. Observe the kinds of sounds that the biggest and the smallest items in each set make. (The larger, longer, or thicker objects will make slower lower sounds when they vibrate, whereas the smaller, shorter, or thinner objects will make faster and higher sounds.)

2. Piano strings

Materials

A piano.

Procedure

1 Have children look inside the piano and at the keyboard. Push some low piano keys and some high piano keys. Have the children observe the inside strings and hammers moving while the piano keys are being pushed in. Discuss the appearance of the strings. Ask the children how the strings on the inside of the piano look different from one another, and how they can tell by just looking at some of the strings whether they will make a higher sound or a lower sound.

2 Ask the children to predict which strings will make a slower, lower, and heavier sound, and which strings will make a faster, lighter, and higher sound.

3 After they predict what the sounds will be like, let them each have a turn choosing a piano key to press down. The other children can try to locate the vibrating string while they wait for their turn to press down a key.

3. Rubber-band guitar

Materials

An empty and lidless cigar box; assorted rubber bands in different thicknesses and lengths arranged in sequence from thinnest to thickest; a wooden dowel; ruler or a long, slender piece of Styrofoam to be used as a bridge underneath the rubber bands.

Procedure

1 Show children the cigar box with rubber bands. Tell them it is called a sound box. Have a child pluck the rubber bands. Listen to the sounds. If they are played in sequence, they will create sounds like those on a musical scale. The sounds will sound like they are moving up or down.

2 Place the bridge made of wood or Styrofoam underneath the rubber bands. Have a child pluck the bands again.

Is the sound the same? If not, why not? (It will sound different because the bridge makes the rubber band shorter by absorbing some of the vibrations and making the length of the rubber band that is able to vibrate shorter.)

3 Move the "bridge" off center or to a diagonal position so that one side of the rubber band is short and the other side is long. Have a child pluck the rubber bands and hear the different sound pitches the rubber bands make. Discuss with the children why they think this happens.

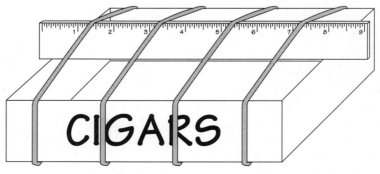

6-23 *Sound box with a wooden bridge.*

(The longer length of rubber band makes a low, long, heavy sound and vibrates at a slower rate or frequency. The shorter length of rubber band makes a high and short sound and vibrates at a faster rate or frequency.)

4. Quality of sound

Materials

Toy cymbals, coffee-can drum or toy drum, a drumstick. (Children can create a cymbal out of a pie tin. With a piece of yarn, just have them add a strap to hold onto in the center.)

Procedure

1 Hit one of the cymbals at the edge with a drumstick, then in the center of the cymbal.

Are the sounds the same? (They are not. The sound from the center has a thinner, less resonant sound. The circle is small. At the edge there is a more resonant tone quality. The circle or area that is vibrating is larger.)

2 Have a child use a drumstick to hit one of the cymbals with a fair amount of force. Then hit the same cymbal very softly.

Can you notice a difference in the sound? (The strong hit creates a louder volume of sound.)

3 Repeat the same procedure with the drum. Have the children test the sound quality at different spots on the drum and the effect the force of the hit has on the volume or relative loudness of the sound.

Fine points to discuss

Does a drumstick hit with a lot of force or a little bit of force? (It depends on how it hits and how much force it is given.)

How does the force in the hit of the drumstick affect the intensity of the sound? (The more force, the louder the sound.)

Does it matter where a drumstick hits a surface? (Yes. If the hit is in the center of a drum, it will sound more resonant. On a flat piece of metal such as the cymbal, however, it will vibrate more if it is hit on the edge because the entire surface is free to vibrate. It will sound like a gong. When a drum is hit near the edge, the framing material of the drum prevents the drumhead from vibrating.)

Do materials made from the same stuff sound the same when they vibrate? (The size of the material and the force of the hit affect the sound.)

X. Up and down the scale

1. Monochord

Materials

A monochord—a thin 1-inch-by-2-inch board that is 36 inches long with an eye-screw at each end securing a nylon fishing line tightly; a small plastic tub or box to use as a resonator; a bridge that can be slid freely up and down the spine of the monochord underneath the "string" of fishing line. See Fig. 6-24.

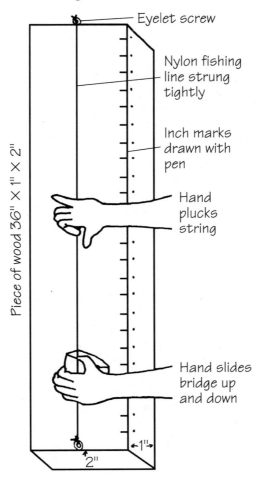

Piece of wood 36" × 1" × 2"

— Eyelet screw

Nylon fishing line strung tightly

Inch marks drawn with pen

Hand plucks string

Hand slides bridge up and down

6-24 *Homemade monochord.*

Procedure

1 Have a child pluck the "string" of the monochord and listen.

Can you think of a way to make the pitch or tone that the string makes sound different? (They will probably suggest that you move the box up or down the spine of the monochord.)

2 Move the resonator bridge box to the very top of the spine on the monochord. Have a child pluck the string on each side of the bridge box.

Does it sound different than it did before? (The sound will be very high on the top side with the short string and very low on the bottom side with the long string.)

3 Have the children move the "box" up and down the spine and listen to all of the different sounds or pitches of sound that can be created on one string.

Fine points to discuss

As the box moves up and the string becomes shorter, what happens to the sound? (It becomes a higher pitch.)

As the box moves down and the string becomes longer, what happens to the sound? (It becomes a lower pitch. It sounds like you are going down a flight of stairs.)

What is a sequence of musical tones called? (A musical scale.) Demonstrate what a scale sounds like on a piano or other musical instrument.

2. Bottle sounds

Materials

A small, empty soda bottle or thin jar; newspaper; water inside a pitcher; a funnel; a wooden spoon.

Procedure

1 Pour a small amount of water into the soda bottle. Have a child tap it with the wooden spoon and listen to the sound.

2 Pour some more water into the bottle. Have another child tap it and listen again.

3 Continue to do this several more times until the bottle is almost full.

Why is the sound able to change? (A different amount of water and air are vibrating each time the amount of water changes.)

Fine points to discuss

How is the bottle being filled with water like the monochord? (The pitch or tone can be changed. A scale can be created by changing the amount of water and the amount of air above the water. Different vibrations create different sounds and can be arranged in an order or sequence.)

How could the bottle be made into a musical instrument? (By using several bottles filled with different amounts of water.)

Note: Bottle organ—You might want the children to create a soda-bottle organ consisting of six to eight bottles filled with different heights of water. The "organ" can be "tuned" by filling the bottles while playing piano keys or xylophone keys to find sequential pitches. If the organ is tuned properly, a musical scale and possibly some simple tunes like "Mary Had A Little Lamb" and "Jingle Bells" can be played. Place a piece of masking tape with a number on it on each bottle to indicate where the water level should remain if it accidentally spills or evaporates. The numbered bottles can be played as "notes" if a melody is written for them.

Going further

What will happen if you blow across the bottles, rather than tapping the bottles?

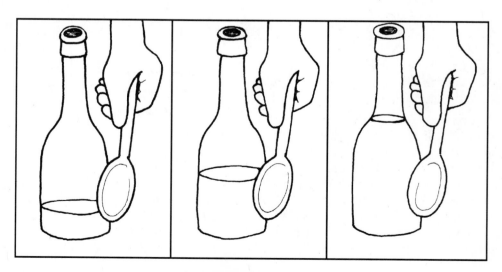

6-25 *Bottle sounds.*

Will the sounds be the same?

When you blow across the top of the bottles, what makes the sound change?

The column of water or the column of air?

How do you know? (The reverse scale occurs with the bottles. The lowest water level makes a high sound when tapped, but makes a low sound when it is blown across.)

3. Wind instrument

Materials

A fluteophone (wind instrument) or recorder.

Procedure

1 Show the children the wind instrument. Cover all the holes with your fingers and blow through the fluteophone or recorder. While you are blowing, cover one hole at a time from the bottom of the instrument. Listen to the sound. It will sound as though you are going up a flight of steps.

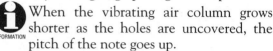 When the vibrating air column grows shorter as the holes are uncovered, the pitch of the note goes up.

2 While blowing, cover the holes one at a time from the top. It will sound as though you are going down a flight of stairs.

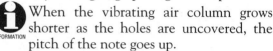 The column of air that is vibrating as you blow is getting longer; therefore, the pitch becomes lower.

4. Plastic straw horn

Materials

Several plastic straws, a pair of scissors.

Procedure

1 Flatten out a plastic straw. Bend the straw about ½ a centimeter down at one end. Then cut off two small triangles from the flattened, bent end. See Fig. 6-27.

2 Blow through the pointed end that has been cut. It will sound like a horn. *Note:* The straw needs to be placed inside your mouth, and you need to blow hard. Your lips need to be stretched and pressed flat around your teeth against the straw. It is not as hard to do as it sounds. Just blow hard and practice a few times.

3 Cut off small snips from the end of the plastic straw while blowing through it. The note or tone will become higher and higher.

6-26 *Changing the length of the column of vibrating air changes the pitch.*

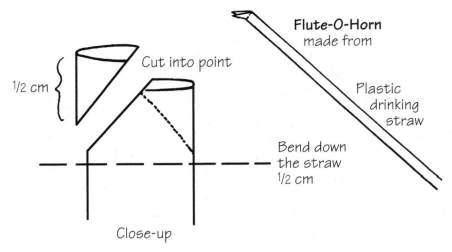

6-27 A plastic straw horn.

Can you think of another way to make the note get higher in pitch without cutting the end off? (They might suggest adding some holes to the straw so that it looks like a flute.)

4 Have children experiment making different sounds with different lengths of pointed plastic straws.

5. Plastic straw flute-o-horn

Materials
Same as above.

Procedure
1 Make another "plastic straw horn" as previously described in Procedure 4.
2 Cut or punch holes in the straw with the scissors.
3 Blow through it and find out if the one straw can produce many pitches if the holes are covered and uncovered one at a time.

(It can be done, but it requires patience.)

4 Have children make their own plastic straw flute-o-horn.

6. Water Trombone*

Materials
For each child or group of children: a plastic drinking straw, a large-size plastic glass (like the ones that are given away at fast food places as souvenirs.)

Procedure
1 Dip the straw horn into the glass of water.
2 Blow across the top of the straw.

* Adapted from *Science Wizardry for Kids* by Kenda.

3 As you blow across the top of the straw, move the straw up and down in the water.

How can you control the sound from the straw? (By raising and lowering the plastic straw into the water while it is being blown through.)

Fine points to discuss

What is vibrating the water or the air? How can you tell? (The air is vibrating. When the column of air is short, the sound is higher than when the column of air is longer.)

How does the water level in the straw affect the sound that is heard? (The water column changes the column of air inside the straw. The tone of the straw changes as it is raised and lowered into the water. As you lower the straw into the water, the tone becomes higher. As you raise the straw in the water, the tone becomes lower.)

Further resources
Dewey Decimal Classification Number for sound is: 534.

Selected books for children
Ardley, Neil. *Sound and Music.* Watts, 1984. (For older children.)

Ardley, Neil. *The Science Book of Sound.* New York: Gulliver (HBJ), 1991.

Brandt, Keith. *Sound.* Mahwah, NJ: Troll, 1985. (For children who can read.)

Brown, Bob. *Science for You: 112 Illustrated Experiments.* TAB Books, 1988. (For children who know how to read and want to do more sound activities.)

Jennings, T. *Making Sounds.* New York: Franklin Watts, 1990. (For children that can read.)

Knight, David. *All About Sound*. Mahwah, NJ: Troll, 1983. (Contains activities related to sound for children who want to do more "experimenting.")

Newman, Fredrick R. *Zounds! The Kid's Guide to Sound Making*. New York: Random House, 1983.

Wood, Robert W. *Physics for Kids: 49 Easy Experiments with Acoustics*. TAB Books, 1991. (For children who know how to read and want to do more sound experiments.)

Wyler, Rose. *Science Fun with Drums, Bells and Whistles*. Englewood Cliffs, NJ: Messner, 1987. (K–3)

Resource books for adults and older children

Berger, Melvin. *The Science of Music*. New York: Thomas Y. Crowell, 1988. (Explains how sounds are processed, produced, and reproduced.)

Brainard, Audrey. NJSTA NEWSLETTER Science for Non-Science Teachers, article on sound, 1981.

Brown, Robert J. *333 More Science Tricks and Experiments*. TAB Books, 1984. (See Chapter 2, Sound & Other Vibrations, for more activities to do with waves and sound.)

Darling, David. *Sounds Interesting*. New York: Dillon, 1991.

Kaner, Etta. *Sound Science*. Reading, Mass: Addison-Wesley, 1991. (Activities for Grades 2–6.)

Kenda, Margaret and Phyllis S. Williams. *Science Wizardry for Kids: Safe Scientific Experiments Kids Can Perform*. Hauppauge, N.Y.: Barrons Educational Series, 1992. (This book is full of great innovative ideas and new ways to do familiar activities.

Lampton, Christopher F. *Sound More Than What You Hear*. Hillside, NJ: Enslow Publishers, 1992. (Explains sound and discusses such topics as how we hear, ultrasound, and sonar. Although this book has very few illustrations, it is a good resource book for older children and adults.)

Rubin, Mark. *The Orchestra*. Buffalo, NY: Firefly Books, 1992. (Introduces children to the orchestra by describing and illustrating each instrument.)

Taylor, Barbara. *Hear! Hear! The Science of Sound*. New York: Random House, 1991.

Selected literature connections for younger children

Keats, Ezra Jack. *Whistle for Willie*. N.Y.: Viking, 1964. (A story about a young boy named Peter who wanted to be able to whistle for his dog.)

Lemieux, M. *What's That Noise?* New York: Morrow, 1985. (Good story for making children aware of sounds. Brown bear hears a noise that he cannot figure out.)

McCloskey, Robert. *Lentil*. New York: Viking, 1968. (A tale about a little boy who saves the day by playing his harmonica.)

Plume, I. *The Bremen Town Musicians*. Garden City, NY: Doubleday, 1980. (A good story for children to hear who are going to make their very own musical instruments.)

Wells, R. *Noisy Nora*. New York: Dial, 1973. (Also as a Scholastic paperback. Good introduction to what makes noise.)

Wood, Audrey. *The Napping House*. San Diego: HBJ, 1979. (A tale about how vibrations keep everyone from sleeping.)

General community enrichment activities

Music store Visit a store that sells musical instruments. Children can touch and feel instruments. They can also stroke some string instruments and perhaps observe a piano being played with the top open, so that the strings would be visible when they are struck by the hammers from the piano keys being pushed down.

Farm Listen to animal sounds and farm machinary.

Nature walk Listen for animals and locate where they are. Listen to water running in a brook, leaves rustling in the wind.

Concert Attend a musical concert with a full orchestra or band.

Music teacher Ask your school's music teacher to demonstrate how sounds are produced and controlled in various musical instruments.

Speech teacher Ask your school's speech teacher to explain how we control our voice and how we produce sound.

Hearing aid store Visit an audiology center and find out about hearing aids and how they work, and about the anatomy of the human ear.

Buildings Observe soundproofing around buildings and on ceilings.

7
Light

Objectives

The objectives of this chapter are for children to become aware of the following:

- Beams of light come from the sun and other sources.
- Light is a form of energy.
- Some materials allow light to pass through them, and some materials do not.
- Shadows are formed when light beams are blocked.
- Light can be reflected.
- Mirror reflections can create multiple images.
- Lenses have a curved surface, and curved surfaces can bend light beams to make objects look bigger, smaller, or upside-down.
- We need light to see.
- Light is made up of many colors.
- When colors are mixed or blended together, new colors are created.

General background information for parents and teachers

Light Any source of illumination is called light. Light can be found in nature or made by humans. We need light to see. If there is no light, there is no sight.

Natural light Sources that are natural, like the sun, lightning, and fire, are natural sources of light. They are very hot and give off their own light.

Artificial light Human-made lights are artificial sources of light. They do not appear in nature. Humans have created the light source from resources. Electric lights are human-made. Electric light bulbs have filaments that give off enough heat to create light.

 Incandescent light Light that produces enough heat to give off light.

Fluorescent light Light produced or created from a source that is cool. Electric sparks flow through a fluorescent tube that contains special gases. Lit fluorescent tubes do not feel as hot to the touch as lit light bulbs with filaments.

Energy Light gives off heat or thermal energy, which can be transformed into energy of motion and/or stored as potential energy.

Transparent Light can pass through materials that are transparent. A clear window pane and a piece of cellophane or clear plastic are examples of transparent material.

Opaque Light cannot pass through an opaque material. Opaque materials are usually solid. Opaque materials can absorb and reflect light. Some examples of opaque materials are tinfoil, cardboard, furniture, and books.

Translucent Some light can pass through materials that are translucent. The light is scattered and images cannot be seen clearly. Examples of translucent materials are waxed paper, frosted glass, tissue paper, a silk scarf, shedded snakeskin.

Diffused light Light that is scattered. Translucent materials give off diffused light.

Reflect Light that bounces off one surface onto another is reflected. Materials that reflect stay cooler than materials that absorb light.

Absorb Light that does not bounce from one surface to another is absorbed. Materials that absorb light become warmer than materials that reflect (for example, a blacktop surface becomes very hot on a sunny day).

Shadows A shadow occurs when a light source is blocked. Opaque materials create shadows. So do translucent materials. Opaque materials make solid shadows because part of a beam of light is entirely blocked. Translucent materials make lighter, less solid-looking shadows because only some light is blocked.

Night Earth's own shadow creates night. The sun can shine only on one-half of the earth's surface at a time. The other half is in the dark.

Light beams Beams of light can cause a direct or indirect lighting effect.

Direct light Direct lighting occurs when a beam of light shines directly from a light source to a surface.

Indirect light Indirect lighting occurs when a direct beam of light reflects or bounces off another surface. For example, a direct light becomes an indirect light if it bounces off a wall or ceiling and throws indirect light into a room.

Reflection A mirror image is called a reflection.

Image An image is an illusion. It looks like the original but it is a duplicate or copy of the original.

Law of reflection A law that helps explain reflections. The law states that the angle of incidence is equal to the angle of reflection. This means that when light hits a surface, it will bounce or reflect off that surface, continuing in a straight line at the same angle as when it hit the surface (before it was reflected). (See Fig. 7-2.)

Angle An angle is formed when two lines meet at a point.

Kaleidoscope A device that allows us to see multiple mirror images by using more than one mirror to cause reflections of reflections.

Periscope A device that uses two mirrors to reflect images. A periscope helps us see things around corners or above our heads.

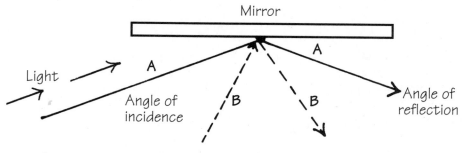

7-2 Reflection.

A periscope helps us see an image of a reflected image.

Refraction The bending of a light beam is called refraction. Refraction occurs when light enters one medium like oil, glass, air, or water on a diagonal. Each time the light enters or leaves one clear substance and travels through diagonally to another substance, the parts of the slanted light beam travel or penetrate the next clear substance at a slightly different angle. This difference in angles creates an illusion that an object like a straw or a spoon is broken or bent. See Fig. 7-3. Light slows down as it enters the surface of a medium that is optically thick or dense. It increases its speed when it leaves the (thick or dense) medium. This difference of speed at surfaces causes the light beam to bend. Refraction sometimes makes objects in liquids appear closer and bigger than their real-life size.

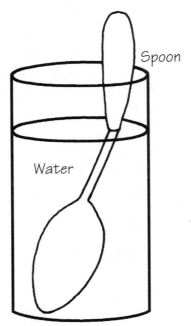

7-3 *Refraction.*

Mirage Mirages are caused by refraction of light in the air. When the layer of air next to the ground is at an extremely high temperature (this often occurs in a desert) and the layer of air directly above that layer of air is at a different temperature, a mirage will occur. Mirages also happen frequently over water on hot sunny days.

Lens A transparent curved surface that causes light to bend or refract. A lens can enlarge an object, make an object look smaller, or make an object look upside-down.

Microscope Two lenses that work together to make objects look much larger. Microscopes magnify.

Telescope Two lenses working together that make things that are far away look closer.

Concave The shape of a lens when it caves in in the center and looks like a valley or the inside of a bowl. The lens causes things to diverge or separate and spread out from a focal point.

Convex The shape of a lens when it curves out in the center and looks like a hill. The lens causes things to converge or come together at a focal point.

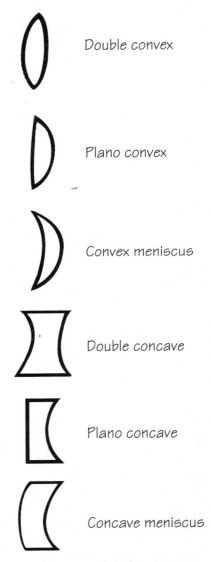

Double convex

Plano convex

Convex meniscus

Double concave

Plano concave

Concave meniscus

7-4 *There are many types of lenses.*

Color The amount of light of different wavelengths reflected off an object gives the object its color. Every color has its own wavelength. The higher the light wave in amplitude, the more energy it has, and the brighter the color is.

Chromatography The separation of complex mixtures (liquid, powders, or other small particles) by the passage through a selectively absorbing filter, resulting in distinct layers or colors.

Prism A triangular piece of crystal-clear material like glass, plastic, or water in a specially shaped glass that is able to bend (refract) a light wave two times and cause a separation of the light beam to occur. The separation of the light beam causes a rainbow effect.

Rainbow The rainbow is a spectrum of all of the colors of visible light. The violet colors bend the most and appear on the inside of a rainbow's arc. The reds bend the least and appear on the outside edge of the rainbow's arc.

Primary colors Red, yellow, and blue are the primary colors. When they are mixed together, they create the secondary colors of orange, green, and purple.

Tint Colors that have white added to them to lighten them are called tints. Red can become a very light pink if enough white is added to it. Colors that have black added to them to darken them are called shades. Red can become very dark and almost black if enough black is added.

Color wheel All of the colors arranged in a circle according to their sequence on a rainbow's spectrum.

Complementary Colors that are opposite each other on the color wheel are called complementary colors. When two complementary colors are blended together they form a very dark-brownish neutral color. Examples of complementary colors are: red and green, orange and blue, yellow and purple.

A comparison of light and sound

To develop a better understanding of light, it is helpful to compare light to sound.

Sound waves Both sound and light travel in waves. However, light travels much faster than sound. Sound travels like a snail, in comparison to light, which travels like a bullet.

Travel Sound needs to travel through something to be heard. Something needs to vibrate. Whereas, light does not need to travel through anything to be seen.

Eyes and ears When our eyes are closed we cannot see, but our ears never close. If our ears are healthy and normal, they cannot be turned off.

Frequency The frequency of light waves affects the hue of color, whereas the frequency of sound waves affects the pitch of sounds.

Hues All of the colors seen in the rainbow. Each color has its own frequency.

Pitch Pitch refers to musical notes. Every musical note has its own frequency.

Mixtures Waves of light can be mixed together to form new hues of color. Two or more different hues of color mixed together will blend to form a new color.

Timbre If one instrument, several instruments, or a complete orchestra plays a tune, the timbre or quality of the sound might change, but the tune will still be the same. If several colors are mixed together, they will blend together, becoming a totally new color. The number of colors added will change the quality of the original color (hue) beyond recognition.

Amplitude The height (amplitude) of a light wave affects the brightness of color. Whereas, the height (amplitude) of a sound wave affects the loudness of sound.

Note: As you do these activities with your children, try to encourage them to keep a science journal of their observations and their thoughts.

Activities and procedures

I. Sources of light

1. Seeing in a dark closet—the more light the more sight

Materials

A well-lighted room and a closet, or several dark-colored blankets to "tent" over a desk or table.

Procedure

1 Promote a discussion about light by asking the children the following questions:

What gives us light in this room? (The sun and/or an electric light.)

What gives us light during the day? (The sun.)

What gives us light during the night? (The moon, stars, candles, electric lights, fire, fireworks, sparks.)

If there were no electricity, how would we have light at night? (Only natural sources like fire, candles, moonlight, and starlight.)

What did cave people use for the light at night? (Natural light.)

If there were no sunlight or any other kind of light, what would a day be like? (Dark.)

 The poles of the earth are in nearly total darkness for six months out of every year.

What can be seen when it is dark?

What could we do now to find out? (Perhaps children will suggest going into a closet, or using the blankets to throw over a table. If not, guide them in that direction.

2 Darken the room, or go to a closet and turn out the lights.

3 Try out their ideas for seeing in the dark. Discuss which of the places they suggested was the darkest.

How did they know it was darker? (Listen to their responses and help guide them to observe that most colors, especially red, are not as bright and brilliant in the dark, unless they have been treated with a luminescent chemical to glow in the dark.)

Why is red a poor color choice for fire engines?

4 Discuss what the best color for a fire engine is so that it can be seen easily at night.

Did the colors of things look as bright as they did when there was more light? If not, why?

What can we do to make the room light again? (Turn the lights on, or open the closet door to let the sunlight in.)

Is there a difference between how much light there is indoors and outdoors?

Where is there more light? (During the day when it is sunny, there is usually far more light outside than inside. When we take photographs inside a room, we usually need to use a flashbulb because there is not enough light indoors for the picture to turn out well.)

Fine points to discuss

What kinds of things give off natural light? (The sun, fire, fireflies, sparks, and lightning.)

How can we create or make artificial light when it is dark and there is no natural light from the sun? (By using human-made lights that use electricity, or lamps that use oil or gas; by making a campfire or lighting candles.)

2. Going further

Investigations for older children

Do different kinds of electric lights make colors look different? How can you find out?

Do different kinds of light bulbs give off more heat energy? How can you find out?

Does the size, color, wattage of a bulb or the kind of gas inside the bulb (halogen, sodium or mercury vapor) affect the heat it radiates? How can you find out?

II. Light reflects and/or absorbs heat

1. Light feels warm

Materials

A small light or tensor lamp, or halogen light.

Procedure

1 Ask the children the following question:

Can you feel, touch, see, or taste light? (They will probably respond that they can see light, but that they cannot feel or taste light.)

2 Turn the light on and have the children feel the heat that the light gives off.

3 Ask the children the following kinds of questions:

Is it as warm at night as it is during the day? (Not usually.)

What makes it warmer during the day? (The sunlight.)

If we stay in the sun on a sunny day, what happens to our skin? (It tans or burns from the heat.)

4 Have the children stick their tongues out under the light. Ask them if they can taste the light. (Light does not have a taste, but it does feel warm on our tongue.)

2. Light can burn a hole

Materials

⚠ A small magnifying glass with a handle, a small pail filled with water (in case a fire starts), sunglasses or pieces of colored cellophane, pieces of black-and-white construction paper, white tissue paper.

Procedure

1 Ask the children the following question:

Can the rays of sunlight burn a hole through a piece of paper? (Listen to their responses.)

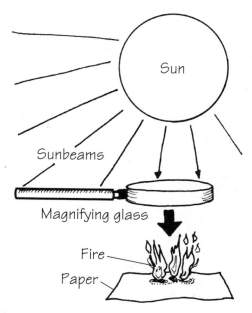

A magnifying glass is a convex lens. A convex lens causes the light to converge or come together at a focal point. The lens of the magnifying glass focuses the sunlight energy onto the surface where the light is absorbed as heat energy. The speed with which this can occur depends upon: the intensity of the sunlight, the material it is shining on, and the size (diameter) of the convex lens.

5 Let each piece of paper sit in the sun for a few minutes. Have the children feel each piece of paper.

Which piece of paper feels the warmest and which feels the coolest? (Black will feel the warmest.)

Fine points to discuss

What can our body tell us about light? (Light feels warm.)

7-5 Sunlight that is magnified can burn a hole in paper.

2 Take the children outside or near a window on a bright sunny day. Have them wear sunglasses or place a piece of colored cellophane in front of their eyes to protect them from the bright light they are about to see.

Have one or two children at a time catch a light beam from the sun with a magnifying glass. I suggest one or two children at a time to avoid the possibility of several small fires starting. The pail of water should be next to the child using the black paper (in the unlikely case that a fire might start).

3 Tell children to:
   a Concentrate a small sunlight beam on a piece of black construction paper (the smaller the beam, the higher the concentration of light).
   b Hold the magnifying glass very still.
   c After about 15 to 30 seconds, you will see and smell smoke.

(If the magnifying glass stays focused longer it will actually burn a hole in the paper.) It is very important not to stare at the bright spot of light because it can harm our eyes.

4 Do the same thing again with the piece of white tissue paper and the piece of white construction paper. (They will burn eventually, but it will take a great deal of patience.)

Do you know why the white pieces of paper do not burn as quickly as the black one did? (Black absorbs light; white reflects light.)

What is the magnifying glass able to do to light? (It is able to concentrate the power or energy of light to show us what light is. It is a form of energy. The energy is a form of heat that we can feel on our bodies and that can affect other materials like paper.)

What does the paper tell us about light? (Different colors absorb light differently. Some colors become very hot, some remain cool.)

What would be good colors to wear on a hot day if you wanted to feel cool? (White or other light colors.)

On a very hot, sunny day, which would feel cooler to walk on: a blacktop surface or a concrete sidewalk? (A sidewalk.)

III. Light can go through some materials and not others

I. Does light go through?
Materials

To be given to each child or group of children as needed: An assortment of paper products: waxed paper, paper towels, aluminum foil, black-and-white construction paper, cellophane in different colors, cardboard, cardboard tube, tissue paper, clear plastic wrap, clear vinyl, a pin, flashlight.

Procedure

1 Turn the lights out and darken the room.
2 Show the children the various materials by holding them in front of the lighted flashlight one at a time.

Do you think the light can shine through the various materials? (Listen to their thoughts, then have the children experiment to find out if they were right.)

3 Have the children pierce their piece of aluminum foil with a pin. Ask the children to predict what the light will look like and whether it will shine through the aluminum foil.

(It will shine through the tiny hole and look like starlight. More pinholes will produce more lights.)

4 Have children shine the flashlight through the cardboard tube and see what happens. (It will appear as a concentrated beam of light with a slight shadow, like a stage light.)

2. Seeing through a balloon

Materials

A large balloon that blows up to approximately 9 inches.

Procedure

1 Hold the uninflated balloon up to a light. Have the children see if they can look through it.

What needs to happen to the balloon for it to become thinner so they can see through it? (It needs to be blown up or inflated with air.)

2 Blow the balloon up with air. Have the children look through it. (They will be able to see things that are close up, but things that are farther away will look hazy and blurry.)

Going further

Let children "mess around" trying to look through assorted opaque and translucent materials for a few days. Ask them to search around their home to find materials to look through to share with their classmates.

Fine points to discuss

Can light pass through all materials? (No, but it can pass through some. Explain to the children that when materials are clear like a window, they allow light to pass through and are transparent. Materials that are opaque do not allow light to pass through. They simply block light. When materials allow some light to pass through in a scattered kind of way they are called translucent. Waxed paper, tissue paper, and frosted glass are examples of translucent material. Translucent materials make objects look blurry or invisible.)

Are translucent materials always translucent? (No. If they become too thick or dense, they lose their translucency and become more solid or opaque. We can see through one thin piece of tissue paper, but we cannot see through several layers of tissue paper. We can see through a blown-up balloon but not through a balloon that has lost its air. Thinness allows a material to become translucent.

 There are some translucent plastics that can be ¼-inch thick, through which you cannot "see" anything except the diffused light.

IV. Shadows

1. Making shadows

Materials

A small halogen light, tensor light, or a film or slide projector; a clear plastic cup.

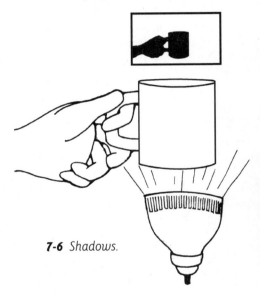

7-6 Shadows.

Procedure

Do you know what a shadow is?

- Have them look for their own shadows.
- Darken the room, and turn the lights off to make it easier for them to see and to make shadows of themselves.

Is it easier to see shadows when lights are on or off? Why?

What makes a shadow?

- Shine a bright light on a wall. Have the children observe the light and notice if there are any shadows. (There will be a shadow if something is blocking the light.)
- Choose a child to hold a clear plastic cup and stand in front of the light. Have the children observe the child's

shadow of a hand holding a cup. Then tell the child to walk toward the screen or walk away from the light.

- Discuss what happens to the shadow of the child's hand.

(The shadow of the child's hand holding a cup grows smaller as it moves away from the light but it becomes gigantic when it is near the light.)

Fine points to discuss

When the light shines on the child's hand holding a clear plastic cup and creates a shadow of the child's hand and the cup, is the whole hand lit up by the light, or just one side of the child's hand? (Just the side of the child's hand that the light shines on is lit up. The other side of the hand remains in the dark.)

Why doesn't the light shine through the child? (The child is a solid object. Light is blocked by solid objects. Solid objects form shadows of themselves when light shines on them.)

Does the clear plastic cup appear as a solid shadow? (No, it appears as a lighter shadow.)

Can a person or an object have more than one shadow?

How could we find out? (Yes. If there are two light sources shining on the object, each light source will create a shadow. Have the children experiment with two lights or flashlights shining on a toy from different angles to check this out.)

Does the brightness of the light affect the shadow? (Yes, when the light is brighter, the lines of the shadows appear sharper and clearer.)

How can you tell how solid an image is by looking at its shadow? (Solid objects do not allow light to pass through. Solid objects appear darker than translucent objects.)

2. Shapes of shadows

Materials

A small, halogen light; tensor light; various-shaped objects such as a small tin can, a pair of scissors, a rectangular block, a pencil, a fat round crayon, a paper cup, a cone shape, a jar lid, a large thin book.

Procedure

1 Darken the room and turn the lights out. Shine the light on a wall. Display the various-shaped objects.

2 Have the child hold up one of the objects in front of the light beam so that the object creates a shadow.

3 Have the children experiment holding and rotating each of the shapes around one at a time to different positions so that the shapes are standing up or lying down, or at a different angle to the light. Ask the children to experiment to find out how many different kinds of shadows each of the differently shaped objects can make. Ask them to make a prediction before they look at the shadow about what the shape of the shadow might look like.

Fine points to discuss

What happens to round and curved objects when they make shadows? (They look flat and lose their roundness. The shadows of some things look very different from what we expect them to look like. A pair of scissors lying flat can look like a straight line; a pencil held horizontally to the light can look like a small circle.)

What happens to shapes or objects when they are very close to the light? (The shadows of the objects get much larger.)

What happens to shapes or objects when they are further away from the light? (The shadows of the objects more accurately represent their true size.)

Which part of the shape or object is always in the light? (The part facing the light source.)

What part of the shape or object is always in the dark? (The part of the object that is not facing the light is in its own shadow.)

V. Night is earth's shadow

1. Day and night model on a globe

Materials

A small model of a globe representing the earth; a flashlight, halogen light, or tensor light; a small piece of clay; a toothpick.

Procedure

1 Turn the lights out and darken the room. Shine the light on the globe.

2 *Explain:* The globe is a model of the earth. The earth is the name of the planet we live on. All of the blue represents oceans of water. Show the children where North America and the United States are on the globe and where their state and city are located. Place a small dab of clay with a

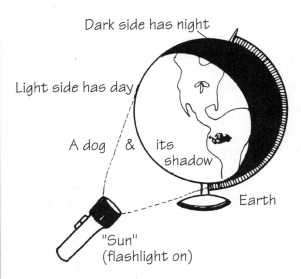

Dark side has night

Light side has day

A dog & its shadow

Earth

"Sun" (flashlight on)

7-7 *Creating a model of day and night with a globe..*

toothpick in it to represent a person on the state in which the children live.

3 Rotate the earth slowly until the light is shining on the dab of clay with a toothpick in it. Ask the children if they know what the bright light that shines on the earth is called. They will probably respond that it is the sun. If they don't, tell them that the light is a model that represents the sun shining on the earth.

4 Have the children observe that one side of the earth is in the dark, and one side is in the light.

Which side of the earth is having night and which side of the earth is having day? (The answer is rather obvious. The lit-up side is having day; the dark side is having night.)

5 Continue to turn or rotate the earth so that the dab of clay with a toothpick in it is in the dark.

6 *Explain:* The earth is continuously moving but we cannot feel it moving because everything is moving with us. The sun stays still.

7 Have individual children continue to shine the light on the globe and to rotate the globe to experience where the light shines and to experience how night is caused by earth's shadow.

2. Child's body as model of the earth

Materials

A flashlight, a globe representing the earth.

Procedure

1 Ask children to pretend that their bodies are the earth. Their chest could represent where they live now. Their back could represent "someplace else" on the earth.

2 Have them look at a globe and see what is on the other side of the earth from where they live. (For example: If you lived in Chicago, Illinois, and made an imaginary line through the interior of the earth, Calcutta, India would be on the other side of the earth.)

3 Tell children also to pretend that the flashlight is the sun. Shine the light on their chests.

Are their backs lit up too? Why not? (The light from the flashlight or sun can only light up one side of their body at a time. The sun cannot go through them. Their body is a solid object. Their body creates a shadow when it is in the light.)

If their bodies are the earth, which part of their body is experiencing day? How can they tell? (Their chest is experiencing day because it is in the beam of light.)

If their chest represents Chicago, and their back represents Calcutta, which part of the earth would be having night? (When the flashlight "sun" is shining on their chests ("Chicago"), then their backs ("Calcutta") would be having night because night is being created by their bodies' own ("earth's own") shadows.

3. Shadows change

Materials

A globe with dab of clay and a toothpick; a tensor light, or halogen light.

Procedure

1 Turn the lights off and darken the room. Shine the light on the earth.

2 As you rotate the earth, have the children observe where the sun is located. Ask the children if the sun is always located in the same spot on the earth or if the sunlight would appear to be moving. (The sunlight would appear to be moving. It would appear to be rising and setting.)

When will the sun that is rising or setting affect shadows? (To find out this answer, have children observe the toothpick's shadow in a beam of light.)

Fine points to discuss

Will our shadows always look alike or will they be different at different times of the day? (Although the sun stays still, it appears to be making an arc in the sky. When the sun is low, our shadows are long. When the sun is directly overhead, our shadows are short.)

How can you tell where the sun is by looking at your shadow? (The sun will always create a shadow in an opposite direction from where it is shining. If you turn your back to the sun when the sun is low, you will see your shadow in front of you. You can always tell where the sun is by looking at where the shadows are.)

4. The sun's "arc"

Materials

A flashlight, halogen, or tensor light.

Procedure

1 Turn the lights out and darken the room.

2 Choose a child to shine a light on, and another child to hold the flashlight.

3 *Explain:* The light from the flashlight is going to represent the sun. Although the sun does not move, it appears to move by rising and setting every day.

4 Have a child hold the flashlight. The child is to pretend that the light coming from the flashlight is the sun rising and setting.

5 Have the child move the light in an arc. (You might need to assist the child in moving the flashlight to form an arc.)

6 Have a child begin the arc on the floor by holding the flashlight parallel to the floor. Slowly have the child create an arc shape by moving the flashlight into an upward position. Be sure the light is shining down onto the other child. Have the child end the arc on the floor on the opposite side from where he or she started.

How did the size and shape of the child's shadow change as the sun "rose and set?"

VI. Light can bounce (reflect)

1. Catch a sunbeam in a mirror

Materials

A small mirror.

Procedure

1 Have a child stand near a window on a bright sunny day and catch a sunbeam with a mirror.

2 Ask the child to shine or reflect the beam onto a wall or the ceiling so everyone can see the beam of light.

Is the light going through the mirror, and if it is not, how can they tell? (The mirror makes a shadow and the light hitting the mirror bounces off the mirror and is thrown to another place.)

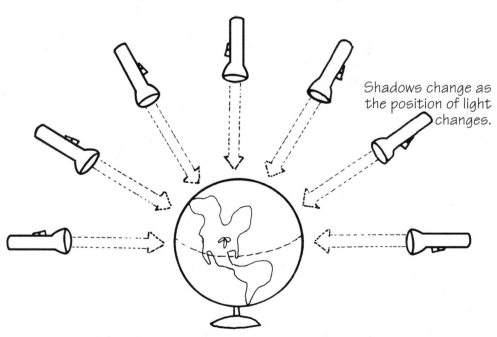

Shadows change as the position of light changes.

The suns are in the sky as seen from the Earth. The flashlight represents the sun.

7-8 *Shadows change.*

Light

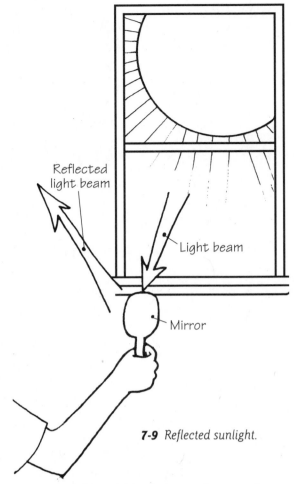

Reflected light beam

Light beam

Mirror

7-9 Reflected sunlight.

3 *Explain:* When light is "thrown" this way by an object like a mirror, then the light is called a reflection.

Can you think of other things that cause mirror like reflections? (Examples: red bike reflector lights, colors that glow in the dark, chrome on cars, shiny surfaces, water.)

2. Making a ball bounce against a wall as a model of a reflection

Materials

A ball, a long hallway wall with no obstructions.

Procedure

1 Have the children roll a ball against a wall. Ask them to predict what will happen to the ball.

Where will it bounce off to when it hits the wall?

2 Have the child roll a ball directly in front of himself or herself so that the ball will hit the wall head-on.

(The ball will roll back to him or her.)

3 Have the child roll the ball at an angle.

(The ball will hit the wall at an angle and roll off at an angle away from him or her.)

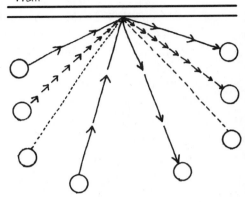

Balls bounce off the wall, or reflect, at the same angle they were sent.

Wall

7-10 Angle of incidence equals angle of reflection.

4 Have the children line up and sit down parallel to the wall a few feet from the wall. Place a marker on the wall for the children to aim at. Ask them to predict which child will receive the ball that they roll at an angle.

(The children should be able to notice how the ball bounces differently according to the angle it is thrown from.)

Note: One child can do this activity by himself or herself by extending and holding his/her arms apart. If the child rolls the ball from his/her extended right arm, the ball will bounce against the wall and roll back to the child's extended left arm.

Fine point to discuss

How is the rolling ball bouncing against a wall and reflecting off it like a light beam hitting a mirror? (Light behaves like a bouncing ball. It reflects or bounces off a surface to another place. Light travels in a straight line, just as the ball does.)

INFORMATION

See the Law of Reflection at the beginning of this chapter, under General Background Information for Parents and Teachers.

3. Black and white— bounce or absorb?

Materials

Black-and-white construction paper, a shiny piece of vinyl material, a shiny piece of glossy paper or aluminum foil, a flashlight.

Procedure

1 Have children shine a flashlight on the different pieces of paper and plastic. Ask them if light bounces off or reflects off each kind of material in the same way. Discuss the differences.

Which kind of surface bounces off or reflects more light? (The shiny surfaces reflect more light.)

What color reflects more light? (White reflects more light than black.)

2 *Explain:* Black absorbs light; that is why the magnifying glass was able to burn the black paper. White feels cool because it reflects light and heat.

4. Water reflection

Materials

A black, flat pan filled with water; photographs from travel magazines that depict pictures of lakes with mirror images of scenery.

Procedure

1 Have children observe their reflection in the pan of water. They will be able to see themselves if they are directly over the pan, but if they look into the water from an angle they will be able to see other children or other things that are in front of them.

2 Show children the travel pictures of lakes with mirror image reflections. Turn the picture upside-down

How can you tell the picture is upside-down? (The reflection will probably have waves in it from the water, or the colors of the reflection might not be as bright.)

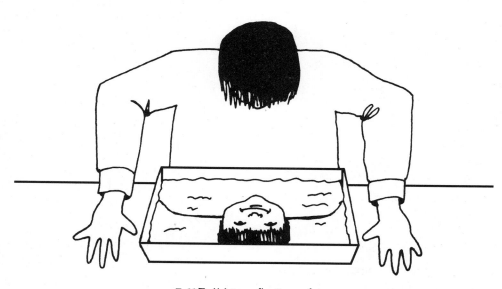

7-11A *Water reflecting a face.*

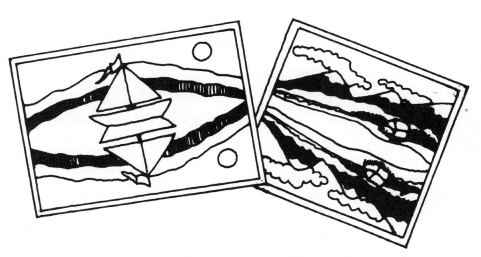

7-11B *Water reflecting a picture.*

5. Mirror writing

Materials

For each child or group of children: a small mirror, a piece of paper for each child, a black marking pen.

Procedure

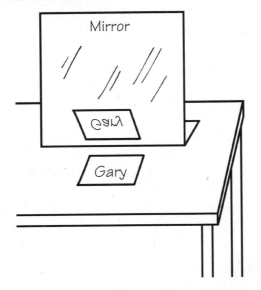

7-12 See letters appear upside down in a mirror.

1 Have each child write his/her own name on the paper and underline it.

2 Instruct the children to place the mirror perpendicular to the paper on top of their own written name.

(The letters will appear to be upside-down.)

3 Instruct children to place the mirror perpendicular to the paper on the bottom of their own written name so that the word is upside-down, and the word will appear to be written backwards in the mirror. (See Fig. 7-12.)

4 Suggest to children that they lift the paper up and turn it over to the other side. The word can be seen through the paper.

5 Tell children to place their mirror next to the word.

(It will appear in the usual form in the mirror.)

Why did the letters appear to be backwards and upside down?

6 *Explain:* A mirror reflects an image. The image is a picture. The real you and the real word are not in the mirror. The mirror creates a reflection of real things. Mirrors can trick you into

7-13 See letters appear backwards in a mirror.

thinking you see things that are "there," that are not really "there."

7 Have the children continue to experiment with the mirror held perpendicular to letters, words, or pictures.

6. Multiple images

Materials

For each child or group of children: one small mirror and access to a large wall mirror.

Procedure

Have children hold a small mirror under their chin while standing in front of a large mirror so that they can focus on their image while holding a mirror under their chin. *Note:* If the mirror is tilted at an appropriate angle to catch their own reflection, the children will be surprised to see a multiple image of themselves that goes on for what appears to be forever inside of the mirror. It will appear to be an endless tunnel. Each image inside the image will appear to be smaller, less clear, and darker. Each time something is reflected it loses some light.

7. Make a periscope model (for older children)

Materials

For each child or group of children: two small mirrors, two pieces of cardboard, some tape, two empty half-gallon milk cartons, a pair of scissors.

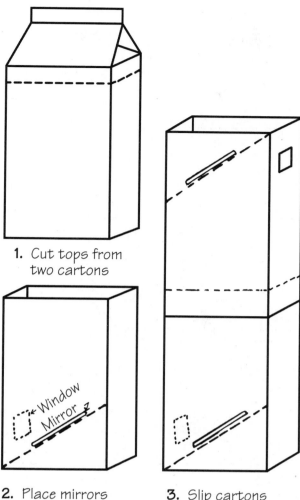

7-14 *Making a periscope.*

1. Cut tops from two cartons

2. Place mirrors and cut windows

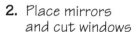
Window
Mirror

3. Slip cartons together

Procedure

1 Show children a model of a periscope.
2 Have children make their own toy periscope. (See Table 7-1.)

Table 7-1 Instructions for making a toy periscope

1 Wedging a piece of cardboard to the bottom of each of the opened empty half-gallon milk containers at about a 45° angle.
2 Mount a mirror to the cardboard.
3 Cutting a two-inch square hole directly in front of where the mirrors are mounted.
4 Secure the cardboard in place with some tape.
5 Secure the mirror in place on the cardboard with some tape.
6 Slip the two cartons together.
7 Be sure that the two holes are "katty-korner" to each other.

How and why are periscopes used? (Periscopes are used in submarines. They are also used for seeing around corners. The mirrors inside them reflect light.)

8. Take apart periscope

Materials

A finished toy periscope; paper; two small, round magnets; marking pens.

Procedure

1 Have the children play with the periscope and experiment with it.

How does the periscope work? (It works because the two mirrors work together to reflect an image. It creates an image of an image.)

2 Have the children disconnect their periscope and connect it so that both holes are on the same side. Then ask them to look through the hole and to explain what they see.

(Everything will appear to be upside-down because the light reflects off the mirrors in

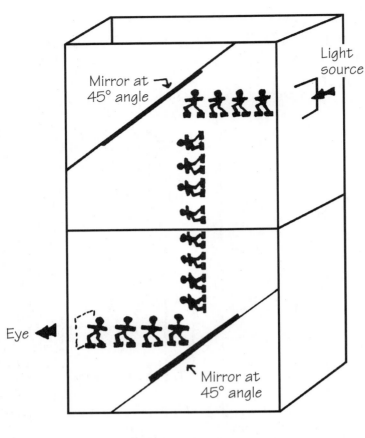

7-15 Periscope angles. Everything appears right-side up.

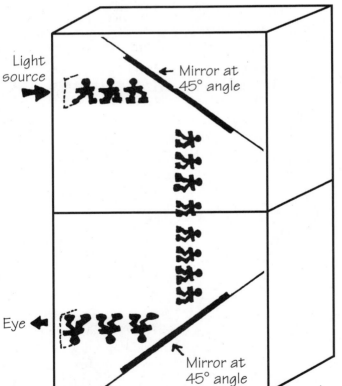

7-16 Periscope angles. Direction changes and everything appears upside down.

straight lines. Light reflects the way it enters the periscope.)

- On a piece of typing paper, draw the two sketches that appear in Figs. 7-15 and 7-16. Use a set of small round

magnets as markers to move on the two sketches.

- Tell children to look at the first sketch and to try to imagine little children or toy soldiers marching on a reflected light beam or boats floating down a reflected light beam inside the periscope. When the toy soldiers or children reach or hit the first mirror, they follow the light beam to the next mirror and continue to march or float out of the periscope on the reflected light beam. The reflected light beam has continued to move in the same direction and moves in a straight line.

- Have the children look at the second sketch and try to imagine those same soldiers marching or the boats floating on the reflected light beam again, but this time when they hit the first mirror, the reflected light beam bounces down to the second mirror and that mirror reverses the direction of the light beam. Because the soldiers or boats follow the light beam as it reverses direction, they are forced to march or float upside-down along the reflected light beam as they leave or exit from the periscope.

9. Curved reflections

Materials

Several shiny metal spoons in different sizes, a curved mirror or shiny pot lid.

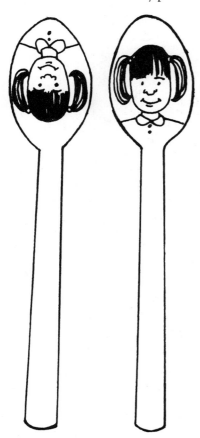

7-17 Reflections on a spoon.

Procedure

1 Have the children look at their reflections in the various curved shapes.

Do your reflections look the way they would in a mirror or do they look different? (Their reflections will be distorted.)

Why do you think you look different? (The surface is curved.)

2 Have them now look at themselves inside of the curve of the spoon (the concave side that caves in). They will notice that they look upside-down.

3 Have the children look at themselves on the convex side of the spoon—the side of the spoon that curves out (the part that children might call the bottom of the spoon).

Fine point to discuss

Why do reflections look so different on the curved or rounded surfaces? (Light that hits a curve reflects or bounces on a tangent of the curve so it appears to reflect light differently from light that hits a flat surface. This causes a twisting and a bending of the images that are reflected and is called a distortion.)

10. Hinged mirrors

Materials

For each child or group of children: two small mirrors of the same size, taped together on one side to form a hinged effect; a pencil.

Procedure

1 Stand the hinged mirror perpendicular to the surface of a table. Have the children look inside the mirrors and count how many mirrors they see.

(There will be a range of four to twelve mirrors. The number will depend on the angle that the mirrors are opened to.)

2 Have the children experiment with the angle of the two mirrors (to be acute and obtuse).

Can you see more images when the mirrors are standing close together or when they are opened far apart? Why? (When the mirrors are held close together, the children will see more images because the mirrors will reflect more images.)

3 Have the children place a pencil in front of the hinged mirror. Ask them to make a prediction about how many pencils they will see before they place

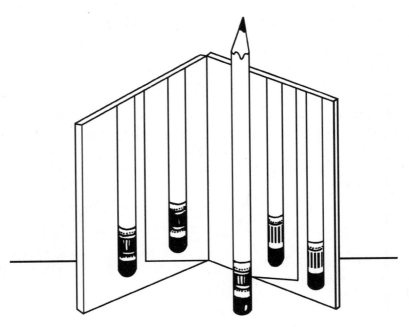

7-18 *Multiple images of a pencil.*

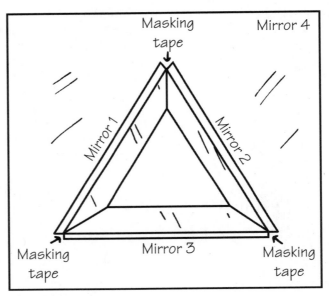

Top view

7-19 *Kaleidoscope of mirrors.*

the pencil in front of the mirrors. (The number will vary depending on how close the mirrors are to each other and how close the pencil is to the mirrors.)

Note: When the mirrors are at a 90-degree angle, the child should look into the hinged mirror. The child will be able to see a real, rather than an inverted left-to-right image. That is, if the child winks with his or her right eye, the image in the mirror will wink with the right eye too.

II. Kaleidoscope model

Materials

Give each child or group of children: three small mirrors that are the same size,

taped together on their sides to form a tri-angular-shaped tunnel; one other small mirror.

Procedure

Have the children look through the home-made kaleidoscope. Have them place the one extra mirror in front of the "triangle tunnel." Then ask them to discuss what they see.

Fine point to discuss

Why do they see so many eyes in the kaleidoscope if only one eye is being reflected? (They see a multiple image of their eyes or images of their eyes in mirrors. The multiple image they see is caused by the reflection or bounce of light. The reflection takes place many times, causing a multiple image. The multiple image is an illusion. It makes it appear that something is there that is not.)

VII. Refraction (the bending of light)

I. "Broken" straw effect

Materials

A clear glass partially filled with water and oil; a drinking straw or a spoon.

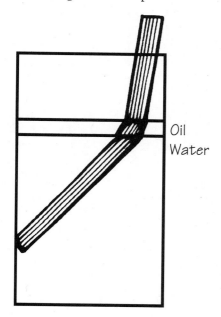

Oil
Water

7-20 Refraction of a drinking straw

Procedure

1 Have the children observe the separation of water and oil. Also discuss the layer of air on top of the oil.

2 Have a child place the drinking straw into the water so that it is resting in a diagonal position.

3 Have the children discuss what they see. (The straw will look strange, as though it has been cut.)

This phenomenon is called refraction. Refraction is the bending of light. For more information, see General Information for Parents and Teachers at the beginning of this chapter.

2. Appearing and disappearing coins

Materials

A clear glass of water, a coin.

Procedure

1 Place a penny on the inside side of a glass of water. (not in the center)

2 Observe the penny from different angles, and slowly rotate the glass.

Do the number of pennies you see change?

Going further

Will the amount of water in the glass or the shape of the glass make a difference to what you see?

What will happen if you place the coin under the glass of water instead of inside the glass?

What affects the number of pennies you see? (The curve of the glass and the angle from which you are viewing the penny.)

VIII. Lenses

I. Water-drop lenses

Materials

A Styrofoam meat tray, a clear plastic zip-lock baggie, used postage stamps, Scotch tape, eye dropper, water, clear plastic vinyl or waxed paper.

Procedure

1 Mount the used postage stamps on the meat tray with Scotch tape. Slip the meat tray into the clear plastic zip-lock baggie.

2 Have a child use an eye dropper to drop a few drops of water onto the clear vinyl or waxed paper. Have the child place the waxed paper or clear vinyl with water drops on top of the Styrofoam meat tray that has the postage stamps mounted on it inside the zip-lock baggie. (See Fig. 7-21.)

3 Have the child slide the vinyl or waxed paper around with the water drops on it, and then observe the postage stamps under the water lens. Discuss what is seen. (The parts of the stamps that are underneath the water-drop lenses will be magnified.)

Why are the postage stamps magnified? (They are magnified because they are seen through a curved surface.)

Fine point to discuss

Does the size of the drop of water affect what you see? (Yes. When the drop of water is smaller, the curved surface of the drop is higher and the magnification effect is

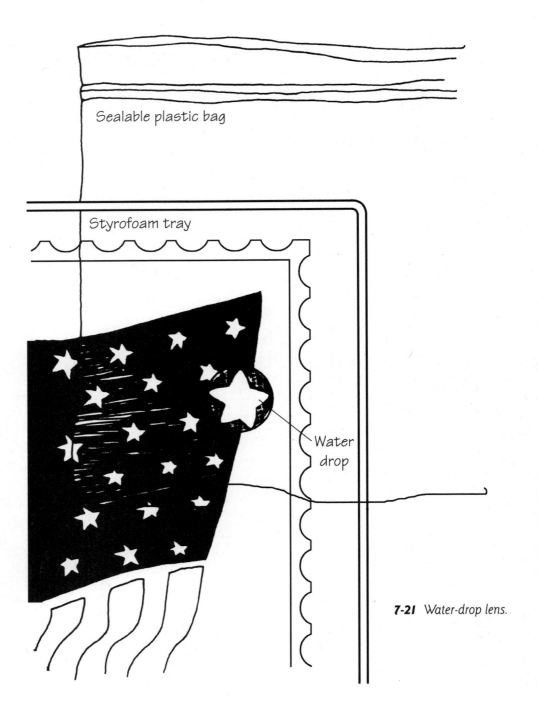

Sealable plastic bag

Styrofoam tray

Water drop

7-21 Water-drop lens.

greater. A large water-drop lens has a flatter surface.)

2. Water magnification

Materials

For each child or group of children: a clear plastic glass filled with water, a page of print from a newspaper or magazine.

Procedure

1 Have a child place a page of print behind a glass filled with water. Ask the children what happens to the print when it is seen through the glass.

(The print becomes bigger or magnified.)

2 Place the glass on top of the page of print and have a child look through the bottom of the glass.

Do the words look as big as they did when they were seen through the sides of the glass? (No, the print will not be magnified. The curve on the side of the clear drinking glass creates a lens effect. A lens needs to have a curve and be transparent to be a lens.)

3 Tell children to place their thumb inside the glass of water.

4 Have children observe their thumb.

5 Tell children to place their thumb on the back side of the glass and look through to see their thumb.

THE JOURNAL

NewsPlu

ISSUE ...UNDED ...BUT NO

re's little ... eace C... me and
hope for p... ...orny is

7-22 Water magnifies objects.

6 Discuss whether their thumbs look as big on the outside of the glass as when their thumbs were on the inside of the glass.

Note: Their thumbs will still look big. Water inside of a glass behaves like a magnifying lens.

3. Magnifying glass

Materials

Magnifying glasses, page of print, other items of interest to magnify.

Procedure

1 Have the children look through a magnifying glass at their skin, fingernails, and clothes, or other items of interest.

2 Have them discuss what they see, and what the magnifying glass is able to do.

Is it is easier to use a magnifying glass to make things look bigger or to use a drop of water? Why? (A magnifying glass gives you more control. It is more stable and can be manipulated easier.)

3 Have children look for and feel the curve on the magnifying glass. Discuss the shape of the lens.

Is it similar to the shape of the water-drop lens? (Yes, they both curve up like a round hill and are called convex lenses.)

4. Convex and concave lenses

Materials

Old prescription lenses from eyeglasses and/or various cheap, defective, or surplus lenses purchased from a science supply house; or lenses from old cameras or binoculars, old watch-face crystals, or clear marbles.

Convex and Concave Lenses

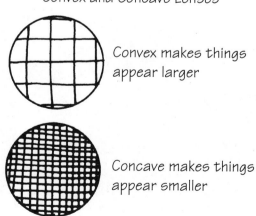

Convex makes things appear larger

Concave makes things appear smaller

7-23 Curves affect what we see.

Procedure

1 Have the children examine the various lenses and see the effect they create. Ask them to observe whether thickness or thinness affects the lens,

and how the curve of the lens affects what they see.

2 Have the children observe how things appear through different lenses. Have the children observe whether all of the lenses are convex or if some of them are concave.

(Concave is shaped like a valley: it caves in, in the center.)

 You might want to show children the spoon again so they can see the difference between a convex and a concave curve.

5. Microscope lens model

Materials

A water-drop lens (see Procedure #1 from this activity section), a postage stamp or other interesting item to magnify, and a plastic magnifying lens.

Procedure

1 Set up the water-drop lens over a postage stamp. Have the children look through a plastic magnifying lens through the water-drop lens at the postage stamp.

2 Have the children discuss what they see.

(It will be like looking through a microscope. The tiny dots and lines on the stamp will become very large.)

6. Seeing through two lenses: microscope effect/telescope effect

Materials

Two plastic magnifying glasses; interesting things to look at with the magnifying glass, like feathers, snakeskin, a grain of salt, a drop of water, a leaf. (See Fig. 7-25.)

Procedure

• Place the items out on display. Have the children observe the items by looking through two magnifying glasses. Have them discuss what they see. *Note:* If the two magnifying glasses are held together on the surface of the object, the two magnifying glasses will act like one strong magnifying glass. However, if the two magnifying glasses are lifted up off the surface, everything will look upside-down and small. If one magnifying glass is removed while it is away from the object being looked at, everything will look blurry and out of focus.

What does a telescope do? (Telescopes make things that are far away look closer.)

How can we create a telescope effect with two magnifying glasses? (See Table 7-2.)

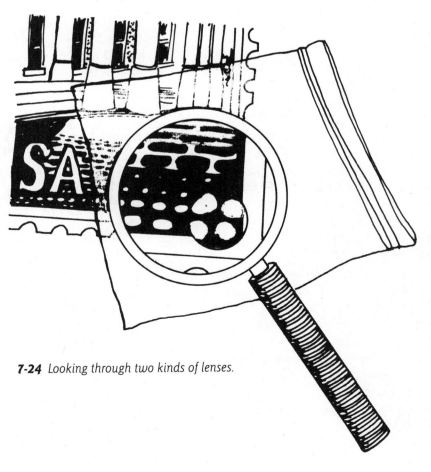

7-24 *Looking through two kinds of lenses.*

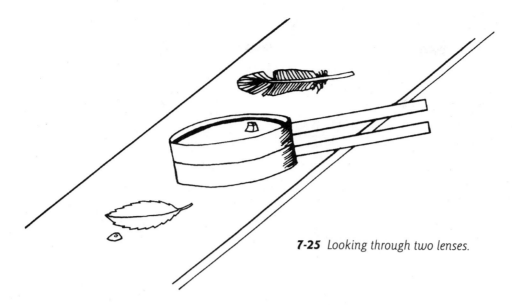

7-25 *Looking through two lenses.*

Table 7-2 Telescope effect

1 Show the children how to focus the two magnifying glasses onto something far away in the room.

2 Have the children close one of their eyes and hold one magnifying glass in front of their opened eye.

3 Move the other glass approximately 3 to 4 inches in front of the first magnifying glass until it looks focused.

* *Note*: It will be focused when things can be seen clearly through both of the lenses. Everything will look upside-down and small, but things will look closer than they really are.

What do microscopes do? (A microscope makes things that are small look bigger.)

How can we create a microscope effect with two magnifying glasses? (See Table 7-3.)

Table 7-3 Microscope effect

1 Show the children how to focus the two magnifying glasses onto something close to their nose.

2 Have them close one of their eyes and hold one magnifying glass in front of their open eye.

3 Have them move the other magnifying glass approximately one inch in front of the first magnifying glass.

4 The second magnifying glass should be about one-half inch away from the material being focused on.

* *Note*: When they are focused, things will look very large.

---

7. Projector magnification

Materials

A small, halogen light, tensor light, or flashlight; a magnifying glass; a clear transparent ruler or shedded snakeskin or piece of transparent film. (See Fig. 7-26.)

Procedure

1 Darken the room. Have a child hold a transparent ruler a few inches in front of a lit tensor light or flashlight.

2 Have another child hold a magnifying glass a few inches in front of the ruler until the light is focused through the ruler and part of the ruler is projected onto the wall or ceiling.

(The ruler will look magnified when it is projected.)

Fine points to discuss

What do lenses do for us? (Lenses help us focus so we can see things better. They also make things look larger or smaller than they really are.)

What is a lens? (A lens is a curved surface that refracts or bends light to help us see better.)

IX. Color

1. No light, no sight

Materials

For each child or group of children: an empty shoe box with a lid; a small, colorful picture; Scotch tape.

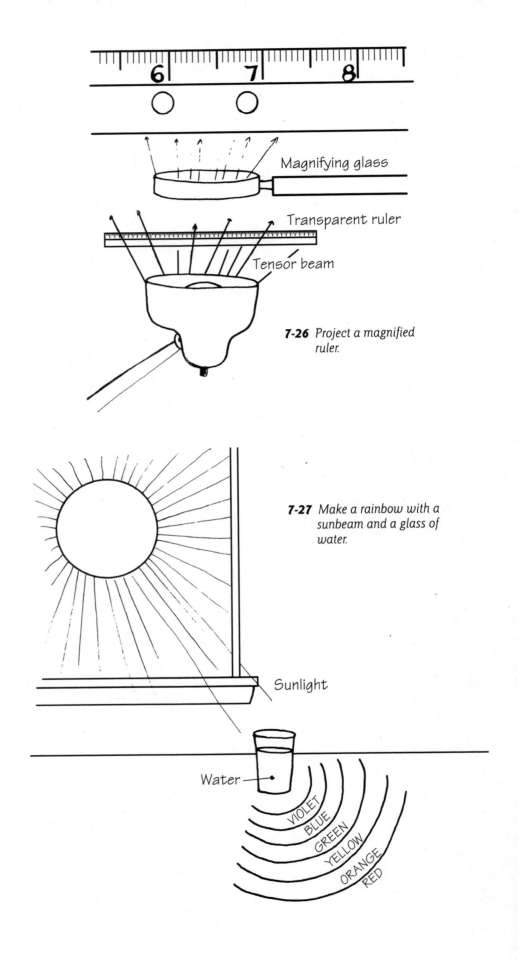

7-26 Project a magnified ruler.

7-27 Make a rainbow with a sunbeam and a glass of water.

Magnifying glass

Transparent ruler

Tensor beam

Sunlight

Water

VIOLET
BLUE
GREEN
YELLOW
ORANGE
RED

Procedure

1 Have children use Scotch tape to mount a colorful picture on the inside of the box.

2 Make a small peephole in front of the picture at the opposite end of the box.

3 Have the children cover the shoe box with the shoe box lid.

4 Tell children to look through the peephole.

Can you see the colors in the picture? (They might be able to, but it will be hard to see.)

5 Have children open the lid of the shoe box while they are looking through the peephole.

Can you see the colors in the picture better when there is light? (The objects will be easier to see, and the intensity and brightness of the colors will be greatly improved.)

Fine point to discuss

Why do we need light to see? (Colors are reflected. If there is no light, there is no reflection of the color to our eyes.)

2. Make a rainbow

Materials

A sunbeam, a piece of white paper, a prism or clear glass partially filled with water (the glass can be made of clear plastic).

Procedure

1 Place the prism in a window that has a light beam shining through it. Discuss the rainbow effect that can be seen. Have the children place the white paper underneath the rainbow to see if the colors become brighter and more distinct. *Note:* The rainbow can be made to look brighter if you shade the area where the rainbow appears with your hand.

2 *Explain:* The light is being bent by the water. It is being bent twice: once when it enters the glass, and once when it leaves the glass. This bending of light twice causes the light to separate. When the light beam separates, we can see a rainbow.

3 Ask the children to name the colors in the rainbow from the top band down to the bottom band. (There are seven colors in the rainbow: red, orange, yellow, green, blue, indigo, and violet.)

Note: A popular mnemonic device for memorizing the order of the colors in the spectrum is to remember the name: ROY G. BIV. The letters in this name stand for the first letters in Red, Orange, Yellow, Green, Blue, Indigo and Violet.

3. Spinning colors

Materials

Toy tops or hand drill; a round cardboard disk, or paper circles; crayons in the following colors: red, orange, yellow, green, blue, purple; a ruler; a pencil.

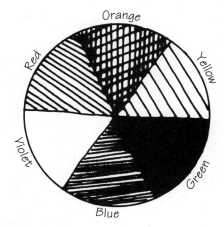

7-28 Colored paper disk.

Procedure

1 Tell the children to divide the disk into six sections with a ruler and a pencil, or have the children fold a paper circle in half three times and draw lines on the folds.

2 Have children color in each of the six sections with one of the crayon colors in the order that the color would appear in a rainbow spectrum.

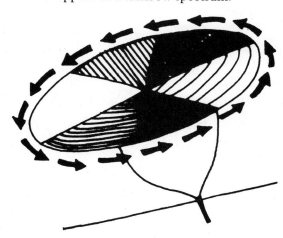

7-29 Colored disk on a spinning top.

3 Have children place the center of the colored cardboard disk or paper circle on top of the toy top or on top of the

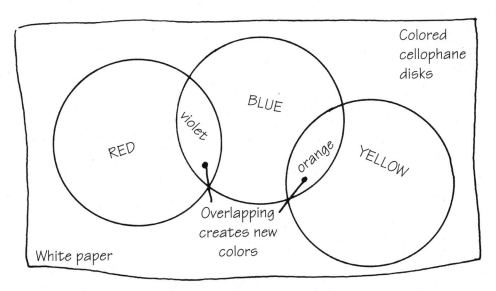

7-30 *Combine and mix colors to make new colors.*

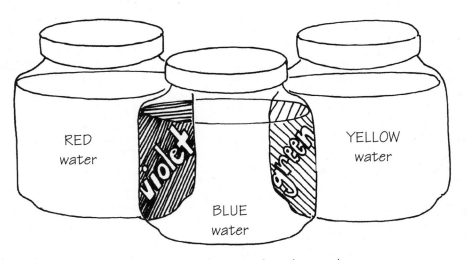

7-31 *See a new color by seeing through two colors.*

hand drill. Then tell children to make the top or drill spin.

What happens to the colors on the spinning disk? (The colors will blend together and begin to look white or have a white cast.)

4. Combining and mixing colors

Materials

Pieces of colored cellophane; pieces of colored transparent plastic; three small jars filled with water; red, yellow, and blue food coloring; red, yellow, and blue poster paint; toothpicks; white paper.

Procedure

1 Have the children arrange the pieces of colored cellophane on top of each other in a random pattern on a piece of white paper, then discuss with the children the new colors that are created by the overlapping pieces of cellophane.

2 Have the children place food coloring in each of the three small jars of water so that one jar has red in it, one jar has yellow in it, and one jar has blue in it. Tell them to use a lot of food coloring in the jars so that the colors are fairly intense. After the colors are fairly intense, tell the children to observe the colors and then observe them through another color.

What are the new colors that can be seen through the overlapping colors?

3 Have the children use toothpicks to lift drops of water from the jars filled with colored water onto white paper.

What are the colors that can be created by combining two or three colors of water?

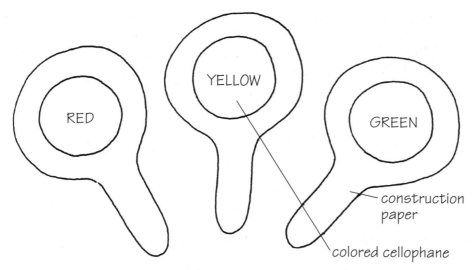

7-32 Seeing colors through filters.

4 Show the children the poster paint colors. Have them predict what colors will be made by combining two colors together. Then have the children mix two toothpick-drops of color together to see the result.

5. Seeing color through filters

Materials

Pieces of red and yellow cellophane; construction paper; staples or masking tape; red, yellow, and blue crayons; white paper.

Procedure

1 Have children place one or two pieces of red (or yellow) cellophane together so that they are able to filter out that color.

(When you look through red cellophane at something red, it will look white or disappear.)

2 Have children staple or tape the cellophane together, and place a frame around it made of construction paper. *Note:* The cellophane can look like a small slide or can be large like a ping-pong paddle. The construction paper frame will make the "cellophane window" easier to hold and more sturdy.

3 Have the children draw simple designs on white paper with red, yellow, and blue crayons. Then have the children look at their drawings through the red or yellow cellophane windows.

What has happened to the colors? (The color yellow in the drawings will seem to disappear when it is viewed through the yellow cellophane. The color red in the drawings will seem to disappear when it is viewed through the red cellophane.)

Fine point to discuss

Why do colors appear to change or to disappear when they are seen through other colors? (All of the colors we see are reflected colors. Colored transparent materials act as filters. They filter out all of the other colors from the light beam except the color of the filter. The crayon colors cannot be reflected back to our eyes when a colored filter absorbs the other wavelengths of color from the light beam.)

 A colored crayon on white paper does not absorb or add to color. It takes out certain wavelengths of light and reflects them back to us. When an object looks blue to our eyes, it is because every other color is absorbed by the object except blue, and blue is reflected back to our eyes.

 Grass appears to be green because the only wavelength of light that grass does not absorb is green. Grass cannot absorb green light so it appears green to our eyes. The grass absorbs or traps all of the other colors in light. A plant in green light would die because all colors would be filtered out except green. The green filter would absorb and trap all of the other colors, but the plant needs the other colors to live.

6. Chromatography

Materials

Give each child or group of children: marking pens in assorted water-soluble colors, a pile of white paper towels cut in

4-inch circles, several clear plastic glasses, water, scissors.

Procedure

1 Have children partially fill the glasses with water. Have them make two cuts into each paper towel "filter." *Note:* The two cuts should be parallel to each other and form a strip or tongue that hangs down from the center of each circle. (See Fig. 7-33.)

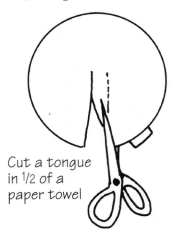

Cut a tongue in ½ of a paper towel

7-33 *Cut a tongue in filter paper.*

2 Have the children color the top near the center of the circles of each "filter" tongue with a color from a marking pen. (See Fig. 7-34.)

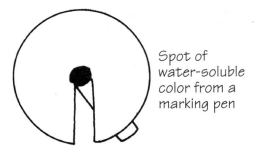

Spot of water-soluble color from a marking pen

7-34 *Mark paper towel with water-soluble ink.*

3 Have the children place the "tongue" or strip in the water and the rest of the paper circle on the rim of the glass.

(The water will rise up the strip onto the colored pen mark.* The colors in the pen mark will separate into all of the component colors or dyes that were needed to create the color made by the marking pen.)

* The water rises up the strip due to capillarity. Capillarity also helps leaves of plants receive water from their roots.

Paper towel filter

Spot of color

Filter tongue

Water

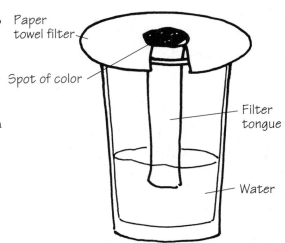

7-35 *Wait to see results.*

(i) **INFORMATION** There should be one filter and one glass with water for each marking pen color used. A comparison can be made afterwards of the results. It will be hard to remember what the original color was before the chromatography process occurred, so you might want to mark the outer perimeter with the original color. The chromatography process takes about 15 minutes per color.

Going further

• Show children the effects after chromatography. See if they can guess the original color that was used to create the colors in the chromatography.

• Is black ink really black? (Adapted from More Science Surprises from Dr. Zed/OWL-TV, edited by Marilyn Baillie, page 29 and 32.) Draw a heavy black or brown dot onto a white paper towel or coffee filter with a water soluble marker.

• Use a drinking straw to drop a drop of water onto the dot of color.

• Observe what happens to the dot of black or brown color. *Note:* The different colors will separate out from the dot of ink. The "heavier" particles in the ink will stay near the center, the "lighter" particles in the ink will spread out beyond the original dot.

• Experiment with different brands and different colors and different kinds of paper to see what the effects will be.

• Experiment with rubbing alcohol. Compare what it does to the dot of color as compared to what the water did to the same color from the same marking pen.

What happens to the original color if you use water and rubbing alcohol?

7. Camouflage

Materials

Magazine pictures of animals that depict camouflage,* colored paper in various colors; crayons in assorted colors.

Procedure

1 Show the children the pictures of animals and discuss what camouflage means and how the coloration of these animals helps protect them in their habitats. (Examples are: the zebras' stripes and tigers' stripes protect them in tall grass; lions' color protects them on the plains; polar bears' white coat protects them in the snow; bright colors on some insects protect them on flowers, etc.)

2 Have the children create a camouflage texture on the colored paper with colored crayons and another that is not as camouflaged but uses contrasts that are easier to see.

(Examples: red spots on red paper and one that shows red spots on white or yellow paper.)

3 Observe the effects of colors on colors and discuss what the children notice about the colors on colors.

* *Ranger Rick* or other wildlife magazines are a good source for such pictures.

X. The energy from light can affect plants and animals

1. Plants and light

Materials

Four plants that are healthy and identical in size and species; one empty half-gallon milk container or other cardboard container; labels: A, B, C, D.

Procedure

1 Ask the children the following questions:

Do plants need light?

How can we find out? (Listen to the children's suggestions.)

Do plants grow toward light?

How can we find out? (Listen to the children's suggestions.)

Note: If they don't think of a box, a closet, or other similar ideas for the plant, it is okay to suggest the following:

2 Have a child or group of children construct two boxes with a "window." (See Fig. 7-36.)

3 Cut a "window" hole about one-inch square on the side of two milk cartons. Open the top of the milk cartons.

4 Place three of the plants in a sunny window. Label them "A" "B" "C." Place an inverted milk carton with a "window" cut on the side on top of one of the plants. Label it "A." Label the

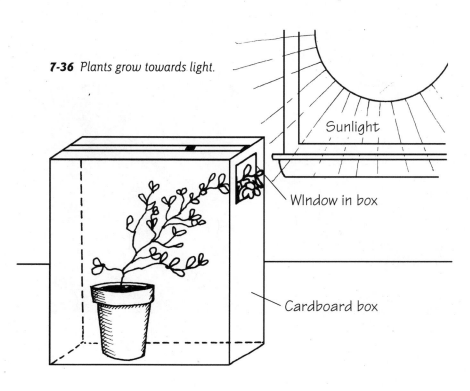

7-36 *Plants grow towards light.*

Sunlight

Window in box

Cardboard box

other plant "B." Be sure the "window" on plant "A" is facing the sun. The "window" on the second box labeled "B" should not be facing the sun. The third plant should be labeled "C" and just be in the sun (as a control) to see if it will grow under regular conditions.

5 Place the fourth plant labeled "D" in a dark closet.

6 Remember to have the children water the four plants daily and to check their growth in a few days.

(After a few days, there will be a noticeable difference in the way the four plants look. The plant that is covered will be twisted. It will be growing in the direction of the "window" on the milk carton. The plant in the closet might start to look a little yellow from lack of sunlight or be very straggly looking.)

Fine point to discuss

Why is the plant growing toward the "window" of the milk carton? (The light enters through the window and the plant seeks light. The plant needs the energy from the light to grow and produce its own food supply.)

2. Invertebrate animals and light
Materials

For each child or group of children: an earthworm or mealworm (beetle larvae), black paper, white paper, halogen light or tensor light.

Procedure

1 Have children place the black and the white papers side by side so that one sheet of paper is tucked slightly under the other.

2 Have a child shine the light on the papers. Place the animal on the paper so that it is touching both sheets of paper.

3 Have the children observe where the animal moves.

Does it move toward the black or the white paper?

4 Have the children repeat the experiment a few times to see if there is a consistency to the animal's response or behavior.

Fine points to discuss

Why do these animals prefer one piece of paper to the other? (The black paper will feel warmer to these animals because the black paper will absorb heat from the light, whereas the white paper will reflect heat off and will feel cooler to them.)

Do these animals prefer black or white? (These animals usually prefer black. They are accustomed to living in or on the ground where it is warm, damp, and dark.)

Further resources

Selected books for children and adults

Dewey Decimal Classification Numbers for light are: 535.6 and 612; 152.1 (optical illusions).

Ardley, Neil. *The Science Book of Color.* New York: Gulliver Books (HBJ), 1991.

Ardley, Neil. *The Science Book of Light.* New York: Gulliver Books (HBJ), 1991.

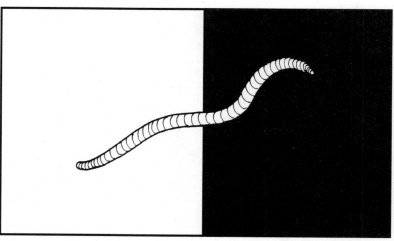

White paper   Black paper

7-37 *Some animals prefer dark surfaces; some animals prefer light surfaces.*

Arvetis, Chris. *What Is a Rainbow?* New York: Checkerboard Press, 1988.

Baines, Rae. *Light*. Mahwah, NJ: Troll, 1985. (For younger children who can read.)

Berger, Melvin. *Take One Mirror*. New York: Scholastic, 1989. (Comes with a small mylar mirror. The book poses questions to the reader and activities to do with the mirror to find out the answers. Grades 2–5.)

Birmingham, Duncan. *"M" Is for Mirror: Find the Hidden Pictures*. Norfolk, England: Tarquin, 1988. (Good for children in grades K–3. Comes with a small mylar mirror that can be used on the pages while the book is being used.)

Birmingham, Duncan. *Look Twice! Use the Mirror to Find Pairs and Opposites*. Norfolk, England: Tarquin, 1992. (Good for children in grades K–3. Comes with a small mylar mirror that can be used on the pages while the book is being used.)

Bliefield, Maurice. *Experimenting with a Microscope*. New York: Franklin Watts, 1988.

Branley, Franklyn. *What Makes Day and Night*. New York: Harper & Row, 1986. (Explains earth's rotation.)

Broekel, Ray. *Experiments with Light*. Chicago: Children's Press, 1986.

De Bruin, Jerry. *Light and Color*. Carthage, IL: Good Apple, 1986. (Good for older children.)

Doros, Arthur. *Me and My Shadow*. New York: Scholastic, 1990. (Activities with shadows.)

Flatow, Ira. *Rainbows, Curve Balls and Other Wonders of the Natural World Explained*. New York: Harper & Row, 1989.

Goor, Ron and Nancy. *Shadows, Here, There and Everywhere*. New York: Thomas Y. Crowell, 1981. (Book of photographs.)

Hoban, Tana. *Shadows and Reflections*. Greenwillow Books, New York, 1990.

Jennings, T. *Light and Color*. New York: Franklin Watts, 1991. (For children who can read.)

Lenssen, Ann. *A Rainbow Balloon: A Book of Concepts*. NY: Cobblehill (Dutton), 1992.

Moore, Frank J. *The Incredible Moving Picture Book*. New York: Dover Publications, 1987.

Moore, Frank J. *The Magic Moving Alphabet Book*. New York: Dover Publications, 1978. (Good for young children to see optical effect that occurs when the piece of "lined" acetate that comes with the book moves up and down across the pictures.)

Moscovich, Ivan. *The Magic Cyclinder Book*. Norfolk, England: Tarquin, 1988. (The book comes with a mylar mirror, that can be rolled into a cylinder.)

Orii, Eiji and Orii, Masako. *Simple Science Experiments with Optical Illusions*. Milwaukee: Gareth Stevens, 1989. (For children who can read.)

Oxlade, Chris. *The World of the Microscope*. London: Usborne, 1989. (For older children.)

Paul, Ann Whitford. *Shadows Are About*. New York: Scholastic, 1992.

Reid, Barbara. *Have Fun with Magnifying*. Toronto, Canada: Kids Can Press, 1987.

Scholastic. *Colors: A First Discovery Book*. New York: Scholastic, 1991. (Grades pre-K through 1st. The book has transparent over-leaf pages that create new colors.)

Simon, Hilda. *The Magic of Color*. New York: Lothrop and Lee, 1981. (Activities for older children.)

Simon, Seymour. *Shadow Magic*. New York: Lothrop and Lee, 1985. (Activities with light and shadows for older children.)

Taylor, Barbara. *Over the Rainbow! The Science of Color and Light*. New York: Random House, 1992. (Color and light experiments.)

Taylor, Barbara. *Seeing Is Not Believing! The Science of Shadow and Light*. New York: Random House, 1992.

Walter, Marion. *The Mirror Puzzle Book*. Norfolk, England: Tarquin, 1988. (Good for children in grades 4–6. Comes with a small mylar mirror that can be used on the pages while the book is being used.)

Walter, Marion. *Magic Mirror Tricks*. New York: Scholastic Book Services, 1971. (Good for children in grades K–3. Comes with a small mylar mirror that can be used on the pages while the book is being used.)

Watson, Philip. *Light Fantastic*. New York: Lothrop, Lee and Shepard, 1983. (Pages filled with numerous colorful illustrations of experiments.)

Wyler, Rose. *Raindrops and Rainbows*. Englewood Cliffs, NJ: Messener, 1989. (Activities with raindrops and making rainbows.)

Selected resource books for more ideas

Asimov, I. *How Did We Find Out About Lasers?* New York: Walker, 1990.

Austry, Siegfreid. *Lenses! Take a Closer Look*. New York: Lerner, 1991.

Broekel, Ray. *Experiments with Light*. Chicago: Children's Press, 1986. (Contains activities for children who want to do more "experiments" with light.)

Wood, Robert. *Physics for Kids: 49 Easy Experiments with Optics*. TAB Books. 1990. (Contains activities for older children who know how to read.)

Zubrowski, Bernie. *Mirrors: Finding Out About the Properties of Light*. New York: Morrow, 1992. (Mirror and light experiments.)

Zubrowski, Bernie. *Tops: Building and Experimenting with Spinning Toys*. New York: Morrow, 1989.

Selected literature connections for younger children

Baum, Arlene and Joseph. *Opt: An Illusionary Tale*. New York: Viking Kestrel, 1987. (A cute tale about optical illusions.)

Lionni, Leo. *Little Blue and Little Yellow*. New York: Ivan McDowel Oblensky, 1959. (A story about color.)

Holl, Adelaide. *The Rain Puddle*. New York: Lothrop, 1965. (A story about reflections in a puddle and the confusion it causes among some farm animals.)

Sonneborn, Ruth. *Someone is Eating the Sun*. New York: Random House, 1974. (The story introduces what happens when an eclipse occurs.)

General community enrichment activities

Visit a shopping mall Observe the lights and displays that are up, especially during the winter holidays.

Visit a paint store Observe paints being mixed. Learn about matching and mixing paints. See paint color "formulas" followed to make new tints and shades.

Visit a theater See a stage production being lit by a lighting crew.

Visit a movie theater Observe the projector light being projected on the big screen.

Visit a planetarium Observe the effect of light coming through holes looking like stars.

8
Air and water

Objectives

The objectives of this chapter are for children to become aware of the following:

- Air is practically everywhere.
- Air takes up space.
- Air has force that can push or pull objects.
- Moving air can create a suction.
- Moving air can cause movement and/or lift. (This lift is a suction.)
- Water has and exerts pressure.
- The surface of still water is "sticky" and can stretch.
- The common properties of water include: Water is transparent, flows easily, has weight, can dissolve things, can act as a filter, and can be absorbed.
- Several kinds of materials can float in water.
- Water affects buoyancy, boat design, and load.

General background information for parents and teachers

Air An invisible gas that does not weigh much. It is all around us. We live in an ocean of air. It is essential to plant and animal life. Air is the fuel of life. We can live for a few days without food, but no more than five minutes without air.

Oxygen A part of the air we breathe in. People use oxygen and give off carbon dioxide.

Carbon dioxide A gas in the air. We exhale carbon dioxide. Our bodies generate carbon dioxide gas from the oxygen we inhale. Plants use carbon dioxide and give off oxygen. Plants help purify our air.

Bubble A small globule of gas that is trapped in a liquid or a solid, as in carbonated soda or in hardened glass.

Displacement of air Air takes up space. When another substance moves in to occupy the space the air is in, the air is displaced.

Displacement of water by air This occurs when air forces or pushes water out of a space it is occupying.

Compressed air Air that has been squeezed and compressed into a smaller volume than it originally occupied. Compressed air has energy. Examples of machines that use the force of compressed air are: spray cans, air hammers, and pneumatic drills.

Air pressure Air pressure is the force of air per square inch. Air pressure increases with depth in our ocean of air. At higher altitudes, the air pressure is less.

Note: Liquids flow easier from closed cans when two holes are punched into the lid. Two holes allow air to flow in and to replace liquid that pours out; air goes in one hole, and liquid comes out the other hole (due to gravity). Air entering the can equalizes the air pressure on the outside of the can, allowing the liquid to flow easier.

An example of liquid and air flow occurring together for an easier flow happens every time you fill your car's tank with gasoline. In order for gasoline to enter the car's gas tank easily, air needs to flow out through a small vent hose; otherwise, an air pocket would prevent the gasoline from entering the tank easily.

When there is only one hole in a can, a vacuum is created. A burp sound will be heard as liquid pours out, because air pressure pushes air into a can at a greater pressure than that created by a liquid coming out of a can. (See Activity III.3, Air Has Force; Air Supports Water and Weight.)

Pressure The amount of force per unit of area. The larger the area over which a force is distributed, the less the pressure is on a given point. The smaller the area over which a force is spread, the greater the pressure will be felt on a given point. For example, the corner of a brick feels heavier resting on the palm of your hand than a brick lying flat on your palm.

Cohesion The ability of a substance such as water to stick to itself.

Adhesion The ability of a substance to stick to another substance or surface.

Surface tension Surface tension is caused by the force per unit of area on the surface of the liquid due to the cohesion of the liquid.

Water pressure The force per unit area in the water. The pressure or force per unit area of water increases with depth. When an object is submerged beneath the surface of water, the water pressure at any given depth is the same in all directions.

Matter Matter refers to anything that has weight and takes up space. Everything that "is" is matter.

Mass Refers to the amount of material or matter in an object or substance. For example, a marshmallow is a marshmallow whether it is thick and compressed, or light and fluffy. The matter in the marshmallow remains that of a marshmallow.

Weight Refers to gravitational pull. It is the force of gravity on an object. Weight is equal to the mass of an object times the pull of gravity.

Volume The amount of space "matter" occupies. It is found by measuring an object or substance by its length, width, and height (or depth).

(V = l times w times h.)

Objects that have the same weight do not necessarily have the same volume.

Density Density is the weight or mass of a certain volume of a substance. If you know the weight and the volume of something, you can determine its density. The formula for finding density is:

$$D = \frac{w}{v}$$

Density is commonly expressed in grams per cubic centimeter. (g/cm^3.) The density of water is one gram per cubic centimeter

(1 g/cm^3), which means that one cubic centimeter (cc) of water weighs one gram.

More-dense liquids, such as saltwater or mercury, have densities larger than one. More-dense liquids buoy up less-dense liquids. That is why oil floats on water and mercury sinks in water or water floats on mercury.

Buoyancy The tendency or ability to stay afloat is caused by the balancing of forces, such as water pressure pushing up and gravity pulling down on a floating or immersed object. An object that is placed in water floats when the buoyant or upward force equals its own weight. It sinks when the force of its own weight is greater than the buoyant force.

Why large steel ships float Large steel ships are able to float because they are filled with passenger and cargo areas. They are not solid steel because passenger and cargo areas are filled with things lighter than water, such as air or oil. Also, the density has no correlation to the size. Large ships have a relatively low density. A ship displaces a weight of water equal to its own weight. The lighter the ship, the higher in the water it will ride. As cargo is added, the ship will ride lower and displace more water. When a ship does not displace an amount of water equal to its own weight, it sinks. A steel ship compacted into a ball would be the same weight but would have less volume and would sink. When ships fill with water, their density or weight increases and the buoyant force from the water cannot support their weight. Therefore, ships that fill with too much water sink.

Why submarines can dive and surface in water When a submarine surfaces, it takes in air, and compressors compress air into bottles. The bottles of compressed air are stored. When the submarine dives beneath the surface, special chambers called ballast tanks fill with water. As the water enters the ballast tanks, the submarine sinks to lower depths. In order to surface, the valves on the bottles of compressed air need to be opened to change the density of the submarine. The compressed air pushes or blows the water out of the ballast tanks. As the water is pushed or blown out by air, the ballast tanks fill up with air and the density changes. This makes the submarine weigh less. When the submarine

weighs less, the net force from the water exceeds the weight of the submarine and it is pushed upward due to its buoyancy.

Volume of water displaced Water cannot be compressed easily. For everyday purposes, we assume it is incompressible. When objects are submerged in water, they displace an amount of water equal to their own volume, and the water level rises. An object with more volume displaces more water. Two objects cannot occupy the same space at the same time. A completely submerged balloon filled with air will displace the same amount of water as a heavy rock with the same volume.

Archimedes A Greek philosopher, mathematician, and scientist who lived in 200 B.C. He made discoveries about mechanics and water at rest.

Archimedes' Principle The weight of water* displaced by a floating object is exactly equal to the weight of the object. For example, because standard measuring cups are calibrated to the density of water, water can be weighed by measuring its volume in a measuring cup. You can find out how many ounces a given amount of water weighs by reading the measuring cup. If you place water in a large-capacity measuring cup and place a piece of fruit like a pear or an orange in the measuring cup, partially filled with water, you can then measure the weight of the piece of fruit by observing how much the water level rises

* Archimedes' principle applies to all liquids.

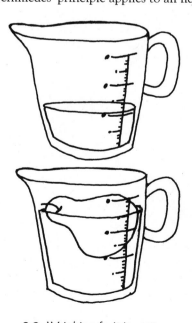

8-2 *Weighing fruit in water.*

in the measuring cup. The actual increase in ounces of water is the weight of the fruit. The fruit will displace an amount of water equal to its own weight.

Note: As you do these activities with your children, try to encourage them to keep a science journal of their observations and their thoughts.

Activities and procedures

I. Air is practically everywhere

1. Catching air

Materials

Plastic bags.

Procedure

1 Catch some air in a plastic bag by pulling the opened bag through the air. Twist the end of the bag so that the air stays inside.

What is inside the bag? (The children will probably respond "air." If they don't, explain to them that air is inside the bag and that we are surrounded by an ocean of air.)

2 Tell children to move their arms around in a swimming style. They should be able to feel their arms pushing air around.

3 Give each child a plastic bag and tell him/her to catch some air.

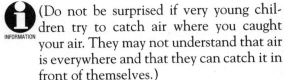

(Do not be surprised if very young children try to catch air where you caught your air. They may not understand that air is everywhere and that they can catch it in front of themselves.)

Fine points to discuss

Where is air? (Air is practically all around us.)

Can we see air? (Not usually.)

Can we feel air? (Yes, if we move around quickly.)

Can we smell air? (Yes, if there are molecules of odors mixed in the air. We can smell odors in the air from such things as food, flowers and plants, animals, decaying materials, moisture, and/or odors caused from some pollutants in the air.)

2. An empty bottle

Materials

For each child or group of children: an empty plastic detergent squeeze bottle, a feather, a bucket of water, newspaper to absorb possible mess from water.

8-3 Catch some air.

Procedure

1 Show the children that the bottle is empty.

Is anything in it? (Some children may respond "air.")

2 Tell them you are going to squeeze the bottle. Place a feather in front of the squeeze hole.

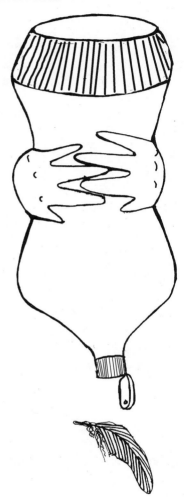

8-4 *The feather will move.*

If you squeeze this empty bottle, will anything come out of it?

If air comes out of the bottle, what will happen to the feather? (It will move.)

3 Choose a child and tell him or her to place the end of the plastic bottle that has a hole into the water, and to squeeze the bottle. Ask children to observe if anything comes out of the bottle into the water. (They will observe little bubbles coming out of the bottle into the water.) (Note: In order for bubbles to appear the bottle needs to hold water.)

Do you know what has caused the bubbles to appear? (Air inside the bottle has made the bubbles appear. Air is inside the bubbles.)

3. Finding air in seeds

Materials

For each child or group of children: seeds like lima beans or peas; a clear plastic glass of water.

Procedure

1 Show the children the seeds.

Is air inside the seeds?

How can you find out? (By placing the seeds in water. If air bubbles can be seen, that means the seeds contain some air.)

2 Have children place the seeds in water and observe whether air bubbles appear.

Going further

Where else can air be? (Adapted from Gega, *Where Air Can Be*, page 529.)

• Have children find other materials: a brick, a rock, fabrics (wool, cotton, leather, fur), unfinished wood scraps, pieces of food (bread crust, dry cereal, banana, apple or orange peel) metal objects (nail, fork, spoon, coin).

• Drop the objects into a clear bowl of water.

Can you observe any bubbles coming out of the material dropped into the water? If so, what does that tell you about air?

• Write down your observations in your science journal.

Can you make any generalizations about what you observed?

Note: Soft objects can be put in water and squeezed to show that they contain air. Hard, solid objects like metal will not contain air even when squeezed with a pliers.

4. Lungs

Materials

None.

Procedure

1 Take a deep breath. Have the children do the same.

What are you breathing in and out? (Air.)

2 Have the children take another deep breath, but this time tell them to hold their breath for as long as they can.

What happens? (We cannot stop breathing. Our body forces us to take another breath.)

3 Ask the children to feel their rib cage as they take a deep breath and let their breath out.

Where does the air go when it enters our body? (It enters our lungs.)

4 *Explain:* Our rib cage protects our lungs. When new air comes into our lungs, our lungs and rib cage expand. When used air leaves our lungs, our rib cage contracts or gets smaller. All living things need air to live.

 Explain to children that plastic bags are dangerous to play with. If a plastic bag is near our mouth, it can prevent us from breathing.

II. Air takes up space

1. Containment of air

Materials

A balloon for each child.

Procedure

1 Ask children to inflate their balloons. (You will probably need to inflate the balloons for the younger children.)

2 Ask the children the following questions:

What is inside the balloon? (Air.)

If the air was not inside the balloon, what would happen to the balloon? (The balloon would be flat. Air takes up space.)

What happens to a tire that loses its air? (It becomes flat. If air does not fill the space inside an object, the object loses its shape.)

2. Displacement of air by water

Materials

For each child or group of children: a large, empty juice can with the top removed and a small hole in the bottom end; a bucket of water.

Procedure

1 Turn the juice can upside-down so that the end with a hole is on top. Have the children place their hands near the hole as the can is pushed down into the water. They will feel a surge of air come out of the can as the can enters the water.

2 Ask the children the following questions:

What do you feel coming out of the can? (They will probably respond, "air.")

What is pushing the air out of the can? (The water is pushing the air out. Two things cannot take up the same space at the same time. As water comes in, it pushes the air out.)

Going further

Beakman's World, a children's television program, demonstrated the following experiment.

Materials

An empty plastic soda bottle; a tiny, mushed-up "spit wad."

Procedure

1 Place the small mushed-up "spit-wad" in the opening of the bottle.

2 Hold the bottle horizontally or place it on a table.

3 Blow into the bottle.

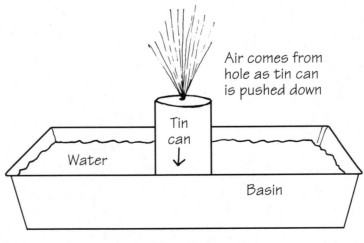

8-5 *Water displaces air.*

What happens to the "spit-wad"? (It will be blown out of the bottle.)

Why does this happen? (Air takes up space. When more air is added to the bottle from your lungs, the "spit-wad" has no place to go but out of the bottle.)

3. Air pocket

8-6A *Dry tissue stuffed into a dry glass.*

8-6B *Glass with tissue is inverted and totally submerged into a bucket of water.*

Materials

For each child or group of children: a bucket of water, a clear plastic glass, a tissue, newspaper to absorb possible mess from water.

Procedure

1 Show children how to push the tissue into the glass so that it stays in place when the glass is turned upside-down. *Note:* If the tissue does not stay in place, use a piece of rolled transparent

8-6C *Tissue remains dry due to air pocket.*

tape to secure the tissue to the bottom of the plastic glass.

2 Tell the children that you are going to choose a child to place the glass with the tissue into the water.

Do you think the tissue will get wet?

3 Have a child hold the glass upside-down vertically and push it down into the water. Have the children observe that the tissue is still dry.

4 After your demonstration, allow the children to repeat the procedure on their own several times to see if the result is the same. Discuss the results and record their findings.

Fine points to discuss

Why can't water enter the glass? (Air has already taken up the space inside the glass. Air and water cannot take up the same space at the same time.)

Why is the tissue still dry? (Air takes up space. The water cannot move into the area that is occupied by the air. The tissue is in the space where the air is, so the tissue stays dry. The air has formed a pocket around the tissue inside the glass. There is no water inside the glass, only air.)

4. Air takes up space

Materials

For each child or group of children: a cork from a wine bottle; a clear plastic glass; a large bowl of water; newspaper to absorb possible mess from water.

Procedure

1 Float the cork in the bowl of water.

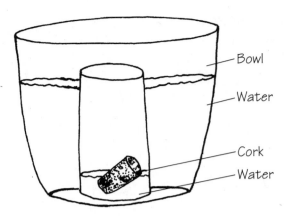

— Bowl

— Water

8-7 *Air takes up space.*

— Cork

— Water

Can you think of a way to make the cork sink? (Listen to their responses and try their ideas.)

2 Turn the empty plastic glass upside-down and place it on top of the floating cork. Have a child push the glass down into the water vertically. (When the glass of air displaces the water, the cork will appear to sink, because the cork goes down with the surface of the water inside of the glass.)

Fine points to discuss

Why does the cork sink? (The air inside the glass pushed the water out of the space it was occupying. The cork sank because the water was no longer lifting it up. Corks do not float in air. Corks float in water because they weigh less than the water. Corks are heavier than air so they do not float in air.)

• Allow children to continue to "experiment" on their own with floating and sinking the cork.

5. Displacement of water by air

Materials

For each child or group of children: a basin filled with water; a glass jar; a piece of plastic tubing or an old garden hose about 3-feet long; newspaper to absorb possible mess from water.

Procedure

1 Tell children to:
a Place the jar inside the basin filled with water.
b Lay the jar on its side so that it can fill with water.
c Turn the jar upside-down in the water so that the bottom of the jar is protruding above the water line in the basin.
d Place one end of the tubing into the upside-down jar filled with water. (See Fig. 8-8.)

2 Choose one child in the group to blow on one end of the tubing.

What do you think will happen when the tube is blown into?

What will be inside of the tube when you blow through it? (Air.)

Where will the air go? (Into the glass jar.)

What will happen to the water inside of the jar? (It will be forced out of the jar because the air will displace the water. Air takes up space.)

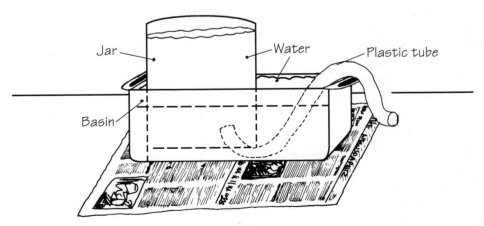

Jar — — Water — Plastic tube

Basin —

8-8 *Air displaces water.*

How will you know that air is going into the jar? (Bubbles will be seen in the water. Then there will be no more water in the jar and the jar will fall over on its side in the water.)

When you drink milk with a straw and blow into your drink, what happens? (Bubbles of air appear.)

III. Air has force

1. "Breath" power

Materials

A pencil for each child.

Procedure

1 Tell children to lay their pencil down on a flat surface (like a table or a desk top).

What will happen to the pencil if it is blown on? (They will most likely respond that it will move.)

2 Have children blow on their pencil. Have the children observe the movement that takes place.

Why does the pencil move? (The air that takes up space is being pushed. The movement of the air from one place to another causes the pencil to move. A push or pull that causes movement to take place is called a force. One of the properties of air is force or pressure.)

2. Air's accelerated force lifts

Materials

Several large books, a long balloon.

Procedure

1 Ask the children the following question:

Can a balloon lift a pile of books? (Listen to their responses. Try out their suggestions.)

2 If children do not make suggestions, demonstrate how the balloon can be used to lift the book by:
   a Placing the balloon near the edge of a table and placing the pile of books on top of the balloon.
   b Inflating the balloon while the pile of books is resting on top of it. (The children might be surprised to see that the balloon can lift the pile of books.)

3 *Explain* to the children that the force from your air added to the air inside of the balloon has lifted the books.

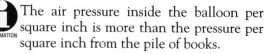 The air pressure inside the balloon per square inch is more than the pressure per square inch from the pile of books.

4 If the children can inflate a balloon, give them one to inflate so they can repeat the experiment by themselves.

3. Air supports water and weight

Materials

For each child or group of children: a clear plastic glass, a bucket of water, newspaper to help absorb possible mess from water, a top from a cottage cheese container or a piece of cardboard.

Procedure

1 Fill the glass with water. Cover the top of the glass with a cover from a cottage cheese container or a piece of cardboard.

2 Tell the children you are going to turn the glass upside-down. Ask the children what will happen to the top

8-9 *Air's force can lift.*

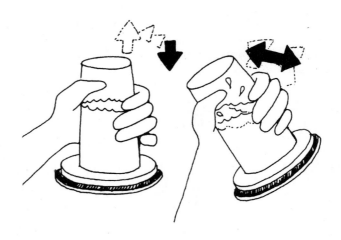

8-10 *Air pressure seals the lid.*

when the glass is turned upside-down.
Listen to their responses.

3 Carefully turn the glass of water
upside-down while holding the lid on
top of the open end of the glass.

4 Remove your hand from the lid when
the glass of water is upside-down. You
can turn the glass on its side and shake
the glass up and down. The water will
not come out.

5 *Explain:* The force of air is pressing the
lid to the rim of the glass. The force of
air pressure seals the lid in position on
the rim. If the air seal is broken, the
water will spill out. If you press hard on
the sides of the plastic glass, it will
break the air seal.

6 After your demonstration, allow
children to repeat the procedure on
their own several times to see if the
results are the same. Discuss the results
and record them.

4. Air lifts liquids

Materials

For each child: One drinking straw, a
drink of water in glasses.

Procedure

1 Have children place their drinking
straws inside their drinks.

*Can you think of a way to lift your drink
without putting your mouth on your straw?*

2 Show the children how to place their
fingers on the top end of the drinking
straw while it is in their drinks. Have
them lift their straws out of the drink;
part of the drink will still be in the
straw.

*What is inside the straw that has helped lift the
drink up and has kept it inside of the straw?*
(The force of air pressure supplies a push
or a pull to keep the drink inside of the
straw.)

5. Jet power

Materials

A balloon.

Procedure

1 Inflate the balloon, but do not tie it
shut. Hold the inflated balloon.

2 Tell the children you are going to let
the balloon lose its air.

*What do you think will happen if I let go of the
balloon?* (Listen to their responses.)

3 Let the balloon go. Have the children
observe what happens. (The balloon
will "fly" around wildly until all of the
air is out.)

4 If children can inflate their own
balloon, allow them to repeat the
procedure.

5 *Explain:* Air is a gas. When the air in
the balloon was squeezed into a tiny
space, the air became compressed gas.
Compressed gas has stored energy.
When air is compressed into a balloon,
it has stored energy. The air in the
balloon was like a fuel. It made the
balloon move forward. When all of the
air was out of the balloon, it was out of
gas and the balloon stopped moving.

Fine points to discuss

Why did the balloon fly? (The air coming
out of the balloon forced the balloon to
move. The air coming out pushed or pro-
pelled the balloon.)

Does the amount of air inside the balloon affect how long it can fly around? (Yes. The more air or fuel there is the longer the flight will last.)

Is there a way to make the balloon fly in a straight path? (Yes, but the design of the balloon has to change. The balloon's force of air has to be controlled for it to fly straight.)

6. Guided jet power (equal and opposite reaction)

Materials

For each child or group of children: a long balloon, a paper bag, two paper clips, two chairs, 15 feet of nylon fishing line.

Procedure

1 Tie the fishing line onto two chairs. Pull the two chairs apart so that the fishing line is fairly taut.

2 Open up two paper clips so that one end of each paper clip can be hooked onto the top side of the paper bag.

3 Place the balloon inside the paper bag and inflate the balloon while it is inside the bag.

4 Mount the "balloon bag" onto the stretched fishing line with the paper clips that have been opened. See Fig. 8-11.

5 Let the "balloon bag" loose. Have the children observe how the balloon travels in a straight line on the fishing line, which acts as a "guidance system" to control the flight direction of the balloon.

6 Give each child a paper bag, a balloon, and two paper clips to do the experiment on his/her own.

Note: With older children, measurements can be taken to see which jet-powered balloon bag travels the farthest, and the variables that affect distance can be analyzed.

Fine points to discuss

Why does the balloon push forward in a straight line? (It moves in a straight line because it is guided by the fishing line. It moves forward because air is being released. Jet engines operate in the same way.)

 Newton's classic Third Law of Motion states that for every action, there is an equal and opposite reaction. The movement is in the direction opposite to that from which the force is applied. In the example of the balloon, the air that is being released is under pressure and the compressed air comes out of the balloon nozzle. This causes a movement to occur in the opposite direction, which causes the balloon to propel itself forward.

Going further

You might want to let the children experiment to see if they can create a design that makes the balloon travel farther or faster. Bernie Zubrowski's book, *Balloons: Building and Experimenting with Inflatable Toys* suggests many interesting activities to do with balloons.

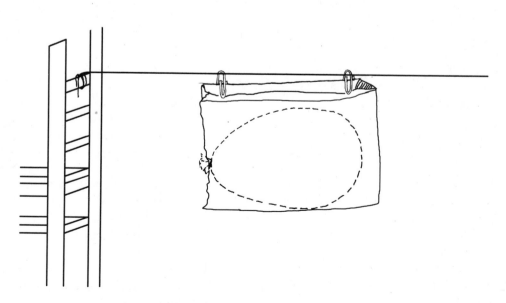

8-11 *Balloon inside a paper bag.*

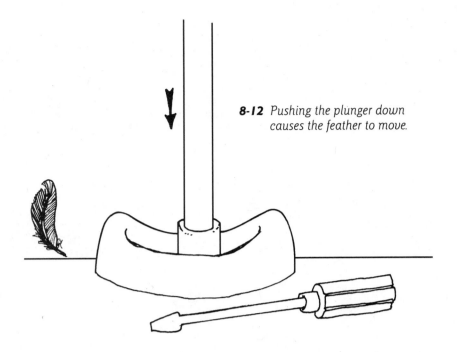

8-12 *Pushing the plunger down causes the feather to move.*

IV. Air pressure

1. "Plunger" power

Materials

Bathroom plunger; a feather or bits of paper; spoon or screwdriver.

Procedure

1 Place the plunger on a smooth surface like a desk or a floor. Do not press down on it. Ask one of the children to lift the plunger up.

2 Place a feather or bits of paper near the suction cup of the plunger. Have a child press down on the plunger.

What has happened to the feather? (It has been moved.)

What caused the feather to move? (When the plunger was pushed down, air came out from underneath the suction cup. Before the plunger was pushed down, the air pressure was equal on both the inside and the outside of the suction cup. When the plunger was pushed down, the air underneath the suction cup was pushed out. This caused the feather or the bits of paper to move.)

3 Now that the plunger has been pushed down, ask a child to lift the plunger up. It is very difficult to do unless the suction seal of air is broken. (To do this, slide a spoon or screwdriver under the plunger's suction cup to break the air seal or suction.)

Fine points to discuss

Why is it so difficult to lift the plunger? (The air pressure on the outside of the suction cup is greater than the air pressure on the inside of the plunger's suction cup. There is no air to push up from underneath the suction cup. So, the downward push of air is stronger and the pressure or force from the outside air is extremely strong. This makes it difficult to lift the plunger up.)

How does air pressure hold things in place? (By pressing in on them.)

2. The ruler breaks

(Pressure from Volume)

Materials

For each child or group of children: a slat of wood from an orange crate or a thin yardstick, large sheets of newspaper, a lightweight hammer.

Procedure

1 Have child place the slat of wood or the yardstick on a desk. Then cover the wood with a few pieces of newspaper.

2 Tell children to allow the edge of the wood slat to stick out beyond the desk. They need to be sure that the newspaper is flat and centered on the wood slat.

3 Tell the children you are going to hit the wood with your fist or with a hammer.

What do you think will happen when I hit the wood with a hammer?

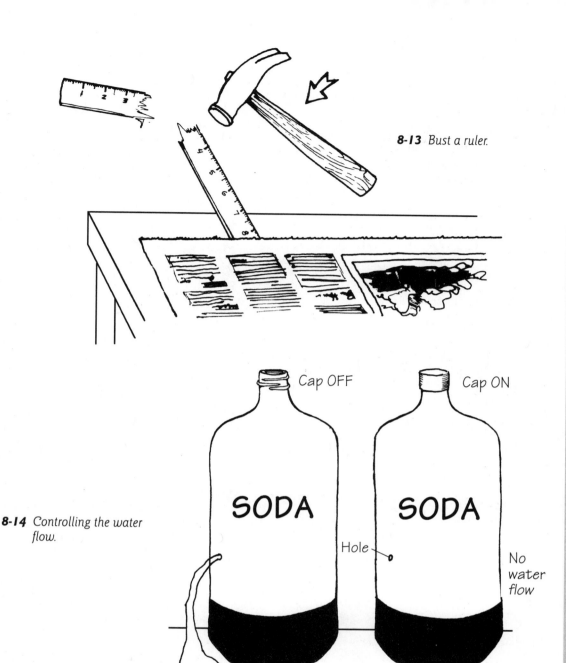

8-13 Bust a ruler.

8-14 Controlling the water flow.

Cap OFF

Cap ON

SODA

SODA

Hole

No water flow

Water flows out

Will the newspaper pop up? (No.)

Will the wood break? (Yes.)

4 Demonstrate the wood slat being broken.

5 After your demonstration, allow children to hit the wood hard and fast with a tight fist or a hammer. (The wood will break.)

Fine point to discuss

Why did the wood break? (The wood broke because the newspaper had a great deal of air pressure pushing down on it. This large amount of air pressure prevented the wood from popping up.)

3. The water stops

Materials

A nail; a hammer. For each child or group of children: an empty plastic liter soda bottle with screw-on cap; water.

Procedure

1 The adult reading this book needs to: Use a hammer to puncture the plastic bottles with the nail. Make the hole on the side of the bottle about 3 inches up from the bottom.

2 Demonstrate how to hold the bottle over the basin. Fill the bottle with water. The children will be able to

observe the water leaving the side of the bottle through the hole.

Can you think of a way to keep the water from flowing out of the hole in the bottle?

3 Tell the children that you are going to screw the cap on to the opening of the bottle. Ask them if they think this will keep the water from flowing out. (It will.) (See Fig. 8-14.)

4 After your demonstration, allow children to repeat the procedure on their own several times to see if the result is the same. Discuss the results and record them.

Fine points to discuss

Why does the water stop flowing out of the hole on the side of the bottle when the cap is screwed on tightly to the bottle? (In order for the water to flow out of the hole, air is needed to displace the water. When the cap is screwed on very tight, it prevents air from entering the bottle. When there is no air to equalize the pressure, the water stops flowing because a vacuum is created within the bottle. A second hole allows air to displace water and equalizes the air pressure.)

 Many children have the misconception that air pushes the water out of the container. Air does not "push out" the water. It merely equalizes the air pressure, takes away the vacuum, and allows the force of gravity to pull the water out due to its own weight.

4. Two holes are needed

Materials

A full can of juice, a can opener, glasses to pour drink into.

Procedure

1 Open the can of juice by puncturing one hole in the top of the can. Try to pour the juice. It will not flow evenly.

Can you suggest what to do to make the juice flow from the can easier?

2 Puncture a second hole in the top of the can. (The juice will flow out faster and easier.)

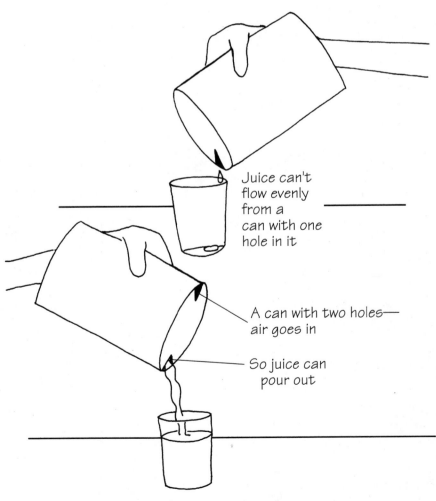

Juice can't flow evenly from a can with one hole in it

A can with two holes— air goes in

So juice can pour out

8-15 With two holes, liquid flows out in a smooth stream.

Fine points to discuss

Why does the juice can make sounds when there is only one hole in the can? (As the juice leaves the can, air enters the can and takes up space in the can.)

Why does the juice flow out more easily when two holes are in the top of the can rather than one hole? (In order for the juice to flow out, air has to enter the can. The first hole allows air to enter the can, but the air flow restriction prevents the air from entering and prevents the juice from flowing out easily. When there are two holes, the flow of air and hence liquid is more even and quiet.)

5. Coins "stick" (holding power from pressure)

Materials

For each child or group of children: a quarter, dime, or penny.

8-16A *Press the coin against the forehead.*

8-16B *When pressed hard against the forehead, the coin will stay in place.*

Procedure

1 Show the children the coin or coins. Tell them that you can make the coin or coins stick to their forehead.

Can you guess how this can be done?

2 Press the coin onto a child's forehead hard and count to ten, or place some moisture on the coin and place it on the child's head. Either way it will stick until the air seal is broken. Air pressure will hold the coin in place.

3 Have children repeat this procedure alone or with another child.

6. Fountain from compressed air

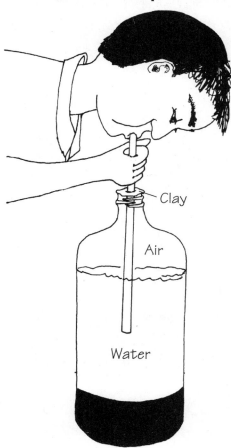

8-17A *Blow air into drinking straw.*

Materials

For each child or group of children: newspaper to absorb possible mess from water, an empty liter soda bottle, a wad of clay, a drinking straw, a large basin of water.

Procedure

1 Have children fill their bottle with about two cups of water. Pack clay around the drinking straw and insert the straw with clay on it inside of the bottle opening. The clay should be

Air and water

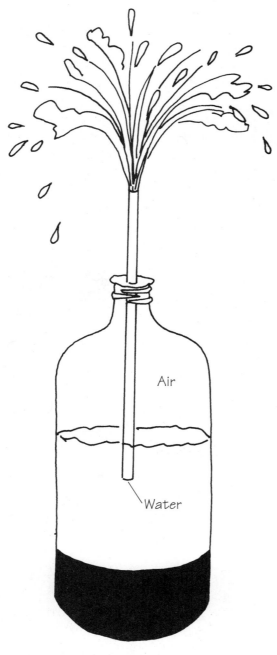

Air

Water

8-17B *Increased amount of air in bottle forces water up the straw.*

packed between the straw and the neck of the bottle opening so that the top has an air-tight seal. The water level in the bottle should be high enough so that part of the straw is underneath the water level.

2 Tell the children that you are going to blow air into the straw. (See Fig. 8-17A.)

When I blow into the straw, what do you think will happen? (Listen to their responses and ask them to observe what does happen.)

3 Blow into the straw with your mouth. Put as much air into the straw as you

can. When you cannot blow any more, step aside quickly, so you will not be sprayed with the water coming out of the straw.

4 After your demonstration, give each child a plastic drinking straw, a plastic soda bottle, and some clay so that he/she can repeat this procedure on his/her own.

Fine point to discuss

What happened to the air inside of the bottle when more air was blown into the bottle? (The addition of more air increased the air pressure inside the bottle. This increase in air pressure was able to push the water up the straw to create a fountain effect. The additional air caused the air inside of the bottle to be squeezed. Compressed air has stored energy.)

7. Pull the bag out of the can
Materials

For each child or group of children: a large, empty juice can; a plastic bag large enough to fit inside of the juice can and hang over the rim of the can; a rubber band large enough to fit over the can.

Procedure

1 Tell children to:
   a Place the opened plastic bag inside the large juice can.
   b Press all the air out of the can so that the plastic bag liner is touching the inner sides of the can.
   c Pull the plastic liner over the rim and secure it with a rubber band.
   d Ask children to reach inside of the can and try to remove the bag from the can without making a hole in the plastic bag.

Note: The force of air pressure pressing in on the plastic bag makes it practically impossible to pull the bag out. The air pressure is too strong. Unless the bag breaks or the rubber band pops, the plastic bag cannot be pulled out.

8. Suction power
Materials

For each child or group of children: two clear plastic cups, a round balloon.

Procedure

1 Tell the children that you intend to lift the two plastic cups up and have them stick to the balloon when it is blown up. Ask them if they can suggest how

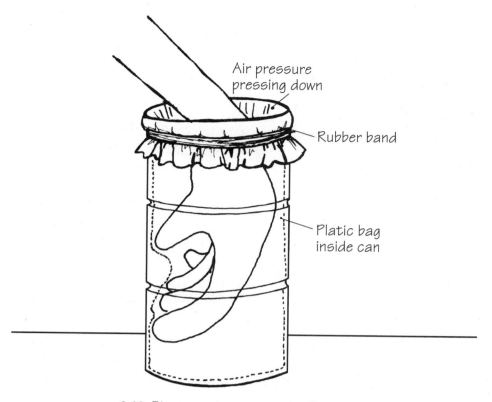

8-18 *Air pressure is too strong to pull the bag out.*

8-19 *The force of air pressure will hold the cups in place.*

this feat can be accomplished. Try out their suggestions.

2 Place the balloon in your mouth so it will be ready to inflate. Hold the two plastic cups in each hand so that the openings of the two cups are facing the balloon. The cups should almost be touching and the deflated balloon should be hanging between the two glasses. (See Fig. 8-19.)

3 As you blow the balloon up, the two cups will stick to the balloon.

4 Give each child a balloon and two plastic glasses so he/she can repeat this procedure alone.

Fine point to discuss

Why do the cups stay put on the balloon? (As the air inflates the balloon, it creates an air seal over the openings of the cups. The force of air pressure holds the cups to the surface of the balloon. If the air escapes from the balloon, the air pressure inside of the cups will become equal to the air pressure outside the cups and the cups will fall off the balloon.)

9. Siphon

Materials

For each child or group of children: two basins, one filled with water; a clear plas-

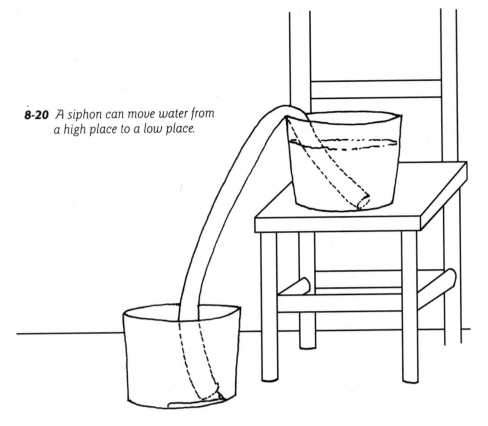

8-20 *A siphon can move water from a high place to a low place.*

tic hose or tubing about 3-feet long; newspaper to absorb possible mess from water.

Procedure

1 Place the basin filled with water on a table or chair. Place the empty basin on the floor near the basin filled with water.

 It is important that the basin filled with water be situated so that the water level is at a higher level than the empty basin. (Water seeks its own level.)

2 Fill the rubber hose with water. Be sure there is no air left in the hose. You can tell when there is no more air left in the hose because air bubbles will stop coming out of the hose. Cover each end of the hose with a thumb.

3 Tell the children you are going to make the water move from the basin filled with water to the basin that is empty. Ask them if they know how that can happen. Listen to their responses.

4 Place one end of the hose into the basin filled with water. Be sure that the end of the hose is in the water and that no air is inside the hose. Keep your thumb on the end of the hose.

5 Place the other end of the hose in the empty basin. Remove your thumbs from the ends of the hoses.

6 Have the children observe what happens to the water. It will move from one basin to the other. The hose or tube is acting as a siphon.

7 After your demonstration, allow each group of children to "experiment" with the siphon on their own. Observe, discuss, and record their results.

Fine point to discuss

Why does the water flow through the tube or hose from one basin to another basin? (The water in the hose flows downward. One basin is lower than the other. Water is pulled down because of the force of gravity. A partial air vacuum is created in the hose. The water is forced up the hose before it flows down to the lower basin. It flows up because air pressure is pressing down on the surface of the basin filled with water. The flow of water will continue as long as the water level of one container is at a higher level than the water level of the other container and as long as there is no air in the hose to break the partial vacuum.)

V. Air streams and air currents can cause movement and/or lift

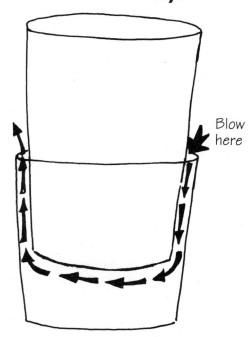

8-21 *A moving air stream causes lift.*

1. Moving air causes lift

Materials

For each child or group of children: two clear plastic glasses that are identical in size.

Procedure

1 Gently put one glass inside the other.
2 Hold the two glasses near your mouth. Blow on the side of the glasses near the top rim. The glass inside the other glass will pop up.
3 *Explain:* The force of air pressure from the air being blown on the rim of the glass creates a current or wind that causes a lift action to take place.
4 After your demonstration, allow children to repeat the procedure on their own.

Materials

A strip of paper 1-inch-by-11½-inches.

Procedure

1 Hold the strip of paper with your two index fingers between your lower lip and chin, and gently blow across the top.
2 Observe what happens to the paper. (It will lift up as you blow.)

Why does the paper lift up? (The air on top is moving faster than the air beneath. This creates an area of low pressure. The air beneath the paper moves up to fill in the area of lower air pressure.)

3 *Explain:* The same kind of thing happens on an airplane wing. As the curved wing moves through the air, the air moves faster on top of the wing than it does on the bottom of the wing. This creates an area of lower air pressure on top of the wing. The air on the bottom of the wing has an area of higher air pressure pressing up on it, and this lifts the wing up.

2. Moving air keeps things put

8-22 *Moving air has pressure.*

Materials

For each child or group of children: a newspaper, an index card.

Procedure

1 Place a flat sheet of the newspaper on your chest. Move quickly, and the newspaper will stay put.

How could this happen? (Moving air helps hold things in place. Gravity pulls the paper down, while frictional force against the chest helps keep the paper up. The frictional force occurs due to the pressure of the paper against the chest, which in turn is due to pressure from the moving air.)

2 Fold the index card so that two of the long sides are folded down to form a tunnel. (See Fig. 8-22.)

3 Blow on the tunnel. Try to make the card tunnel turn over. Blow very hard, then blow softly.

4 Ask the children if they can blow hard enough to make the paper tunnel blow up and/or over. *Note:* (It cannot be done. The air coming from your breath is blowing a strong wind. The wind is pushing the air forward and lowering the air pressure. The top or roof of the paper tunnel is caving in due to a loss of air pressure inside the tunnel. This causes the paper tunnel to stay in a fixed position.)

5 Give each child a sheet of newspaper and allow them to repeat on their own.

3. Bernoulli effect

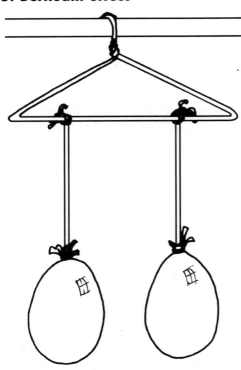

8-23 *Blow air between the two hanging balloons.*

Materials

Two apples with stems or two inflated balloons, string, a metal clothes hanger; a drinking straw or tube to blow through for each child.

Procedure

1 Cut two pieces of string about 2-feet long. Tie a piece of string to each apple stem or to each of the inflated balloons. Tie the other end of each string to a metal clothes hanger. Hook the clothes hanger onto the wood molding of a doorway or other suitable object. Separate the two strings on the hanger so that the two hanging apples or balloons are about one inch apart. (See Fig. 8-23.)

2 Wait for the two apples or balloons to be hanging motionless. Tell the children you are going to choose a child to blow air through the straw between the two apples or balloons.

What do you think will happen to the two apples or balloons when air is blown between them?

Will the balloons move away from each other or will they move closer together? (They will move closer together. When the air between the two apples or balloons is pushed away by the air coming out of the drinking straw, the air pressure in the middle will be lower. The lower air pressure in the middle will cause the two apples or balloons to bounce together.)

3 After your demonstration, allow each child to use his/her straw or tube to blow between the apples. Have children observe, discuss, and record the results.

4. The "card" stays up

Materials

For each child or group of children: a spool of thread, a 3-by-5 index card, a straight pin.

Procedure

1 Have a child push a straight pin through an index card. Place the card with the pin going through it on the hole of a spool.

2 Tell the children that you are going to place your lips on the other end of the spool's hole and that you will be blowing air through the hole of the spool onto the index card with the pin going through it.

3 Hold the card in place while you blow. Then let go of the card while you are blowing. It will stay next to the spool. (See Fig. 8-24.)

 To avoid germs: Have each child repeat the experiment on his/her own with a different spool of thread.

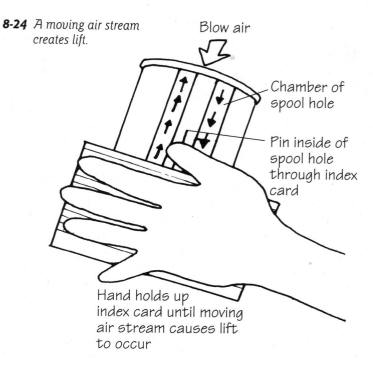

8-24 *A moving air stream creates lift.*

Blow air

Chamber of spool hole

Pin inside of spool hole through index card

Hand holds up index card until moving air stream causes lift to occur

Fine points to discuss

What happens to the index card? (The card stays close to the spool. The air pressure becomes lower because there is a stream of moving air coming through the spool's hole.)

When does the card fall? (The index card falls when the air stream stops flowing because you stop blowing.)

5. Atomizer model

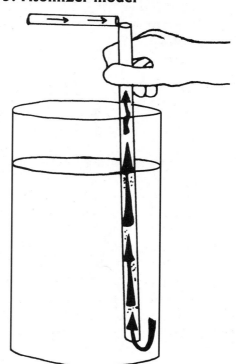

8-25 *The moving air stream lowers air pressure, causing the water to rise up the straw.*

Materials

For each child or group of children: newspaper to absorb possible mess from water, a clear plastic glass, one drinking straw, a pair of scissors.

Procedure

1 Cut a straw in half.
2 Place one straw into a glass of water.
3 Hold the straw vertically in the water with your fingers. The straw should not be touching the bottom of the glass.
4 Place the other straw in your mouth and blow through it hard, directly over the top end of the straw that is in the glass of water. (See Fig. 8-25.)
5 Have the children observe what happens to the water. It will rise up the straw and be sprayed or atomized.
6 After your demonstration, give each child a straw to cut in half so the children can repeat the procedure on their own.

Fine points to discuss

Why does the water rise through the straw? (The water rises through the vertical straw because the moving air stream from the horizontal straw lowers the air pressure in the vertical straw.)

Why does the water become a spray? (When the water reaches the top of the vertical straw, it is met with fast-moving air. This fast air current causes the column of water to break into little water drops, which

Air and water

form a mist or spray. The faster the air moves, the finer the mist formed by the water droplets.)

Additional points to discuss

Spray bottles and some perfume bottles use the same principle. You might suggest to the older children that they examine a few to find out how they work and where the air comes from that helps create the mist.

VI. Water pressure

I. The difference between pressure and weight

Materials

For each child or group of children: about two cups of clay or play-doh (see Table 8-1); a plastic liter soda bottle capped tightly and filled with water or soda; a small, unopened can of tomato sauce or soup.

Table 8-1 Homemade play-doh recipe

Ingredients

1 cup salt	2 cups water
food coloring	2 cups flour
4 teaspoons of cream of tartar	2 tablespoons vegetable oil

Mix salt and water. Add a few drops of food coloring. Add flour. Stir until mixed. Add remaining ingredients. Cook over a low flame, stirring until thick. Put mixture on a floured surface and knead.

1. Bottle sinks into clay

2. Bottle leaves a deep dent in clay

3. Bottle sits on clay

4. Bottle leaves a shallow dent in clay

8-26 The difference between pressure and weight with a bottle.

(This play-doh will last several months if it is stored in an air-tight container.)

Procedure

1 Tell children to:

a Shape their clay or play-doh into a round ball and then flatten it out to make a circle about 4 inches in diameter.

b Place a bottle filled with liquid on top of the clay circle.

c Lift the bottle up.

d Observe the indentation the bottle has made on the surface of the clay (shallow imprint).

e Turn your bottle filled with liquid upside-down and place it on top of the clay. You might have to help balance the bottle with your finger. (See Fig. 8-26.)

f Lift the bottle up.

2 Have the children notice the indentation in the clay made by the filled bottle when it was upside-down (deeper dent).

Was the bottle heavier when it was upside-down? (No, but more of the weight was concentrated on a smaller surface so the bottle made a deeper imprint into the clay. There was more pressure from the small area of the filled bottle on the clay than there was from the larger surface of the bottle on the clay.)

3 Place an unopened can on the clay.

4 Lift the can up.

5 Observe the imprint from the can on the surface of the clay.

How can the imprint be changed? (Have them suggest other ways to place the can in the clay so the dent will be deeper.)

6 Place the can in the clay at an angle so that only part of the can's rim touches the clay. (The can will not stay in this position unless you help balance it with your finger.)

Fine points to discuss

Why was the imprint deeper in the clay? (The imprint was deeper when there was more pressure. The imprint had nothing to do with weight, but rather with the amount of force coming down on one area. The more force that comes down, the more the pressure is on a given point.)

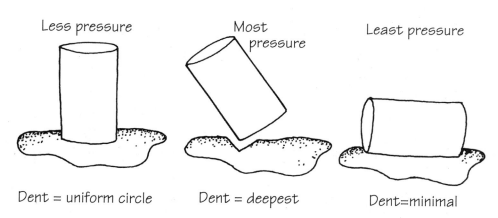

Less pressure — Dent = uniform circle

Most pressure — Dent = deepest

Least pressure — Dent=minimal

8-27 *The difference between pressure and weight with a can.*

Tall book less pressure

8-28A *The difference between pressure and weight with a book.*

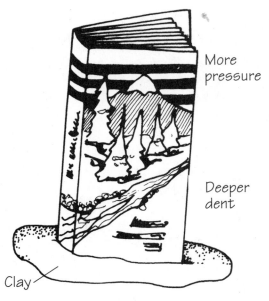

8-28B *The difference between pressure and weight with a book.*

If you are holding a book, is there less pressure if you hold it flat and horizontally, upright and vertically, or on a corner at an angle? (The least pressure would be in a flat, horizontal position. The most pressure would be felt if the book were held on its corner because more of the book's weight would be felt on one small section of your finger.)

2. Water pressure increases with depth

Materials

A nail; a hammer. For each child or group of children: a large, open juice can with one lid removed or an empty plastic liter soda bottle; water; a basin; newspaper to absorb possible mess from water; a marking pen.

Procedure

1 As the adult reading this book, you need to: use a hammer and nail to

Most pressure

puncture the can and/or the plastic bottle with holes. Place three or four holes in a vertical line about two inches apart from the bottom of the container up the side to the top of the container. Number the holes with a marking pen. The hole next to the bottom should be numbered one.

2 Tell children to:
a Hold the container over the basin.
b Fill the container with water.
c Observe the water streams coming out of the can.

Which "numbered" hole has water shooting out farther than the other streams? (Number one on the bottom.) (See Fig. 8-29.)

Which stream of water is shooting out the least? (The one near the top of the can.)

Fine point to discuss

Which stream has the most water pressure pushing on it? (The stream at the bottom of the bottle has the most water pressure. The weight of the water [and air] sitting above the hole opening is pressing down and making the water shoot out farther. Whereas, the top hole is a mere dribble. It does not shoot far from the container.)

3. Water pressure is the same in all directions

Materials

Same as materials for preceding procedure.

Procedure

1 As the adult reading this book, you need to: use the hammer and nail to puncture the can and/or plastic bottle with holes. Place three or four holes in a horizontal line about one or two inches apart near the bottom of the container.

8-28C *The difference between pressure and weight with a book.*

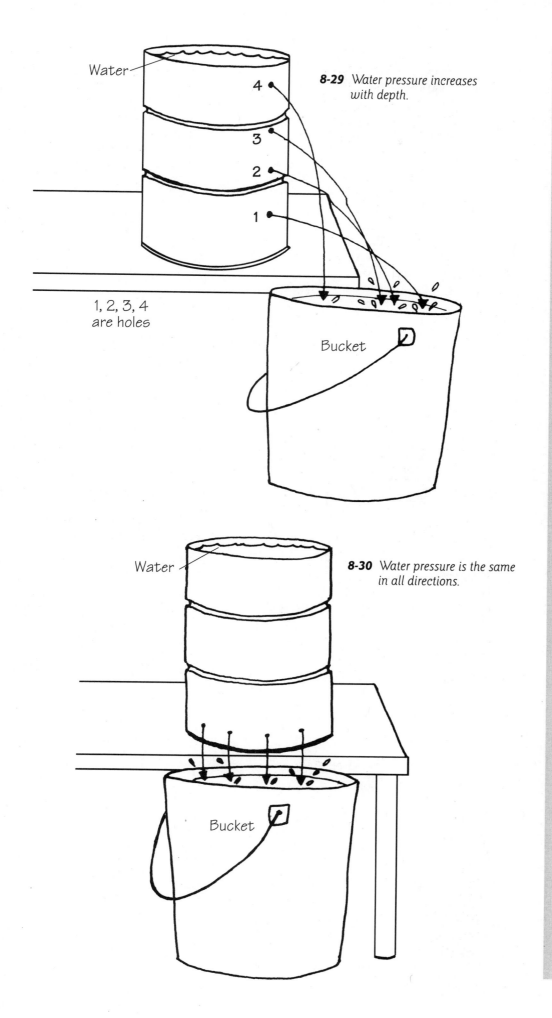

Water

8-29 Water pressure increases with depth.

4

3

2

1

1, 2, 3, 4
are holes

Bucket

Water

8-30 Water pressure is the same in all directions.

Bucket

2 Tell children to:
a Hold their container over the basin while they fill the container with water.
b Observe the water streams. (They will all be shooting streams of water out in different directions. Each stream of water will be shooting out the same length from the can.)

Fine point to discuss

Why are the streams of water all the same length? (Each stream of water starts its flow from the same water depth. The pressure of water [and air] pushing down is the same in all directions.)

4. Water seeks its own level

8-31 *The water in the tube stays at the same level at each side of the tube.*

Materials

For each child or group of children: a clear plastic tube or hose, a basin filled with water, newspaper to absorb possible mess from water, food coloring to color the water, a funnel.

Procedure

1 Choose a child in the group to add food coloring to the water so it can be seen more easily inside the hose.
2 Tell children to:
a Attach the funnel to the hose.
b Fill the hose with water.
c Lift the hose out of the water.
d Hold the hose so that it forms a "U" shape.
3 Tell children to observe the water level in each side of the tube.

What do you notice? (The water level remains the same in each side of the tube, even when the tube is raised or lowered.)

4 Tie a loose knot in the center of the tubing.

5 Fill the knotted tube with water. (The water will still be at the same level in each side of the hose.)
6 Tie the knot tighter while the water is in the hose.
7 Raise and lower the tubing.
8 Tell the children to observe what happens to the water level. (The water level will even out on both sides of the tube, but the water will move more slowly because of the tight knot.)

Fine points to discuss

Why does the level of water on both sides of the tube stay the same? (The air pressure on both sides of the tube is the same. This "sameness" of air pressure keeps the water level the same on both sides. When the water level is not the same, but the pressure from air is the same (as in the example of the tightly knotted tube) the water will "seek" to be at an equal level with itself.)

In which direction does water flow? (Water tends to flow down. The force of gravity pulls it down. When water is not in a container, it flows down toward sea level. When water is enclosed in a container like a hose, it can move or flow up if there is water pressure to push it up.)

VII. Surface tension

I. How full is full?

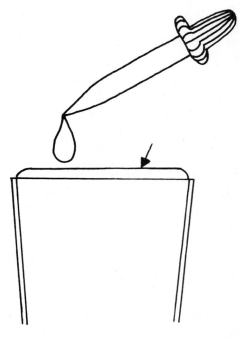

8-32 *Drop drops of water into a very full glass of water.*

Materials

For each child or group of children: two clear plastic cups, water, a basin, newspaper to absorb possible mess from water, an eye dropper or a straw, paper towels.

Procedure

1 Tell children to:
   a Slowly pour water into a cup until it is full. Keep the rim of the cup dry.
   b Fill an eye dropper or use a straw to lift water one drop at a time.
   c Drop drops of water into the full glass of water.

How many more drops do you think will be able to drop into the full glass of water without making the water overflow from the glass? (Listen to their responses and have them record their responses onto the chalkboard or in their science notebooks, so that they can compare their results later.)

2 Continue to drop additional drops of water into the glass. (Many drops can be added to the full glass.)

Fine points to discuss

What happens to the surface of the water as more drops are added to the cup? (The surface begins to look curved, like a lens.)

Why is the full glass able to hold so many additional drops of water after it is already full? (Water has a surface tension. This property of water allows water to stick to itself.)

2. Water is sticky

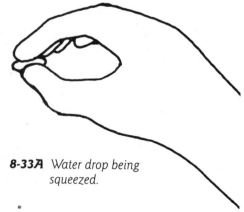

8-33A *Water drop being squeezed.*

Materials

For each child or group of children: a cup of water, an eye dropper or a drinking straw, waxed paper, newspaper to absorb possible mess from water.

Procedure

1 Tell children to:

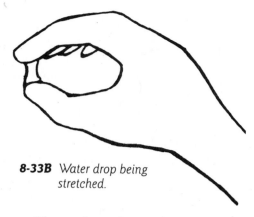

8-33B *Water drop being stretched.*

   a Place a drop of water between their thumb and index finger. *Explain:* The shape of the water drop can be changed by moving your thumb and index finger. It will appear as though the drop of water is being stretched or squeezed.

ⓘ INFORMATION Water itself cannot be stretched or squeezed. It is basically incompressible. However, the shape that water assumes can be changed or deformed. (See Fig.8-33.)

   b Drop several drops of water onto their hands.

Is the water sticking to their hands?

   c Shake their hands.

Is the water still there? (Some of the water will be there. For the water to come off, it has to be wiped off or evaporate.)

   d Drop a drop of water on waxed paper.
   e Observe what happens to the drop. (The drop forms a round curved shape like a ball and can roll on the paper.)

2 Have a child add some more drops of water to the waxed paper.

3 Observe what happens to the drops as they are rolled on the paper. (Some of the drops will combine or stick together to form a larger drop.)

Fine point to discuss

Why do the water drops combine to form larger drops of water? (Water is sticky. It sticks to itself. When water drops meet, they combine.)

3. Capillarity

Materials

For each child or group of children: a cotton washcloth, a shallow pie pan filled with water, newspaper to absorb possible mess from water.

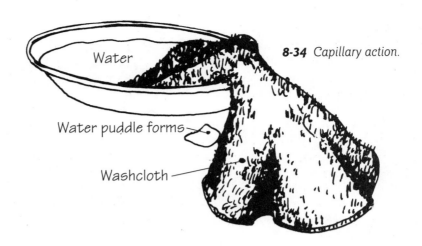

8-34 Capillary action.

Water

Water puddle forms

Washcloth

Procedure

1 Tell the children to place the corner of a dry cotton wash cloth into a shallow pie pan filled with water.

What do you think will happen to the water and the washcloth? (Listen to their responses and wait a while to see the results. It will take time!)

2 *Explain:* If water naturally sticks to itself and to other materials like cotton, the water will travel up the strings in the washcloth and out of the pan. The strings in the washcloth act like tubes for the water to flow through.

 The capillary action helps liquids flow through veins of plants and animals.

4. A water rope

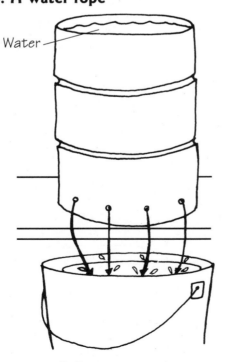

Water

8-35A Four separate streams.

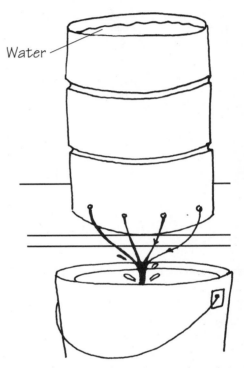

Water

8-35B When streams are pinched, they form a "rope."

Materials

A nail, a hammer. For each child or group of children: an empty can with the top removed, a basin, water, newspaper to absorb possible mess from water.

Procedure

1 The adult reading this book needs to use the hammer and nail to punch out four holes in a horizontal line around the side of the can, very close to the bottom rim. The holes should be very close together, about ¼-inch apart or less. As you pour water into the can to fill it, hold it over the basin. Have the children observe how the water pours out of the can in four separate streams of water.

2 Ask the children if they think it is possible to make all the streams of water combine into one stream. Listen to their responses.

3 Either pinch the stream of water together with your thumb and index finger or twist them together and the four streams will appear as a rope of streams flowing together. To separate the streams, rub your finger horizontally across the holes on the can. The surface tension of the water causes the streams of water to stick to each other and form a water rope.

4 After your demonstration, allow children to repeat the procedure several times with their can and basin of water to observe water streams on their own. Have them discuss and record their observations.

Going further

Beakman's World, a television program for children, demonstrated a different kind of water rope which is described in the following.

Materials

A piece of yarn about 3-feet long, a basin with water, a glass to pour water.

Procedure

1 Place the yarn in the basin filled with water, so that the rope becomes wet.

2 Have one child stretch the yarn up and hold it at a slant.

3 Choose another child to slowly pour the water down the yarn.

4 Observe what happens.

Why does this happen? (Water is cohesive and sticks to yarn itself. It is also adhesive and sticks to other surfaces. The yarn attracts the water, and the water attracts itself. So the yarn becomes a conduit or channel for the stream of water to ride down.)

5. The hairs form a point

Materials

For each child or group of children: a round-tipped easel paintbrush, a clear plastic cup of water, newspaper to absorb possible mess from water.

Procedure

1 Tell the children to:
   a Dip their paintbrush into a clear plastic cup of water.

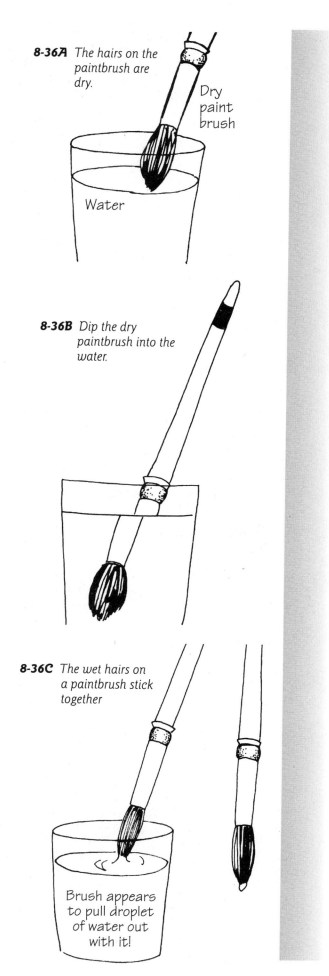

8-36A The hairs on the paintbrush are dry.

Dry paint brush

Water

8-36B Dip the dry paintbrush into the water.

8-36C The wet hairs on a paintbrush stick together

Brush appears to pull droplet of water out with it!

b Observe how the hairs on the paintbrush separate and fluff out in the water.

c Pull the paintbrush out of the water.

d Observe that the brush hairs are now held together and form a point.

2 Ask the children:

Do you know why the hairs are sticking together? (The surface tension from the water is causing the hairs to stick together.)

6. A waterproof handkerchief

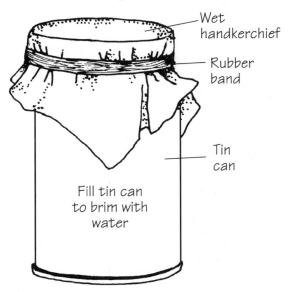

8-37 *Turn the can filled with water upside down.*

Materials

For each child or group of children: a handkerchief, a rubber band, an empty tin can without a lid, a basin of water, newspaper to absorb possible mess from water.

Procedure

1 Tell the children to:
   a Fill water to the top of the can.
   b Wet the handkerchief.
   c Place the wet handkerchief on top of the tin can and secure it on the can with a rubber band.
   d Turn the can of water with the handkerchief on it upside-down.

When the can is turned upside down, will the water stay in the can, or will the water pour out? (It will stay in the can.)

   e Hold the can sideways.

What happens? Why do you think this happens? (The wet handkerchief has swollen threads. When the can is held upside-down, the surface tension of the water and the outside air pressure keep the water from pouring out of the can through the handkerchief. When the can is held on its side, the water dribbles out because the surface tension of the water is broken.)

2. Allow children to repeat the procedure several times to observe if the result is the same. Discuss the results.

7. Water drops

(Adapted from Audrey Brainard.)

Materials

For each child or group of children: work trays; a sponge for each work tray to clean up possible spills; a small, plastic container to hold water; flat, wooden toothpicks; a 6-inch square of wax paper; optional—a 4-inch square of graph paper.

Procedure

1 *Explain:* You will be experimenting with water drops to find out more about water.

2 Drop several water drops onto your wax paper with a toothpick.

3 Observe the water drops.

What does a drop of water look like on a piece of wax paper?

Describe its shape.

Can you see through a water drop?

Is it possible to pull your water drops apart?

Can you form one big drop of water?

Can you separate a large drop into two drops?

Can the two drops be made the same size?

Can a water drop be pushed?

*Can a water drop be pulled?**

What happens when you drop a water drop on a water drop?

What happens when you drop a water drop into the water container?

(You will see concentric circles, a wave is formed.)

How do the ripples change when the drop comes from a high place or a low place?

What happens to a water drop if you drop it from a higher place?

What happens to water dropped on construction paper?

....a paper towel? ....tin foil? ....the plastic tray?

* For fun, "Project Aims" suggests pulling a water drop around on a laminated maze.

Fine point for older children

What measurement can you use to see if two drops are the same size? (A square on graph paper.)

Going further

Controlling water flow from a water dropper

Materials

For each child or group of children: a plastic eye dropper; a small, plastic container of water; a penny.

Procedure

1 Distribute an eye dropper to each child.

2 Let each child experiment to find out how to squeeze the eye dropper to control the drops that come out.

3 Demonstrate how to make just one tiny drop of water come out at a time.

4 *Explain:* In order to do the next activity, you need to be able to measure (count) and record the number of drops that come out of your eye droppers. When scientists do an experiment, they record their results so that they can repeat an experiment to see if the results are the same. Today, I want you to keep a record in your science journals of what your results are.

5 Drop water drops from your eye dropper onto a penny.

6 Predict how many drops of water your penny will hold before it overflows.

How many drops of water will the heads side hold?

How many drops will the tails side hold?

If the amount of drops are different, what would be the reason for this difference? (Different area and configuration of art work on both sides of the coin as well as a difference in the amount of dirt or grease on each coin.)

Will a hot penny hold as many drops as a cold penny?

If not, why not? (A colder surface increases the surface tension.)

See Water drop lenses, Chapter 7, Activity VIII., 1.

8. Soap reduces surface tension

Materials

For each child or group of children: ground black pepper, a bar of soap, a basin of water, a bowl, newspaper to absorb possible mess from water, a ruler, a baking pan under the basin to catch water after it is skimmed off the top.

Procedure

1 Tell the children to:
  a Fill the bowl with water.
  b Sprinkle pepper on top of the water.
  c Observe what happens to the pepper. (Some of it will sink, but most of the pepper will float on the surface of the water.)
  d Dip the corner of a bar of soap into the water.
  e Observe what happens to the particles of ground pepper. (The particles will scatter and move away from the bar of soap.)
  f Add more water and skim the top layer of water off with a ruler or your hand.

2 Allow the children to repeat the procedure several times. Have them observe whether the result is the same. Discuss the results.

Fine points to discuss

Why does the pepper float? (The pepper is lighter in weight than the water.)

Why does some of the pepper sink? (As the particles of ground pepper absorb water, they become heavier and sink.)

Why does the soap make the pepper scatter and move away? (Soap has oil in it. Oil and water do not mix. Oil feels slippery to the touch and it breaks down the sticky, cohesive quality of water. Oil disconnects the surface tension or "skin" of water. The rupture of surface cohesion by the soap causes the pepper to scatter.)

VIII. Description of water

1. Water is transparent

Materials

A hand mirror, a clear plastic fish-bowl or cup filled with water, newspaper to absorb possible mess from water.

Procedure

1 Tell the children to:
  a Look through a clear plastic container filled with water. (It is clear.)
  b Place their hand behind the container of water and look at their hand through the container.

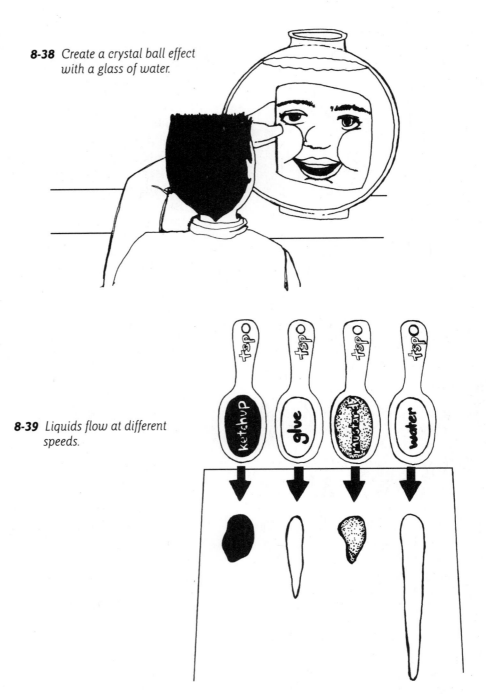

8-38 *Create a crystal ball effect with a glass of water.*

8-39 *Liquids flow at different speeds.*

c Place the mirror behind the clear water container. (See Fig. 8-38.)

d Look through the container into the mirror.

2 Ask the children:

What do you observe? (The children will see their reflection through the curved lens of the container. It will appear as though their face is inside the container, like the image in a crystal ball.)

2. Water flows easily

Materials

For each child or group of children: water and other heavy liquids such as thick ketchup, glue, mustard; a piece of coated cardboard; teaspoons.

Procedure

1 *Explain:* Water is a liquid. Liquids are able to flow. Some liquids flow faster than other liquids.

2 Have the heavy liquids on display and let the children experiment with each of the liquids to see if they flow and how fast they flow.

3 Tell the children to drop a teaspoon of each liquid onto the piece of cardboard. Then have them tilt the cardboard at a slight angle.

4 Observe what happens.

Which liquid moves the fastest or appears to flow the easiest? (Water will be an obvious answer.)

3. Water has weight

Materials

For each child or group of children: two empty soup cans that are the same size, a basin of water, newspaper to absorb possible mess from water.

Procedure

1 Tell the children to:
   a Fill up one can with water. Leave the other can empty (filled with air).
   b Lift both cans.
2 Ask the children:

Which can is heavier and why? (The can filled with water is heavier because water is heavier than air.)

4. Water can dissolve things

Materials

For each child or group of children: Alka-Seltzer, a clear plastic cup of water, a basin filled with water, newspaper to absorb possible mess from water, several clear plastic cups, salt, flour, sugar cube, granulated sugar, teaspoons for stirring and tasting water.

Procedure

1 Tell the children to:
   a Drop the Alka-Seltzer into the glass of water.
   b Observe the large white pill disintegrate in the water and let out bubbles of air. (The bubbles of air are carbon dioxide.)

What happens to other things that are placed in water—for example, powder that makes punch drinks, frozen lemonade, powder for Jello?

   c Place several cups of water on a table.
   d Put a different "powder" into each cup.
   e Stir the various containers filled with water and powder until the powder is dissolved.
   f Observe how the various powders of sugar, flour, salt, and the cube of sugar mix with the water.
2 Discuss the results.

Does the cube dissolve as quickly as the granulated sugar? (No.)

What happens to the water? Is it still clear? (Flour and salt make the water appear less clear.)

How can we tell if the water has the powder in it? (Taste it.)

 Some powders can be dangerous. Children should be reminded that when they experiment, they should never taste substances that are known to be dangerous or that are unknown to them

What happens if a lot of powder is added to the water? (The powder will float and eventually sink to the bottom. The solution will become saturated.)

What happens if the "powder" does not dissolve? (If the solution is left undisturbed, the water will eventually become clearer. The sediment of the undissolved powder will settle to the bottom of the container.)

5. Water can be purified

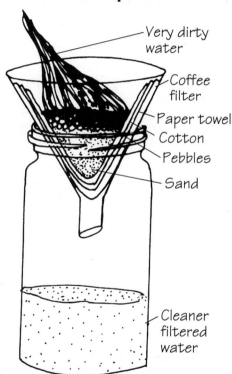

8-40 *Dirty water can be filtered.*

Materials

For each child or group of children: small pebbles, sand, soil, paper towels, coffee filter, cotton, a basin of water, newspaper to absorb possible mess from water, a large funnel, a large pickle jar, paper and pencils or children's own science journals.

Procedure

1 Create some dirty water in the basin by mixing soil into the water.

Do you think the water can be made clean again? (Listen to their responses, and encourage children to discuss and record their predictions and thoughts in their science journals.)

2 Tell children to:

a Create a filter by arranging layers of materials inside the large funnel.

b Place the coffee filter in first, then a paper towel and some cotton, and a layer of sand; the top layer should be pebbles.

c Each group should choose a child to pour a cupful of the dirty water solution slowly from the basin into the funnel.

Note: The funnel with filters should be resting on top of the large empty pickle jar. The dirty water will enter the pickle jar through the filter system in the funnel. When it enters the jar, it will be much cleaner. To get the water still cleaner, continue to refilter the water through the filter system from the pickle jar. It might be necessary to reassemble the filtration system with a clean coffee filter, paper towel, and cotton.

6. Water can act as a filter

Materials

For each child or group of children: a clear plastic cup, salt, sand, pebbles, a large pickle jar with a lid, a measuring cup, a basin of water, newspaper to absorb possible mess from water.

Procedure

1 Tell children to:

a Mix the sand and salt together.

Is there a way to separate these two "powders?"

b Add water to the mix and stir. (The salt will dissolve in the water and the sand will sink to the bottom of the container.)

c Mix: pebbles, sand, and soil together in a pickle jar so that it is not more than half full.

d Fill the remainder of the jar with water.

e Screw the lid on the pickle jar.

f Shake the filled jar vigorously.

g Let the jar sit for several hours.

2 Observe what happens and discuss why. (The heavier materials will sink to the bottom.)

7. Water can be absorbed

Materials

For each child or group of children: assorted objects that absorb water, like paper towels, sponges, cotton, a washcloth, yarn, a handkerchief; assorted objects that do not absorb water, like a plastic lid, a paper clip, tinfoil, a painted pencil, a bottle cap, a feather; a basin of water; newspaper to absorb possible mess from water; an eye dropper or an atomizer to spray water; paper and pencils or children's own science journals.

Procedure I

1 Show the children the assorted materials that can and cannot absorb water.

2 Have the children predict, discuss, and record their thoughts in their science

Will absorb water   **Won't** absorb water

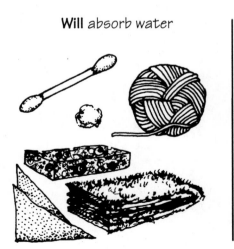

8-41 Observe water being absorbed or repelled.

journals about which materials will absorb water and which will not.

3 Have the children experiment to find out if their predictions were right by using an atomizer to spray water or an eye dropper to drop drops of water on the various materials.

What happens to water that is absorbed? (It spreads out flat.)

What happens to water when it is not absorbed? (It forms little beads and it rolls.)

Why do we wear a material that will not absorb water in the rain? (So we will not get wet.)

What kinds of materials are good to wear in the rain? (Plastic and rubber materials, or materials that have been treated not to absorb water.)

Do bird feathers get wet in the rain? (No, the outer feathers on birds do not absorb water because birds have natural oils in their feathers. These oils repel water.)

4 Tell children to compare their actual results with what they predicted and recorded in their science journals before they conducted their investigations.

Materials

For each child or group of children: a marking pen, dried lima beans, pebbles, two empty juice cans.

Procedure 2

1 Tell children to:
   a Fill one large can half-full of beans and the other can half-full of pebbles.
   b Place a line on the containers with a marking pen to show where the top

of the beans are and where the top of the rocks are. Fill the remaining half of the cans with water.

2 Ask the children:

What do you think might happen to the beans and pebbles if they stay in the water for awhile? (The beans will absorb water and will become practically twice their original size. Nothing much will happen to the pebbles, but their color will become more intense when they are wet.)

8. Water can be distilled
(Adapted from Gega, page 528.)

Materials

Water mixed with chicken broth, an electric hot plate, a tea kettle, an aluminum baking pan, an empty tin can, toothpicks for tasting the water.

Procedure

This is a demonstration for the adult reading this book to do for a child or group of children. It involves boiling water and hot steam, and could be dangerous for children to do on their own. Children should observe what happens and actively participate in the activity by thinking, predicting and answering thought-provoking questions posed by the adult doing the demonstration.

1 Pour the chicken broth diluted with water into a tea kettle. Place the aluminum baking pan underneath the tea kettle onto the electric hot plate.

2 Place the tin can loosely on the tea kettle spout so that the steam can come out freely, condense in the tin can, and fall into the baking pan.

3 Bring the broth to a boil.

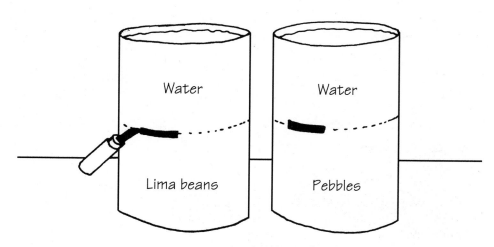

8-42 *Lima beans absorb water; pebbles do not.*

What will happen to the steam that comes out from the kettle? (It will condense inside of the tin can and drip into the aluminum baking pan.)

How can we find out if the steam that condenses into water will have a taste? (By tasting it.)

What does the water that collects in the aluminum pan look like? (Pure, clean water.)

What happened to the water that was mixed with the chicken broth? (It evaporated, turned into steam, condensed, and fell like rain into the collecting pan.)

4 *Explain:* When a liquid is heated and the vapor condenses it becomes purified, or refined. The impurities are left behind. This is called distillation. When water is distilled it becomes pure.

Note: A similar process happens at oil refineries to oil and gas. The refineries remove the impurities from oil and gasoline to create a refined product. The various oils like kerosene and gasoline are then further treated chemically for the desired product.

IX. Boats and buoyancy

1. Floaters and sinkers

Materials

For each child or group of children: basin of water; newspaper to absorb possible mess from water; assorted materials that will float or sink when placed in water (for example: seeds, feather, plastic materials, bar of soap, sponge, comb, crayons, pen, golf ball, popsicle sticks, marble, grapes, buttons, penny, drinking straw); paper and pencils or children's own science journals.

Procedure

1 Place the objects that are to be tested on the floor or table near the basin of water.

2 Tell the children that each object will either sink or float in the water.

3 Have them make a prediction about each object, discuss and record their thoughts in their science journals, and then test their prediction by placing each object, one at a time, into the basin of water.

4 Have them compare the actual results to what they predicted would happen.

Were there any surprises?

2. Floating and sinking cans, bottle caps, and closed containers

Materials

For each child or group of children: a basin of water; newspaper to absorb possible mess from water; bottle caps; empty tin cans that come with plastic lids, in assorted sizes: tuna fish can, coffee can, soup or vegetable can (or other nonplastic containers with removable lids).

Procedure

1 Place the objects on the table or floor near the basin of water.

2 Tell the children that each item can be made to sink or to float.

3 Have them experiment to find out how each item can be made to sink or float.

4 Discuss their findings. Table 8-2 lists some of the things they will be able to observe from their experimenting:

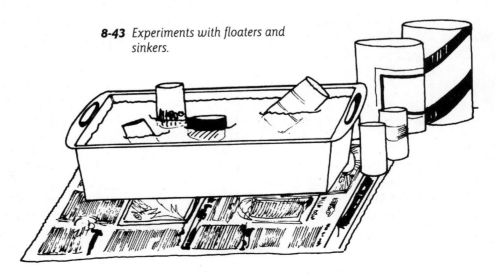

8-43 *Experiments with floaters and sinkers.*

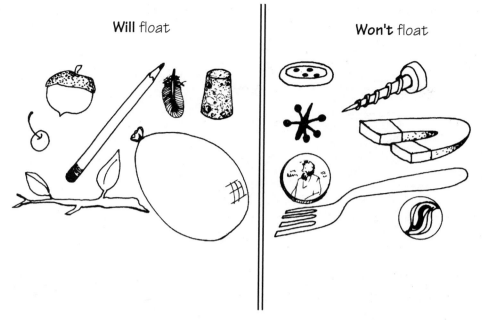

Will float   Won't float

8-44 Experiment to find out which items will sink and which will float.

Table 8-2 Observations that can be made from experimenting with floating and sinking cans

1 When most containers are filled with air and shut tight with a cap, they will float.
2 When metal containers fill with water, they usually sink, whereas plastic containers continue to float.
3 A metal cap can be made to float if the top (flat side) touches the water.
4 An upside-down cap (flat side up, rim in water) will float if a layer of air is between the flat side and the water.
5 A can with short sides (tuna can) will float if the bottom (the flat side) touches the water.
6 A can with tall sides will float at an angle.
7 A can with tall sides floats upright if water is added to the inside of the can.
8 A can with tall sides filled with some water rests or floats deeper in the basin.

3. Will a sieve or colander float?

Materials

A colander or sieve without a handle, a basin of water, newspaper to absorb possible mess from water, plastic wrap like Saran Wrap, Crisco or other solid shortening.

Procedure

1 Place the colander in the water. (It will sink.)

Can you think of a way to make the colander float? (Listen to their ideas, and try out their suggestions.)

2 Rub the holes with shortening to fill in the holes. Place the colander in the water. (It will sink. The water will still seep through the holes.)
3 Cover the colander's holes with two long strips of plastic wrap. The plastic wrap will stay in place with the shortening that is on the colander.
4 Place the colander in the water. (It will float. The plastic wrap will keep the water from seeping through the holes.)
5 After your demonstration, allow children to repeat the procedure on their own to see if they can make the colander float. (See Fig. 8-45.)

4. What makes a boat sink?

Materials

For each child or group of children: small toy boats or homemade barge boats made from pie tins, tin cans, Styrofoam, cardboard, or plastic meat trays from the grocery store, or empty half-gallon plastic ice cream containers; a basin filled with water; newspaper to absorb possible mess from water; a large can of pebbles, rocks, or marbles to be used as weights. (See Fig. 8-46A, B, C.)

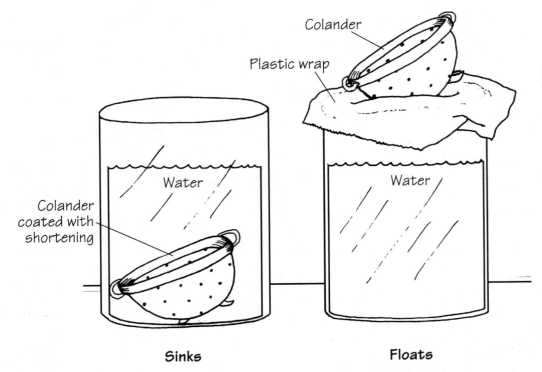

Colander

Plastic wrap

Colander coated with shortening

Water

Water

Sinks

Floats

8-45 *A metal sieve will sink unless its holes are made waterproof.*

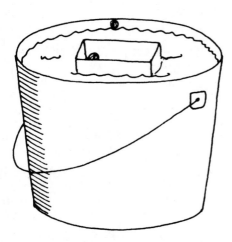

8-46A *Add marbles one at a time.*

8-46B *An unbalanced load causes the boat to be unstable.*

8-46C *A heavy, balanced load causes the boat to float low in the water.*

 Note: If rocks or pebbles are used, their weights will vary. If marbles are used, their weights will be more consistent and constant. Children might discover that if they use only marbles to load their tin boats, it might be easier for them to make predictions of how many marbles a tin boat can hold.

Procedure

1 Tell children to:
   a Load the barge boat with pebbles, one pebble at a time.
   b Predict how many pebbles the barge boat might be able to hold.

c Record your thoughts in your science notebooks.

d Continue to add pebbles until the boat sinks.

2 Ask the children:

What made the boat sink? (It will sink because of too much weight.)

Are there any other reasons a boat would sink?

3 Tell the children to add pebbles to the boat again, but this time tell them to add them to only one side of the barge boat.

How many pebbles will the boat be able to carry when the load is not balanced?

What do you think will happen to the boat from the uneven load? (It will eventually tilt, fill with water, then sink. If it is a Styrofoam boat barge, it will spill its load and then right itself in the water or turn upside-down (capsize).

4 Punch holes in the bottom of the barge boat.

5 Add pebbles to the barge boat.

When pebbles are added to the tin "boat," sediments will probably fall from the pebbles. It would be helpful for the children if an adult made them aware of the sediment and where the sediments came from.

6 Observe the reaction of the barge boat as the pebbles are added. *Note:* This is especially interesting to watch if the barge boat is a tinfoil pie tin. When the tinfoil pie tin "boat" starts to sink, stop adding pebbles. The sinking will continue very slowly, but once it starts to sink, it will continue to sink until it hits the bottom of the basin.

5. Shaping clay to float

Materials

For each child or group of children: clay, plasticine or play-doh; a small, round-bottomed bowl; a rolling pin; a basin filled with water; newspaper to absorb possible mess from water; wax paper; paper towel; paper clips.

Procedure

1 Tell children to:
 a Shape the clay or play-doh into a round ball.
 b Drop the clay into the basin of water.
 c Observe what happens to the clay ball.

2 Ask the children:

Is there a way that you could change the shape of the clay to make it float?

3 Blot the clay on a paper towel.

4 Use the rolling pin to flatten out the clay.

5 Roll out the clay on a piece of wax paper.

6 When the clay is fairly flat and thin, turn a small bowl upside-down and use the bottom of the bowl as a mold to shape the clay into a bowl-shaped boat.

7 Place the bowl-shaped boat into the basin of water. Be sure there are no holes in the clay and that the edges of the clay are pinched together to be solid. (The clay bowl will float. It will be able to carry a small, light load like a paper clip or two.)

8 Let children continue to experiment with the clay to see if they can improve their design for the clay boat, and to experiment with how many paper clips it will be able to hold.

6. Making a clay ball float
Materials

For each child or group of children: clay, play-doh or plasticine; drinking straws; scissors; paper towels; basin filled with water; newspaper to absorb possible mess from water.

Procedure

Tell children to:

1 Roll clay into a ball.

2 Blot the clay onto a paper towel to absorb any extra water that it might be holding.

3 Cut about five or six drinking straws in half.

4 Pierce the clay ball with the pieces of drinking straws.

5 Place the straws around a perimeter on the clay ball. (See Fig. 8-47.)

6 Place the clay ball with straws protruding from it in the water. (It will float. If not, add more straws or use less clay.)

Fine points to discuss

Why is the clay ball unable to float without straws supporting it, but able to float when it is thin and shaped like a bowl? (The clay ball is very thick and dense. The clay bowl

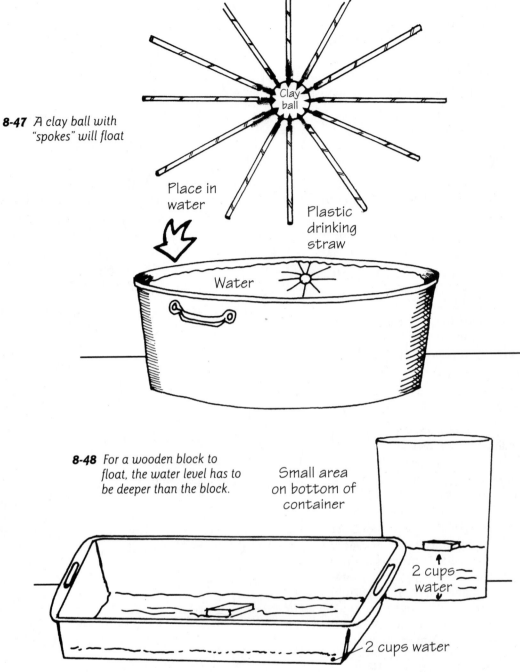

8-47 *A clay ball with "spokes" will float*

Place in water

Plastic drinking straw

Water

8-48 *For a wooden block to float, the water level has to be deeper than the block.*

Small area on bottom of container

2 cups water

2 cups water

Large area on bottom of container

is much thinner than the ball shape. The water is able to support the clay when it is shaped like a bowl because the bowl holds a lot of air. The water is unable to support the clay when it is shaped like a ball because the clay ball contains less air. An object can float when the object has less density than the water has.)

i **INFORMATION** The density of the clay remains the same, but the shape and enclosed volume of air changes the density as the shape of the clay "boat" is changed.

How do straws help the clay ball stay afloat? (The drinking straws contain air; the straws are less dense than the clay.)

7. When does something float?

Materials

A bucket filled with water; a newspaper to absorb possible mess from water; an empty, half-gallon plastic container; a large, flat basin; a measuring cup; two blocks of wood that are the same shape, size and weight; paper and pencils or children's science journals.

Procedure

1 Place a wooden block inside the basin and a wooden block inside the half-gallon plastic container.

2 Tell the children you are going to add water to each of the containers, one cup at a time.

How much water do you think needs to be added to the container before the wooden block will float?

Will the blocks in each container float with the same number of cups of water? If not, why not?

3 Tell them to discuss and record their thoughts in their science journals.

4 Test out their ideas. (The smaller and deeper container will need less water to create a depth of water deep enough to lift the wooden block.)

5 Let children continue to experiment with the wooden blocks, the basins, and the water.

Fine point to discuss

Why does the wooden boat float in the small container with less water? (The wooden block could not float in the water until the water was deeper than the wooden block.)

8. A balloon in water

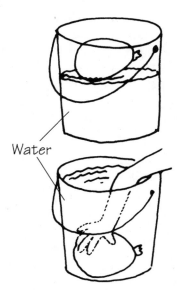

8-49 *When the balloon is submerged, the water level rises. Air in the balloon takes up space, and the balloon displaces water.*

Materials

A bucket half-filled with water; an inflated balloon; newspaper to absorb possible mess from water.

Procedure

1 Tell the children that you are going to choose one of them to place an inflated balloon into the bucket.

2 Ask the children:

What do you think will happen when the balloon is placed into the water? (The balloon will float on the water.)

What will happen if the balloon is pushed into the water? (The water will rise. The volume of space taken up by the air in the balloon will displace or push away the water that is occupying that space. As the balloon is pushed down, the water pushes up.)

Fine point to discuss

Why does the balloon push back up from the water? Isn't the water heavier than the balloon? (The water is heavier than the balloon, but the air inside the balloon is less dense than the density of the water. The water pushes up the balloon with great force because the density of water is much greater than the density of air inside the balloon.)

9. Water makes a brick feel lighter

Materials

A bucket half-filled with water; a brick or heavy rock; a piece of rope or twine about 18 inches long; newspaper to absorb possible mess from water.

Procedure

1 Tie the rope to the brick.

2 Give the free end of the rope to a child.

3 Ask the child to lift the brick up.

4 Have the child observe and feel how heavy the brick feels on the end of the rope. Then have the same child lift the brick and gently lower it into the bucket of water.

5 Tell the child not to let the brick touch the sides of the bucket or the bottom. (As the brick enters the water, the child should notice an immediate difference in the weight of the brick.)

How does the brick feel? (Lighter.)

Why does the brick feel less heavy? (The brick feels lighter because the weight of the water is pushing up against the brick and is supporting some of the brick's weight.)

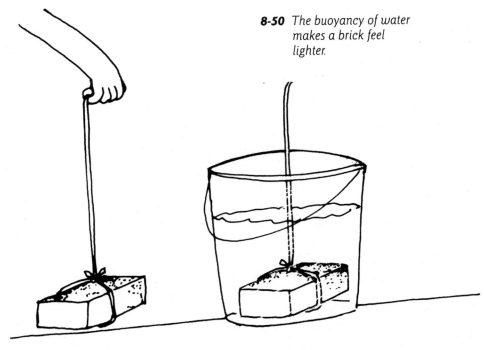

8-50 *The buoyancy of water makes a brick feel lighter.*

Feels heavy   Feels lighter

6 Let each child experience the weight of the brick in water and out of water.

10. Eggs float in saltwater

Materials

Two clear plastic cups filled with water; an egg; salt; a teaspoon.

Procedure

1 Have a child pour salt into one of the cups of water and stir it with a teaspoon. Continue to have the child add salt until the solution is saturated. (It will be saturated when the water cannot hold all of the salt and some of the salt will sink to the bottom of the cup.)

2 Place an egg into the clear water. (It will sink.)

3 Remove the egg and place it in the salty water. (It will float.)

Fine points to discuss

Why can an egg float in saltwater but not in clear water? (Salty water is heavier or more dense than clear water. The increased density of the salt water makes it possible for the egg to float.)

Do ships float higher in saltwater than in clear water? (Yes, the ship displaces less water if the water is denser.)

Further resources

Selected books for children and adults

Dewey Decimal Classification Number for air and water is: 507, 533, and 551.

Ardley, Neil. *The Science Book of Air.* San Diego: Harcourt Brace Jovanovich, 1991. (This book has lots of beautiful color photographs.)

Ardley, Neil. *The Science Book of Water.* San Diego: Harcourt Brace Jovanovich, 1991. (This book has lots of beautiful color photographs.)

Barkan, Joanne. *Water, Water Everywhere.* Morristown, NJ: Silver Press, 1990.

Bennett, David. *Water.* New York: Bantam Little Rooster Book, 1992. (A picture book.)

Better Homes and Gardens. *Water Wonders.* Des Moines, IA: Meredith Corporation, 1989.

Branley, Franklyn. *Air Is All Around You.* New York: Harper and Row, 1986. (Appropriate for children who can read.)

Brandt, Keith. *Air.* Mahwah, NJ: Troll, 1985. (Grades 3–6.)

Cole, Joanna. *The Magic School Bus at the Waterworks.* New York: Scholastic, 1988. (For children grades 2–6.)

Edom, Helen. *Science with Water*. London: Usborne Publishing Ltd., 1990. (For children who can read.)

Ingoglia, Gina. *The Big Book of Real Airplanes*. New York: Grosset, 1987. (For children who can read.)

Jennings, Terry. *Junior Science, Floating and Sinking*. New York: Glouster Press, New York. 1988. (For older children.)

Krensky, Stephen. *Snow and Ice*. New York: Scholastic, 1989. (For children who can read.)

Smith, Henry. *Amazing Air, Science Club*. New York: Lothrop, Lee and Shepard Books, 1983. (Appropriate for children in grades 3–6.)

Taylor, Barbara. *Sink or Swim! The Science of Water*. New York: Random House, 1991.

Taylor, Barbara. *Up, Up and Away! The Science of Flight*. New York: Random House, 1991. (For children who can read.)

Watson, Philip. *Liquid Magic, Science Club*. New York: Lothrop, Lee, and Shepard Books, 1983. (Appropriate for children in grades 3–6.)

Wilkins, Mary Jane. *Tell Me About Air, Light, and Water*. New York: Random House, 1990. (For children that can read.)

Wyler, Rose. *Science Fun with Toy Boats and Planes*. New York: Simon & Schuster, 1986. (For children who can read.)

Young, Caroline, Miles, John, and King, Colin. *Ships, Sailors, and the Sea*. London: Usborne Publishing Ltd., 1988. (Grades 3–6.)

Selected resource books for adults and older children

Agler, Leigh. *Involving Dissolving, Teacher's Guide*. (Grades K–3.) Great Explorations in Math and Science (GEMS.) Berkeley, CA: Laurence Hall of Science, Univ. of Calif, 1989.

Agler, Leigh. *Liquid Explorations, Teacher's Guide*. Grades K–3. Great Explorations in Math and Science (GEMS.) Berkeley, CA: Laurence Hall of Science, Univ. of Calif, 1987.

Arvetis, Chris, and Carole Palmer. *Why Does it Float?* Chicago: Rand McNally, 1983. (Contains buoyancy activities for children who want to do more "experiments.")

Barber, Jacqueline and Carolyn Willard. *Bubble Festival, Teachers Guide*. Great Explorations in Math and Science (GEMS.) Berkeley, CA: Laurence Hall of Science, Univ. of Calif, 1986. (Grades 5–9.)

Kaner, Etta. *Balloon Science*. Reading, Mass: Addison-Wesley, 1989. (Good resource book for adults.)

Lewis, James. *Rub-a-Dub-Dub Science in the Tub*. Deephaven, MN: Meadowbrook Press, 1989. (Children can learn about "water" science while they play in the tub. Activities for children ages 2–5.)

McGlathery, Glenn and Malone, Larry. *Tons of Scientifically Provocative and Socially Acceptable Things to do with Balloons Under the Guise of Teaching Science*. Englewood, CO: Libraries Unlimited, 1991. (K–6.)

Nichols, Wendy and Kim. *Wonderscience*. Santa Fe, N.M.: Learning Expo, 1990. (Contains lots of interesting easy to do activities for grades pre-K through K.)

Pearl, Louis. *Sudman's Bubble-ology Guide*. San Francisco: Tangent Toy Company, 1984.

Seed, Deborah. *Water Science*. Reading, Mass: Addison-Wesley, 1992. (K–3.)

Zubrowski, Bernie. *Balloons: Building and Experimenting with Inflatable Toys*. New York: Morrow, 1990. (Better for older children.)

Zubrowski, Bernie. *Messing Around with Water Pumps and Siphons*. Boston: Little, Brown, 1981. (Better for older children.)

Zubrowski, Bernie. *Wheels at Work: Building and Experimenting with Models of Machines*. New York: Morrow, 1986. (Shows how to make a water wheel.)

Selected literature connections for younger children

Allen, Pamela. *Who Sank the Boat*. NY: Putnam, 1990. (A cute picture story involving a boat that sinks.)

Calhoun, Mary. *Hot Air Henry*. New York: Wm. Morrow, 1981. (A story about a Siamese cat that takes a fur-raising flight in a hot air balloon.)

Cebulash, Mel. *The Ball that Wouldn't Bounce*. New York: Scholastic, 1972. (A story about a ball that needed air in order to bounce.)

Zion, G. *Harry the Dirty Dog*. New York: Harper & Row, 1956. (A story about a dog that gets so dirty no one recognizes him, but water comes to his rescue.)

General community enrichment activities and resources

Visit the airport There are lots of things to observe: the direction the wind blows by observing the flags; the control tower; the preparation before an airplane leaves the ground; the direction the airplanes take off; the designs of airplanes and their wings; the luggage being loaded on and the luggage coming off; the conveyor belts; the design of the airport; the special equipment that workers use and wear; etc.

Visit a boat harbor Observe the going and coming of boats; the safety rules that are followed; the size and shape of the various boats and ships; the materials that the boats and ships are made of; the colors of the ships; the kinds of sails that boats use; the designs of the boats and ships; the special tools and machinery that are visible for hauling and lifting and cleaning; the sounds and smells around the water; how does the wind or lack of wind affect how fast the sail boats travel?

Visit a car wash Observe the sequence of events in the car wash. Observe what each machine does to the car. Observe the kinds of water that hit the car, from a gentle spray to a hard pressure. Observe where all of the water goes from the car wash. Observe what wind does to the water that is left on the car.

Visit a laundry Observe a laundromat. Listen to the sounds the machines make when they fill up and empty out. Where does the water come from and where does it go? How do the clothes get dry? Where does the water go? How do the clothes feel when they are wet? How do they smell when they are dirty? How do they smell when they are clean?

Watch hang gliding Observe the gliders. What keeps the hang gliders up? What controls the flight? Where do the hang gliders land? What special equipment and safety gear do the flyers use? What do the weather conditions need to be like? What designs work best? Which glider design stays in the air the longest? What kinds of material are they made of?

Watch a blimp or hot-air balloons Observe how a hot air balloon takes off. What are the ropes for? Can a hot-air balloon land by itself? What controls how high or how low the hot-air balloon goes? What controls the direction in which the hot-air balloon travels? How much cargo can a hot-air balloon carry? How is a hot-air balloon different from a blimp?

Visit a gas station with a service garage and an air pump Observe the hydraulic lift. Observe the large metal cylinder go up and down with a car on it. Observe the control that controls the lift action. Feel the air come out of the air pump. Unscrew the air valve on a tire and feel the air come out of the tire. Use an air gauge to refill the tire with air at the air pump.

Bibliography

The American Heritage Dictionary of the English Language. Morris William, ed. Boston: Houghton Mifflin, 1976.

Brainard, Audrey, and Denise H. Wrubel. *Literature-Based Science Activities, an Integrated Approach.* New York: Scholastic, 1993. (Appropriate for grades 1–4. This book is filled with creative and innovative science experiences using children's literature as a springboard for science investigations and activities.

Bruner, J.S. *The Process of Education.* Cambridge, Massachusetts: Harvard University Press, 1960. (See especially chapter 2, "The Importance of Structure," and chapter 3, "Readiness for Learning.")

Beakman's World. A Universal Press Syndicated television program, distributed by Columbia Pictures for the Learning Channel. Various programs.

Children's Television Workshop, 3, 2, 1, Contact. Educational Television Series. Various dates.

Davis, Barbara. Science Supervisor, Virginia Beach City Public Schools. Making Inferences about Animals. A lecture given in her course: Topics in Life and Physical Science for Kindergarten Teachers, Spring, 1993.

Fee, Sally. A Child's Real World-Developing Science Within the Program. A workshop presented in Washington, D.C. at the National Association for the Education of Young Children (NAEYC), Washington, D.C.: November, 1982.

Gagné, Robert M. *The Conditions of Learning, 4th edition.* New York: Harcourt, Brace Jovanovich, 1985.

Hewitt, Paul G. *Conceptual Physics, 7th edition. A New Introduction to Your Environment.* Boston: Little, Brown & Co., 1992.

Merrit Student Encyclopedia. New York: Macmillan Education Co., 1991.

Tryon, Bette. Science, A Practical Approach. A workshop presented in Washington, D.C., at the National Conference of the National Association for the Education of Young Children (NAEYC), Washington, D.C., November, 1982.

Williams, David, "Science" for Young Children—Gathering Experiences. 16th Annual Conference sponsored by the Maryland Council of Parent Participation Nursery Schools, Montgomery College, Rockville, Maryland, March 7, 1984.

World Book Encyclopedia, 1979 ed. Chicago: World Book-Childcraft, 1979. (See especially: Sound, Light, Color, Air, Water, Weather, Volcanoes, Atoms, Animals, Plants, Leaves, Flowers, Ecology.)

Series

How and Why Wonder Books. New York: Grosset and Dunlap (various dates).

Selected generic resource books for parents and teachers

Brown, Sam Ed. *Bubbles, Rainbows and Worms: Science Experiments for Preschool Children.* Mt. Rainier, Maryland: Gryphon House, 1981.

Druger, Marvin, ed. *Science For the Fun of It: A Guide to Informal Science Education.* Washington, D.C.: National Science Teachers Association, 1988.

Exploratorium Teacher Institute Staff. *Exploratorium Science Snackbook: A Teacher Resource for Hands-on Science Exhibits & Activities.* San Francisco, CA. 1991.

Goldman, Jane F. *The Curiosity Shop: A Sciencing Sampler for the Primary Years.* Minneapolis: T.S. Denison, 1988. (Has an extensive list of free and inexpensive materials, as well as a chart listing assorted small creatures and how to care for them.)

Ontario Science Center Staff. *Science Express.* Reading, Mass: Addison-Wesley, 1991.

Ontario Science Center Staff. *Scienceworks.* Reading, Mass: Addison-Wesley, 1986.

Ontario Science Center Staff. *Sportsworks.* Reading, Mass: Addison-Wesley, 1989.

Poppe, Carol A. and Nancy A. Van Matre. *Science Learning Centers for the Primary Grades.* West Nyack, N.Y.: The Center for Applied Research in Education, 1985. (Instructions for setting up learning centers, plus 40 activities to do at the learning centers. Better suited for beginning teachers than parents.)

Strongin, Herb. *Science on a Shoestring.* Reading, Mass: Addison-Wesley, 1992.

Wolfgang, Charles H. and Mary E. *School for Young Children: Developmentally Appropriate Practices.* Needham, Mass: Allyn and Bacon, 1992.

Additional generic science books for children and their parents

Althea. *What Makes Things Move?* Mahwah, NJ: Troll, 1991.

Ardley, Neil. *The Science Book of Gravity.* New York: Gulliver Books (HBJ), 1992.

Ardley, Neil. *The Science Book of Machines.* New York: Gulliver Books (HBJ), 1992.

Ardley, Neil. *The Science Book of Energy.* New York: Gulliver Books (HBJ), 1992.

Ardley, Neil. *The Science Book of Motion.* New York: Gulliver Books (HBJ), 1992.

Challoner, Jack. *The Science Book of Numbers.* New York: Gulliver Books (HBJ), 1992.

Cobb, Vicki, and Kathy Darling. *Bet You Can! Science Possibilities to Fool You.* New York: Avon Books, 1983.

Cobb, Vicki, and Kathy Darling. *Bet You Can't! Science Impossibilities to Fool You.* New York: Lothrop, 1980.

Cobb, Vicki. *Chemically Active!* New York: Harper and Row, 1990.

Cobb, Vicki. *More Science Experiments You Can Eat.* New York: Harper and Row, 1979.

Forte, Imogene. *Science Fun: Discovering the World Around You.* Incentives Publications, Inc., Nashville, Tennessee. 1985.

Gardner, Robert. *Kitchen Chemistry.* Morristown, NJ: Silver Burdett, 1988.

Hann, Judith. *How Science Works.* New York: Reader's Digest, 1991. (Better for older children.)

Hazen, Robert M. *Science Matters.* New York: Doubleday, 1991.

Herbert, Don. *Mr. Wizard's Super Market Science.* New York: Random House, 1980.

Herbert, Don. *Mr. Wizard's Experiments for Young Scientists.* New York: Doubleday, 1990.

Jennings, Terry. *Bouncing and Rolling.* New York: Gloucester Press, 1990.

Kenda, Margaret and Williams, Phyllis S. *Science Wizardry for Kids: Authentic, Safe Scientific Experiments Kids Can Perform!* Hauppauge, N.Y.: Barrons Educational Series, 1992.

Mandell, Muriel. *Physics Experiments for Children.* New York: Dover, 1968.

Mandell, Muriel. *Simple Science Experiments with Everyday Materials.* New York: Sterling, 1990. (For older children.)

Mandell, Muriel. *220 Easy-to-Do Science Experiments for Young People: 3 Complete Books.* New York: Dover, 1985.

Mollenson, Diane, and Sarah Savage. *Easy Science Experiments.* New York: Scholastic, 1993.

Penrose, Gordon. *Dr. Zed's Science Surprises.* New York: Simon and Schuster, 1989.

Penrose, Gordon. *More Science Surprises from Dr. Zed.* New York: Simon & Schuster, 1992.

Penrose, Gordon. *Magic Mud and Other Great Experiments*. New York: Simon & Schuster, 1987.

Stein, Sara. *The Science Book*. New York: Workman Publishing, 1980.

Stetten, Mary. *Let's Play Science*. New York: Harper and Row, 1979.

Van Cleave, Janice. *Physics For Every Kid*. N.Y.: John Wiley & Sons, 1991.

Van Cleave, Janice. *Chemistry For Every Kid*. N.Y.: John Wiley & Sons, 1987.

Weiner, Esther. *Dirt Cheap Science: Activity-Based Units, Games, Experiments & Reproducibles*. New York: Scholastic, 1992. (Great activities for an after-school science program).

Wood, Robert W. *Physics for Kids: 49 Easy Experiments with Heat*. TAB Books, 1990.

Wyler, Rose. *Science Fun with A Homemade Chemistry Set*. New York: Julian Messner, 1987.

Index

About the Author

Elaine Levenson brings a rich blend of professional and life experiences—and her own unique educational perspectives—to *Teaching Children about Physcial Science.* An early childhood educator, Elaine has held a variety of teaching assignments: in New York, Maryland, Virginia, and the District of Columbia, working in nursery school through graduate-level venues.

As a Projector Director for the National Science Foundation through the University of the District of Columbia, (1985–1987), she trained and assisted teachers in grades K–6 to be more confident and effective in doing science activities with young children.

Her higher education began at San Diego State College, then continued at Boston University and New York University. She completed her B.S. in Elementary Education and her Masters Degree in Early Childhood at Queens College, City University of New York.

Elaine's teaching career began in a second grade, at P.S. 50, an inner-city, special-services school in the Bronx, New York City. (Subsequently, she took a ten-year leave of absence after her children were born.)

Later, in 1977 when her youngest entered The Franklin Montessori School in suburban Washington, D.C., she was asked to become that school's art and science teacher. The director, Lynn Oboler, knew that Elaine had majored in early childhood, and Lynn was anxious to develop a science teacher for her school. Lynn Oboler suggested that Elaine study some children's science books in the belief that Elaine would surely know more than enough to answer the questions of four-year-olds. The Director of the Montessori school, as well as the parents and other teachers, realized that Elaine had a natural talent for teaching early childhood science, and so they encouraged her to take additional science courses. After completing a series of graduate- level science classes in life, earth, and physical sciences, Elaine was able to start her own visiting science teaching service, known as Science-on-Wheels. For six years, Science-on Wheels offered weekly sequenced science lessons at private schools and day-care centers throughout the Washington, D.C. suburbs.

Today Elaine continues to enjoy developing awarenesses in children and extending their curiosity. She relishes open-ended activities and likes to ask lots of questions, as well as to play.

Her first book, Teaching Children about Science: Ideas and Activities Every Teacher and Parent Can Use (first published in 1985), attracted widespread notice—in reviews, college and university education departments, museums, and in the media. That book went through four printings and is used in college classes and in many homes across the country.

Elaine currently resides with her husband, Hal, a media consultant, in Virginia Beach, Virginia. She teaches kindergarten at Linkhorn Park Elementary School, a public institution.

Other Bestsellers of Related Interest

Nature through Science and Art

Susie Gwen Criswell

A how-to book for teachers, parents, and other educators who spend time exploring nature with children. Instills a deep awareness of the environment in children in grades 3-6 through hands-on science investigations and art activities.

Paper 0-8306-4576-4 $12.95
Hard 0-8306-4575-6 $22.95

The Little Scientist: An Activity Lab

Jean Stangl

This book encourages young children to view the world around them as a giant experiment in progress, to explore their surroundings in search of knowledge about how and why their environment works. Forty stimulating hands-on science experiments physically involve children ages 4-6 in the learning process. Projects include measuring temperature, caring for small animals, studying insects, and recycling garbage. Safety icons.

Paper 0-8306-4102-5 $9.95
Hard 0-8306-4101-7 $17.95

A Teacher's Science Companion

Dr. Phyllis J. Perry

A carefully researched bibliography, organized by topic, of more than 2,000 children's science and math books in print. Includes step-by-step activities that provide instant "lessons" on the subject. Perfect for teachers of grades K-6.

Paper 0-07-049519-X $14.95
Hard 0-07-049518-1 $24.95

Teaching Children About Life and Earth Science

Elaine Levenson

Companion science survival guide for teachers and parents, with activities for grades K-3. The idea-filled edition incorporates the latest teaching techniques to stimulate kids' interest in science.

Paper 0-07-037655-7 $16.95

Science Toolbox: Making and Using the Tools of Science

Jean Stangl

How to recycle everyday items into useful science discovery tools. A step-by-step activities guide for children in grades 1-3. Includes safety icons.

Paper 0-8306-4352-4 $9.95
Hard 0-8306-4605-1 $17.95

Toys in Space: Exploring Science with the Astronauts

Dr. Carolyn Sumners

An unparalleled resource for elementary and middle-school science teachers and parents. Contains dozens of toy-building activities that simulate experiments NASA astronauts perform on space missions, teaching children the principles of physics through play.

Paper 0-8306-4534-9 $10.95
Hard 0-8306-4533-0 $17.95

Prices Subject to Change Without Notice.

Look for These and Other Windcrest/McGraw-Hill Books at Your Local Bookstore

---

To Order Call Toll Free 1-800-822-8158
(24-hour telephone service available.)

or write to Windcrest/McGraw-Hill, Blue Ridge Summit, PA 17294-0840.

Title	Product No.	Quantity	Price

☐ Check or money order made payable to Windcrest/McGraw-Hill

Charge my ☐ VISA ☐ MasterCard ☐ American Express

Acct. No. _____ Exp. _____

Signature: _____

Name: _____

Address: _____

City: _____

State: _____ Zip: _____

Subtotal $ _____

Postage and Handling
($3.00 in U.S., $5.00 outside U.S.) $ _____

Add applicable state and local
sales tax $ _____

TOTAL $ _____

Windcrest/McGraw-Hill catalog free with purchase; otherwise send $1.00 in check or money order and receive $1.00 credit on your next purchase.

Orders outside U.S. must pay with international money in U.S. dollars drawn on a U.S. bank.

Windcrest/McGraw-Hill Guarantee: If for any reason you are not satisfied with the book(s) you order, simply return it (them) within 15 days and receive a full refund.

BC

Other Bestsellers of Related Interest

DATE DUE

APR 1 2 '97	OCT 0 8 2002	
FEB 1 4 '97		
AUG 2 1	OCT 1 3 2002	
MAY 1 6 '97	OCT 1 3 2002	
JUN 2 7 '97	SEP 2 4 2003	
JUL 3 0 '97		
MAR 1 0	NOV 0 9 2003	
APR 0	SEP 0 2 2004	
JUL 0 7 '98	NOV 0 1 2005	
AUG 1 4		
MAY 1 9		
NOV 1 6 '99		
FEB 2 '00		
APR 0 5 '00		
DEC 0 5 '00		

How to Coach Teachers Who *Don't* Think Like You

For Superintendents Dr. Linda Henke and Dr. Cheryl Compton.

To Dennis, Sheila, Sue, Megan, and Mike, and all my colleagues and friends at Cooperating School Districts (CSD), and especially to Doug Miller, of the Missouri Department of Elementary and Secondary Education (DESE)—you made it all possible.

In memory of my mother, my first teacher, Helen M. Schnurbusch.